Resolution of the Senate for the appointment of the Committee of inquiry.

STATE OF NEW-YORK,
In Senate, March 28, 1853.

Resolved, That the report of the majority, and of the minority of the commissioners, heretofore appointed by the Senate, to investigate the pecuniary affairs of Union College, be referred to a committee of three members of the Senate, to investigate the matters specified in the Senate resolutions, of June and July, 1851; with power to send for persons and papers, and if necessary, to sit after the adjournment of the present session of the Senate; and, after a full and fair hearing of all parties and persons desiring to be heard before them, to report the results of their inquiries, and their opinions thereon; and the said committee shall make up and sign their report, by the first day of August next, and shall deposit the same with the Attorney General of this State, by that day, whose duty it shall be, forthwith, thereafter, (if, in his opinion, there are good reasons therefor,) to take such legal proceedings against the Trustees of Union College, or against the President thereof, or against all or any, or either of them, or against any person connected with said college, who may have been guilty of improper conduct, or of any unlawful acts.

Resolved, further, that the Attorney General, present any report, so left with him, to the next Legislature, on the first day of its session, in order that they may take such further action in the premises, as may seem to them right.

By order of the Senate,

IRA P. BARNES, *Clerk.*

In Senate, March 29, 1853.

Ordered that Messrs. Vanderbilt, Jones and Ward, constitute the committee, provided for in the foregoing resolution.

By order, IRA P. BARNES, *Clerk.*

[By subsequent resolutions, the time for depositing the report of the committee with the Attorney General, was extended to November 1, 1853.]

Synopsis of the following Argument.

ARGUMENT

In defence of the Rev. ELIPHALET NOTT, President of Union College, and in answer to the charges made against him by Levinus Vanderheyden and James W. Beekman: presented before the Committee of the Senate appointed to investigate certain pecuniary affairs of Union College, by JOHN C. SPENCER.

I return you gentlemen, the thanks of my friend and
client, for whom I am a volunteer here, and my own, for 1
the great patience you have evinced during this intricate,
protracted, tedious and extraordinary investigation.

It involves the character of some of the most distinguished, and most able men of our State. The Executive
officers, the Governor, Lieut. Governor, Secretary of State,
Comptroller, Attorney General and Treasurer, are and for
more than thirty years have been, by virtue of their respective offices, Trustees of Union College. Judicial officers 2
of high rank, and other distinguished citizens, have been
Trustees. If the charges now brought forward are sustained, it is impossible to screen any of these Trustees from
the charge of the most gross and culpable inattention to
their duties, and ignorance of the fiscal affairs of the College; or a willful and wicked abandonment of its rights
and interests to the cupidity of its President. The first al- 3
ternative is disproved by the most abundant evidence, furnished by the books of minutes of the Trustees, which show
numerous reports of most thorough and searching investigations into the pecuniary condition of the College, by such
men as the late William James, a well known merchant
of this city, the Hon. William L. Marcy, the Hon. Silas
Wright and A. C. Flagg, former Comptrollers of the State,
the Hon. John A Dix and the Hon. John P. Cushman, now 4

deceased. Their reports show on their face the labor
which preceded their preparation. Yet they all exhibited a condition of the College, utterly incompatible with
the alleged robberies and frauds, and they all speak in the
highest terms of the ability, zeal and disinterestedness of
the President and his entire devotion to the interests of the
5 College. Besides these special reports, the minutes show
that there was a standing financial Committee of the Trustees, to watch over the College funds, and an auditing
committee appointed each year to examine the accounts of
the Treasurer, and finally that the Treasurer annually submitted to the Board, a summary of the fiscal affairs of the
College during the year in detail.

Ignorance of the true condition of the College, and inat-
6 tention to their duties, can not then be imputed to the
Trustees, and certainly not to the gentlemen who made the
reports above mentioned.

Before you will adopt the other incredible alternative,
that these Trustees willfully and wickedly abandoned the
rights and interests of the College to the cupidity of its
President, you will demand such clear, unequivocal evidence, as shall amount to demonstration; such as you would
7 require if you were yourselves subjected to such atrocious
charges.

There is another individual, whose reputation is still
more deeply involved in these charges. A venerable man
who has passed his eightieth year, occupied for sixty years
of that time, in the offices of a minister of the gospel,
whose whole private life has never been tarnished, even by
the suspicion of crime, whose exemplary conduct has won
8 him the esteem, the veneration of his cotemporaries, who
has for fifty years been engaged in the instruction of thou-
sands of the youth of our country, in science, morals, and
the principles of the christian religion, and around whom
the warmest affections and the deepest sympathies of those
youths, now become men, and many of them old men, in
all the professions, departments and walks of life, gather
and cluster as around a father; this venerable man, whose
9 early manhood and mature age, have been exclusively de-

voted to this college, is now arraigned on charges of fraud and robbery, and systematic plunder of the child of all his love and hopes.

Gentlemen, it is monstrous; it is against the whole course of nature; it belies all our experience. And what degree of evidence will you, and every man who is not
himself a rogue, and judges others by himself, what degree 10
of evidence should be required to sustain such charges, under such circumstances?

And by whom are these charges brought forward? No man that is, or ever was a trustee, or in any way connected with the college, instigated or abetted these charges, or the enquiries which led to this investigation. No man having any interest in the college, from his associations or his
residence, stirs in the matter. But strangers, from remote 11
parts of the State, or recently removed to this State, who never lifted a finger for the college, and never expressed the least interest in its welfare, have suddenly become its only friends and protectors against the alleged rapacity and guilty confederacy of its natural and official guardians; and have found a subordinate ready and anxious to help them in their chivalrous enterprise. Direct proof of
secret motives is not to be expected. But before we finish 12
our labors, sufficient will appear to cast a dark shade on the justice, honor, and good faith of the conspirators.

Such are the prominent circumstances in which you enter upon this investigation. There are intrinsic and extrinsic difficulties and obstacles in arriving at results, of uncommon character. Most of the men who were engaged in the transactions which are now re-opened after a repose
of thirty, forty and fifty years, sleep with their fathers; of 13
those that remain, the infirmities of age disqualify most of them from giving any explanations. Even my venerable client, whose reasoning faculties has been so wonderfully preserved, cannot be expected to possess a memory that could recall the circumstances which might relieve from obscurity many of these complicated transactions.

And unfortunately the books and papers of the college, 14

of the periods referred to, afford little light. Literary institutions were never famous for strict book-keeping; their
officers have duties, and are engaged in pursuits of a different character. The same test cannot be applied to them,
as to the books of account of bankers and large mercantile
concerns. And Union College seems to have been particularly unfortunate in this respect. The person who was
15 treasurer for twenty-six years, after 1807, has himself furnished us good evidence in his books, that he was far from
being a good accountant. During the latter years of his
service, he was engaged at New-York as a partner with the
contractors, and his interests were not those of the college.
He left his books and papers in the hands of an incompetent clerk, and when he resigned, a committee of the trustees found great irregularities in his accounts, and a con-
16 siderable balance against him from that cause. The present treasurer and acting treasurer, have testified that no
vouchers or papers of the long period referred to, are to be
found, after the most diligent inquiry. The treasurer who
succeeded Mr. Yates is dead, and young men occupy the
place.

I have a right to ask, whether from such materials, any
evidence can be expected of such a character as is demand-
17 ed, to overcome the presumptions against the truth of
these charges, stated in the commencement of these remarks? I trust that this question will be borne in mind
during the discussion upon which I am about to enter.

A history of the events that led to your appointment
as a committee, will be found useful in our subsequent
progress.

In 1849, March 12, the Assembly adopted a resolution,
18 requiring a full report of the condition of the college, to
which a full answer was made April 5, 1849, purporting
to be the result of an examination of the fiscal transactions
of the college for the last twenty-five years.

This report was, on the 11th of April, 1849, referred by
the Assembly to its committee on colleges, academies and
common schools, of which Mr. Beekman, a member from
New-York, was a member, with instructions to examine
19 into the financial condition of Union College, with power

to send for persons and papers, and to report to the next Legislature. (See beginning of Assembly Document, No. 190, 1850.)

On the 19th of March, 1850, Mr. Beekman and three others of the committee made a report, concluding that "the financial condition of Union College is unsound and improper."

The majority say that they met at Schenectady, on the 20
15th of May last, (1849,) and held their meetings at the
college. "Very full explanations of the financial transactions of the college, were made by the President and
Treasurer, both being always present;" page 1 of report.
This report contained very serious charges against the officers of the college, particularly the President, which had
never been specified to them, and of which no answers or
explanations had been required. On the 23d of March, 21
1850, Mr. Pruyn, one of the committee, made a minority
report—Document No. 190. He says, p. 1, that on the
meeting of the committee, "the President, immediately,
placed at the disposal of the committee, a room in one of
the college edifices, and devoted his whole time to facilitate the investigation, and make it as thorough as possible." "The President and Treasurer of the college were 22
examined on oath."

After a very elaborate examination of all the points made by the minority report, Mr. Pruyn, the chairman of the committee, and who had moved the resolution of enquiry, entirely dissents from the conclusions of the majority, and expresses his confidence in the soundness of the pecuniary condition of the college.

On the 8th of April, 1850, the Treasurer of Union Col- 23
lege made the annual report to the Legislature, and appended to it, a reply to the report of the majority of the
Assembly committee.

This reply shows great inaccuracy in the statements of facts and the testimony by that majority.

In conclusion, in behalf of the resident Trustees, he asks,
that if his report be not satisfactory, a judicial proceeding
may be directed, to investigate the misconduct charged by 24

the committee, "with all the advantages of a legal procedure, in which the parties are brought face to face."

No action, however, was taken by the Assembly, although a motion was made, at the request of the officers of the college, to refer the reports to a committee, which was negatived. The inference is strong, that the answer of
25 the Treasurer was satisfactory.

I call attention to the facts, that the committee was appointed 11th April, 1849, that they assembled and made their investigations on the 15th of May, 1849; but that their report was withheld until the 19th of March, 1850, and that 21 days thereafter, the Legislature adjourned, viz: on the 10th day of April, 1850; and I submit whether there was not an intentional delay in making their report, so as
26 to prevent any answer to its fallacies and misstatements; and whether the omission to direct any further proceedings, was not an acknowledgment that their accusations had been repelled? Yet, the report of the majority of the committee was profusely scattered, not only in this State, but into adjoining States.

On the 12th of April, 1851, the same Mr. Beekman, who had figured, as already stated, in the Assembly of 1849
27 and 1850, being a member of the Senate from one of the New-York districts, and chairman of the Literature Committee of that body, made a report on his own responsibility, on the financial condition of Union College, without any new examinations, and founded wholly on that which had been made the preceding year, by the majority of the Assembly committee, entirely *ex parte*, without giving any opportunity to the Trustees or officers of Union
28 College to answer or explain. This miscalled report, was mainly a repetition of the charges in the report of the majority of the Assembly committee in 1850, with some new variations to escape the conclusive replies which the Treasurer had made.

This report, also, was extensively circulated, through the instrumentality of Mr. Beekman and his friends, and a large number of copies were left at the office of a daily
29 newspaper in Albany, for gratuitous distribution, through

the agency, and with the approbation of Mr. Beekman;
and the publisher of the paper, in coarse vituperative terms,
invited people to call at his office for these copies.

In this report, Mr. Beekman proposed that the Comptroller, Attorney-General and John N. Campbell, a Regent
of the University, should be appointed to employ an accountant, to send for persons and papers, to examine into 30
the pecuniary affairs of Union College, and report upon the
same to the next Legislature. (See Senate Journal of 1851,
page 526.) This proposition, put in the form of a resolution, was adopted without debate. Mr. Beekman, the accuser, who had become committed by his reports to serious
accusations, thus himself named the commissioners who
were to investigate.

The Legislature adjourned on the 17th of April, 1851.
With all his materials before him for more than a year, 31
Mr. Beekman thus waits until the close of the session to
bring forth in another form his accusations, evidently for
the purpose of precluding reply. The indefinite and unlimited scope of the enquiry "to examine into the pecuniary affairs of Union College," was calculated to afford
abundant opportunity for the indulgence of prejudice and
animosity in the investigation of the transactions of half a
century, with every person and on every subject, whether 32
connected with the legislative grants or not.

And I will not refrain from remarks on the complexion
of the commission named by the accuser, without any opportunity being afforded to the parties accused to state any
exceptions they might have against the persons named,
and to endeavor to procure an impartial tribunal.

The two executive officers of the State, the most burthen-
ed with official duties, and the least likely to be able to 33
devote any time to the subject, were selected to conduct an
enquiry of such great magnitude and complexity, and embracing a period of fifty-five years. To them was added,
a clergyman, named in the resolution, "a Regent of the
University," as if that were the reason for selecting him
out of twenty-three gentlemen, most of them accountants
and men of business. Probably the least competent member of the Board of Regents was thus selected by Mr. 34

Beekman. Whether the motive for this selection is to be
found in the notorious fact that an unfriendly state of feeling towards Dr. Nott, amounting to animosity, had long
existed and continued to exist in the mind of the individual
selected, must be left for the judgment of those who shall
become acquainted with the subsequent history of this in-
35 vestigation.

Fortunately, an extra session of the Legislature of 1851
was held, commencing in June of that year. The opportunity was used by some senators to correct to some extent
the former proceeding. Two additional members, David
Buel and Philip S. Van Rensselaer, two other Regents of
the University, were added to the commission, and a resolution was passed by the Senate, defining the purposes and
objects of enquiry, and restraining the commissioners within
36 the range of legislative authority; and the commission
were directed "themselves, or a majority of them, personally to visit the college and '*re-examine* the proceedings
heretofore had in relation thereto" (Senate Journal, 28th
June, 1851). On the 27th of May, 1851, the commission
appointed Mr. Levinus Vanderheyden accountant, and on
the 14th of October they appointed Mr. Philip Ford his
37 assistant, with an allowance to the former of $150 per
month, and to the latter of $75 per month. (See report
of commission: Document No. 40, Senate documents of
1852.)

On the 27th of February, 1852 (Sen. Doc. No. 40.), the
commission made a report pursuant to two resolutions of
the Senate, of June 21st and June 23d.

This resolution of June 23d, was calculated to bring out
38 a mutilated and partial report of particular transactions
which, unexplained, would appear unfavorable to Dr.
Nott and the college; and although the commission say
in their report in answer to it, that the examination had
extended only to the year 1820, from the year 1795, yet
they obligingly comply with the resolution, and make a
report which embraces transactions down to 1849, and
presents statements quite different from those subse-
39 quently reported by them, and prepared by the same ac-

countant. This report was wholly *exparte*, no opportunity having been given to controvert or explain the transactions, and being made even without the knowledge of the officers of the college. Its main object seems to have been to prejudice Dr. Nott, by representing him as having borrowed and used the funds of the college to the amount of $560,000.

Before we finish the investigation, you will have learned
to your entire satisfaction, that Dr. Nott was not a borrow- 40
er of the funds of the college for his own use, or for his
private benefit; that the only loans made to him were of
moneys laid out in purchases of property for the college, and for improvements of its real estate and buildings,
and that the other advances were made for the purpose of
saving to the college the utmost amount of interest on the
money paid to the treasurer. He was in the habit of withdrawing such moneys with the sanction of the finance com- 41
mittee, temporarily upon his own notes or obligations on
interest, until he could safely invest them permanently,
and then substituting the securities which he had received
for his own. And in addition to his personal responsibility and the collateral securities he temporarily left with
the treasurer, there was always on deposit with the treasurer, private and individual funds belonging to him, far 42
exceeding the amounts thus temporarily withdrawn. Yet
these transactions, most of which carry on their face evidence of their being of the character described, were thus
promulgated as personal loans for speculative purposes;
and an impression was produced that Dr. Nott had wantonly violated all the duties of his station, and jeoparded
the very existence of the college by such an illegal and
wicked perversion of its funds. And this report too, was 43
circulated with great activity throughout the country, by
Mr. Beekman and his friends.

Previous to the making of this last report, a committee
of the Trustees of Union College, consisting of R. H. Walworth, R. M. Blatchford, A. Hunt and B. R. Wood, had,
on the 23d of July, 1851, addressed a respectful letter to
the members of the commission, requesting the appointment of a time and place for the investigation, that they 44

might attend it in behalf of the college, for which purpose they had been appointed. Without notice to them, or to any Trustee or officer of the college, the calumnious report above mentioned was prepared by the accountant, and transmitted by Mr. Campbell, in behalf of the commission, to the Senate.

Our history now brings us to the report of the majority
46 of the commission, made March 5, 1853, containing the
voluminous statements of the accountant referred to you.
These statements were never submitted for examination to
the treasurer or any officer of the college, nor was an opportunity ever given to them or to the Trustees to examine
them. Such an opportunity had been respectfully requested by a portion of the Trustees who were resident in and
about Albany, who addressed a letter to each of the com-
47 missioners, previous to the meeting of the board, to receive
and consider the statements of the accountant, "soliciting
an opportunity of being heard by the board, in explanation of the said statements, and to correct them if necessary before they should be acted upon by them and sent to
the Senate." (See Memorial of Trustees, March 12,
1853.)

Mr. John N. Campbell, the chairman of the Board assured
48 the President of the College and another Trustee that "when
the accountant was through with the books, the commissioners would visit the College and make the requisite personal
enquiries, and give the Trustees an opportunity of meeting
the charges made against them, and of explaining the difficulties which might arise," and that the proposed answer
of the Trustees should be presented with the report of the
Commission, to the Senate. Similar communications
49 were made to other members of the Commissioners, and
similar assurances were made by them to different Trustees.
(The memorial of Dr. Nott, March 14, 1853, and statement
of the Rev. Dr. Van Vechten, Doc. XXIII.) The manner in
which these engagements were fulfilled, will be shown by an
extract from the report of Messrs BUEL and VAN RENSSELAER,
of March 3, 1853. After stating the application of the trustees of the college for a hearing, these gentlemen say: "the
50 undersigned were desirous of affording them such an oppor-

tunity, but the two members of the commission above refer-
ed to (J. N. Campbell and J. C. Wright) *refused* to afford
such an opportunity, and insisted on transmitting to your
honorable body the statements and schedules, proposed by
the accountant." The accountant Vanderheyden, also
promised repeatedly that he would visit the College and
submit to the President for examination, his schedules, be- 51
fore they were submitted to the Commissioners for their
action thereon. (Memorial of Trustees, March 12, 1853 and
of Dr. Nott, March 14, 1853, and testimony of Gen. George
R. Davis, (Doc. XLIV.) Have I not a right to say, that there
could be no motive or reason for such a gross violation of common justice and of solemn engagements sufficient to overcome
all sense of propriety, other than the apprehension that an
impartial and thorough investigation would overthrow fore- 52
gone conclusions, and add immeasurably to the difficulties
of presenting to the Senate, the materials that had been
collected?

The value of the report as *authority* for any thing it contains, may be determined by the following considerations.
Two of the Commission, Messrs Buel and Van Rensselaer,
say in their report, "these statements and schedules are quite
voluminous, and the undersigned have had no sufficient
opportunity to examine them, and form any opinion of the 53
principle on which they have been made out, or the data
on which they are founded; *nor was there any explanation
of those principles and data given to the commission.*" Mr.
Wright, the Comptroller, from the multiplicity of his official labors, could not possibly have devoted the necessary
time to examine, comprehend and compare these voluminous statements of 190 printed pages, and it is understood
that he has repeatedly declared that he never did examine 54
them, but signed the report in full faith in the intelligence
and integrity of the accountant.

Mr. J. N. Campbell, from his profession and pursuits is,
notoriously incapable of such an investigation, and it is
understood that he also has declared that he knew nothing
about these statements, but took them on the word or oath
of the accountant.

The Attorney General, Mr. Chatfield, has given a very 55

cautious certificate, and simply "concurs in the above report." In fact, as I am informed, Mr. Vanderheyden, the
accountant, repaired to New-York city, where the Attorney General was officially employed, with the balance
sheets, schedule No. 2 and statement No. 1, at pages 8, &c.,
and 81, &c., of the majority report, and awaking Mr. Chat-
56 field from his slumbers at or after midnight, showed these
two statements to him, that he spent perhaps fifteen minutes in looking at them, and then wrote and signed the
cautious concurrence which appears in the report.

There is quite strong evidence on the face of the statements, that the three commissioners who transmitted them
to the Senate never read them. At page 133 of the report,
after giving his views of the transactions respecting the
57 Hunter farm and the Stuyvesant Cove property, the accountant remarks: "The accountant respectfully submits
to the commission the propriety of making the proper
charge for both these parcels of land, with the accruing
interest, to the account of Eliphalet Nott." As all his
charges to the account of Dr. Nott were subject to the approbation of the commission, this particular designation
indicates his own doubts of the correctness of these items,
58 and he therefore specially invokes the judgment of the
commissioners respecting them. The majority of the commissioners, in their preliminary abstract of the results of
the accountant's statements, set down, at p. 2, the President's indebtedness for the Hunter and Stuyvesant property, ... $184,256 06
Interest, ... 184,770 13

The accountant however states at p. 133, the principal of
59 the Hunter farm at, ... $100,000 00
And of the Stuyvesant Cove property at, ... 58,632 15

Making, ... $158,632 15

Instead of the $184,256.06 of the commissioners.

The accountant, also, at p. 133, states the interest on the
Hunter farm at, ... $99,555 54
And on the Stuyvesant property, ... 57,847 12

60 Making, ... $157,402 66

Instead of the $184,770.13 of the commissioners.

But if it be supposed the commissioners intended to include in the interest the incidental charges on the Hunter farm at p. 134, amounting to, ... $8,657 91

And the payments on the Stuyvesant property at p. 135 to 138, amounting to,....... 52,991 39 61

Making,.......................... $61,649 30

Adding the above interest,............... 157,402 66

Makes,............................ $219,051 96

Which is still more wide of the mark.

Nor will the total of the sums given by the commissioners agree with the total of the accountant's items.

The total of their two items of principal and interest is,................................ $369,026 19 62

The total of the accountant's, exclusive of the incidental charges, is,................. 296,034 81

Including those charges it is,............. 377,684 11

So that in no way do they agree.

A similar instance is furnished at p. 188, where the accountant submits to the decision of the commission, the propriety of crediting Dr. Nott with $29,430.92, a supposed 63
balance of the $150,000 bond.

No opinion appears any where, to have been expressed on this question by the commissioners.

All sanction or authority for the accuracy of the statements and accounts in the report, must therefore be derived from the accountant alone. The value of this authority may be determined from the following considerations:

1. He was appointed an *accountant*, an office which, by
the name, implies the duty only of examining existing 64
items of account, reducing them to form, and stating the result. And so the commissioners regarded the duty, for they say his statement is believed by them "to be a true and full exhibit of the pecuniary condition of that institution, as presented by said books and vouchers, as authenticated annually by the treasurer thereof." (p. 1 Report.)

Now, it has appeared to the committee, and is avowed
by the accountant in his testimony, that he has wholly dis- 65
regarded the books of the college on the most important

question involved in the investigation, namely, the amounts
received from lotteries; has derived them from the pleadings
in a suit in chancery between Yates & McIntyre and
the Trustees of the college; and that he has in other instances
wholly set aside the entries in the college books,
and has resorted to the private books of its adversaries in
66 litigation, for amounts paid the treasurer, of which the
books furnish no evidence. And he declares, in his testimony,
that he acted as "vice chancellor," as he terms it;
of which there is abundant proof in numerous instances
where he has made arbitrary charges upon his own crude
and ridiculous notions of equity, and has set aside the most
formal acts, settlements and agreements of the Trustees,
made with the President and other parties. In all this,
67 he has palpably violated his duty, and in doing so, has
evinced a determination to sustain a foregone conclusion
at all hazards.

2. During his examination before you, he has performed
in the alternate characters of accountant, counsel and
prosecutor, and witness; so that it was often difficult to determine
in which he was speaking. In all these characters
he has evinced an intemperate zeal, a tenacity to his own
68 statements, which have resisted all criticism on them
and all scrutiny of his accounts as a personal indignity.
Instead of being solicitous for the development of pure
and simple truth, he has aimed only to maintain his own
infallibility.

3. After his duties as accountant were at an end, by his
final report, and its transmission to the Senate, he volunteered
to transmit to that body, his own affidavit and the
69 statements and affidavits of others upon collateral subjects,
and not sustaining a single item in his account, but calculated
and intended to asperse Dr. Nott and represent him
as a swindler; every one of which aspersions has been triumphantly
refuted before you, as will be shown in the
course of this argument. These papers were never submitted
to the Commission, never passed upon by them, and
of course formed no part of their report. Yet, by the co-
70 operation of his co-adjutor, Mr. James W. Beekman, they

were ordered to be printed, without any opportunity to meet and contradict their calumnious contents, and they were made the theme of declamation by Mr. Beekman in the Senate for days, as if they had been recorded verdicts of impartial juries. The Senate was made instrumental in their publication, and they were actually ordered to be attached to the official report of the Commissioners. Is it
not evident that these affidavits and statements thus fur- 71
nished, were prepared in pursuance of a settled plan, to give an opportunity for a Senator to abuse the privilege of his station, by stabbing in the back a man whom he wished to destroy? And the accountant thus became a party or a tool in the accomplishment of this unworthy design.

While there was pending in the Senate, a proposition to
give the accused Trustees and President of Union College, 72
one opportunity to meet the atrocious charges against them, by the appointment of an impartial Committee, this same accountant, with the view of defeating that proposition, made the voluntary communication of affidavits and statements above mentioned; and also published in two daily papers of the city of Albany, a wanton, scurrilous attack and libel upon Dr. Nott, rehashing some of the
most venomous and unwarrantable charges in his accounts, 73
and adding one of a diabolical character, imputing to Dr. Nott a deliberate and persevering attempt for many hours to induce him, Mr. Vanderheyden to commit a direct and palpable forgery of the books of Union College. That his charge has been proved by himself to be atrociously false, only aggravates the malevolence with which it was made. (See Doc. XLIV.)

His conduct before you has exhibited, especially when 74
put off his guard by his passions, the most spiteful malignity against Dr. Nott. He has sought occasions, not required in defence of his accounts, to malign and insult him in the most offensive terms, and has scarcely been restrained by intimations that it would not be permitted with impunity. He has taken every opportunity and made oppor-

75 tunities, to insinuate and make charges of personal misconduct in matters with which he had no concern.

The conduct described under the three last heads, proves this man to be a most dangerous and unreliable witness in any matter affecting Dr. Nott.

4. He has stated the accounts of the college in a manner
utterly unintelligible, the result either of incapacity or of
the difficulty of making error consistent. I appeal to the
76 recollection of every member of the committee for corroboration of the remarks, that it has required the most tedious
and protracted examination of the accountant to comprehend the reason of his charges and credits, and his manner of stating them; and that he has entered important
items which were the results of complicated deductions
and off-sets, of which no trace is furnished by his accounts
or his tables, so that if he were not present to explain
77 them, no mortal could comprehend them; indeed, this
very remark was made to him by one or two of the committee during the investigation.

5. He has, himself, stultified his own account, for after
spending eighteen months in making it up, he insists, at
this late day, that he has committed errors to the amount
of $65,000, which he says he omitted to charge against
Dr. Nott. He seems to be wholly indifferent to or incapa-
78 ble of perceiving the utter derangement of all his balances
by such additions; and that if true, they exhibit debts due
to the college without any corresponding means on which
they could be founded. Besides those omitted charges
which he now claims to make, he, as counsel has admitted,
that there are charges against Dr. Nott which are erroneous to a considerable amount. He has been convicted, by
proof before yon, of making charges directly in the face
79 of facts recorded in his own report and in the minutes and
books of the college. I allude to his charge against A.
Holland, for dividends on Mohawk bank stock, which he
claimed to belong to the college, when his own statement
showed that it belonged to Mr. Freeman, to whom Mr.
Holland had paid it, and for similar payments to Dr. Nott,
when the books of the college showed the stock had been

transferred to him ; and I particularly allude to his charge
of $400 against Dr. A. Potter, when the very resolution of 80
the trustees to which he referred, showed that it was a repayment for money advanced in the purchase of books.
There are other undeniable errors, but these are selected
because he seemed to admit their inaccuracy.

And yet, he had the rashness, to use the most moderate
phrase, at the very end of the investigation, to volunteer
a statement on his oath as a witness, that the accounts and
statements in his printed report, excepting the new claims 81
he set up against Dr Nott, were accurate and true!

Gentlemen, can this man be relied on for fairness and
truth?

You might indeed give him full credence where his
statements are sustained and corroborated by the books of
the college, as remarked by the chairman of the committee. But in that case, you believe the books, not him. 82
He cannot be sustained by the books of the college in these
accounts, because he avows himself that he has repudiated
those books, and sought information elsewhere, and on that
information has made charges. But besides, he has in
many instances stated large amounts, embracing incalcula-
bly numerous items which are not given, and the accuracy of which amounts it is impossible to test by the books
without a year's labor. Instances are found, of enor- 83
mous amounts of interest received on various accounts for
the last twenty-five years, amounting to $303,661.38; in-
terest paid amounting to $232,500; tuition or term bills
amounting to $335,041.50; salaries, regular and extra,
paid to the president and professors, $526,275.26, besides
many others of less amount. In respect to these you have
no evidence but his own assertion. It is impossible either
to sustain or contradict him. His credibility then, becomes 84
a point of the last importance in determining on the results he has stated.

6. As to his capacity and skill as an accountant. I deny
that there is any such difficulty or mystery in the science
of book-keeping as he pretends. An entry in an account
is a verdict upon facts, or a judgment upon the law and

the facts. Common sense, an impartial mind, and a
85 knowledge of sound legal principles, when they are involved in the case, will enable a man to state truly and
intelligently any account and its results. A drudging
patience and labor, which characterize an ox, are not the
only qualifications for an accountant. The mere man of
figures, may correctly sum up and arrange admitted items.
But when the items are disputed, when the question is
whether they are chargeable at all, or to any particular
86 person or party, it passes beyond the domain of the accountant and becomes matter for judicial decision. The
utter incompetency of Mr. Vanderheyden for such an office
has been most apparent throughout the whole of this investigation.

I do not claim that his character for truth as a man or
for integrity as an accountant has been impeached by the
testimony. On the contrary, I cheerfully concede that the
87 preponderance of evidence on that subject is decidedly in
his favor.

But I do claim what your own observation must have
established in your minds, that he is a man of violent feelings and prejudices, without sufficient moral or intellectual
force to restrain them: that he is therefore an unsafe witness in any case. And further, that the existence of such
feelings and prejudices against Dr. Nott has been abundantly
88 shown, and that they have been manifested in the modes
already described, especially in the admitted falsity of his
publications, and in his final, unasked and reckless oath
to the entire accuracy of his accounts.

I now propose to pursue the investigation in the order indicated by the resolution for your appointment, and to furnish answers to each of the objects of enquiry therein specified.

89 The resolution for your appointment directs that the report of the majority and of the minority of the commission be referred to you "to investigate the matters specified in the Senate resolutions of June and July, 1851," and to report "the results of their enquiries, and their opinions thereon."

The following are the resolutions of June and July, 1851:

"*Resolved*, That the commission appointed by the Senate 90
on the 12th of April, 1851, to employ a skillful accountant
to examine the pecuniary affairs of Union College, and to
report upon the same, be instructed, themselves, or a majority of them, personally to visit the College, and re-examine the proceedings heretofore had in relation thereto, and to investigate and to report to the next Legislature upon the following subjects connected with said College:

1. Whether the funds granted by the State to Union Col- 91
lege have been duly applied to the objects specified in the respective grants;

2. Whether the permanent funds so granted remain entire, and are safely invested;

3. Whether any funds belonging to the College have been applied to any personal purpose by the president, or any other officer or person;

4. Whether any and what losses have occurred in the 92
management of the College, and the causes of such losses;

5. Whether the president or any other officer has, while in the employment of the College, participated individually in the profits of any lotteries which were appropriated by the acts granting such lotteries to Union College; and that the commission appointed by the resolution referred to, or a majority of them, be empowered to employ some person
authorised by law to administer an oath to persons ex- 93
amined by such commission."

The first inquiry is, whether the funds granted by the State to Union College have been duly applied to the objects specified in the respective grants?

It will be observed that this inquiry relates exclusively to the grants made by the State.

A full and accurate statement of these grants is contained in a book herewith presented, called Fund Book. The 94
several amounts may be compared with the different acts of the Legislature making the grants, which are printed in the appendix to the report of the accountant, p. 191 to

200. An account is opened with each one of those grants, and with each object of the several grants.

Under the act making the grant will be found a reference to the account, with the object, where the amount of
95 the grant will be found properly charged to the college,
and accounted for. Each of these will be found clear, distinct, and unquestionable; and no special remark is necessary in relation to them, except, perhaps, the account under the act of 1814, granting $200,000 and six years interest.

At folio 77 will be found an account of the interest received, and the place in the ledger where it is credited in
96 the general account of the college, and accounted for by
the general expenses.

In the middle of the page, fol. 8, each sum is accounted for by reference to the account, with the object to which it was appropriated; and by recurring to that account it will be found credited there, and accounted for; and the committee will see that not only every dollar granted by the State has been applied to the objects specified in the re-
97 spective grants, but that in most instances the monies now
appropriated to these objects exceed the grants.

The second inquiry is, whether the *permanent funds* so granted remain entire and are safely invested?

The permanent funds referred to, are those which were directed to be invested, yielding income which was to be applied to the specified object.

These permanent funds are the following:

1. That for the aid of indigent students.

98 Pages 23, 24, of the Fund book, show that the whole
sum, $50,000, appropriated for that object, is invested in bonds and mortgages, except $5.89.

Pages 30, 31, show that the *income* of this fund has been applied to the object, and an excess of $16,523.93.

2. That for the support of the President and Professors.

The principal of this fund is $78,483.93

The accounts at pp. 35, 36, 37, show investments to
99 the amount of $78,705.78.

The application of the income is shown at pp. 38, 39,

and which exhibit an excess of expenditures on 1st January, 1849, of $292,432.30.

It appears from the accounts presented to you, that the income received from the fund appropriated for the sup-

port of the President and Professors,......	$193,966 72	
From tuition, ...	335,041 50	
And from the income for indigent students,	108,505 61	100
Amount to,................	$637,513 83	

While the expenditures for the President and Professors, and for indigent students, was $652,425.69; showing an excess of expenditures $14,911.86.

With regard to the second branch of this inquiry, whether these permanent funds are *safely* invested?

1. That for the aid of indigent students is proved to be 101
perfectly safe in undoubted bonds and mortgages.

2. That for the support of the President and professors, is also shown by the testimony to be safely invested in bonds and mortgages of undoubted security and in sound stocks.

The third inquiry is, whether any funds belonging to the college have been applied to any personal purpose by 102
the President, or any other officer or person?

Of course, the funds have been applied to the payment of salaries of the President and officers, and their official expenses; and they have been invested, to some extent, in loans to officers of the college, and to others.

It cannot be supposed that the inquiry relates to these. It is supposed to mean, whether any funds have been di-
verted from their legitimate purposes, and *improperly* ap- 103
plied to mere personal purposes—to the private benefit of the President or other officer or person, in fraud, and to the injury of the college.

Of course, the President and officers of the college stand upon the defensive, and can have nothing to say, except to make a general and emphatic denial, until some misapplication of the kind is pointed out.

The zeal of the accountant has presented two instances, 104
which he claims are of this character, the use of the two

and a quarter per cent fund, for supervision and management of the lotteries, sometimes called the President's fund, and the use of twenty-two notes given on settlement by Yates & McIntyre. These will be examined hereafter in their proper order.

So far as respects the pecuniary interest of the College
105 the discussion of the validity of the claims thus set up, is quite immaterial. The funds which are the subject of those claims, are already devoted to the College, an instrument to that effect, and his will confirming the same, drawn under the best legal advice, have been executed by the President, and deposited with the Treasurer. (See Holland's testimony in doc. XXXIV, folio 250.) The execution of the instrument was delayed until the laws should be
106 passed, which the President was advised were necessary to render the proposed trusts, legal and valid. (Doc. XXXIV, folios 245, 248.)

To understand fully, and particularly the questions now to be discussed, it becomes absolutely necessary to give a history of the College and of Dr. Nott's connexion with it, and his exertions for its benefit; of the laws passed for its relief, of the proceedings under those laws, and of the agree-
107 ments and stipulations entered into at different times, the settlements made with Yates and McIntyre and with their representatives, and between the College and the President.

The want of such a connected history has doubtless caused the difficulty that has been felt in comprehending transactions of a diversified and complicated character, occurring during a term of more that half a century.

108 A number of gentlemen in the then county of Albany, associated together in 1795, for the purpose of establishing a college, and having procured subscriptions for its endowment to the amount of thirty thousand dollars only, obtained a charter from the Regents of the University incorporating Union College, and establishing it at Schenectady, which bears date July 7, 1795.

The Rev. John B. Smith, was chosen the first President
109 in 1795, when he repaired to Schenectady, and opened the

college to a few students, who recited in the old academy. From the papers that are left, particularly the remnants of accounts, it is evident that the college made very little progress, and was much embarrassed. Dr. Smith resigned in 1799, in consequence, it is understood, of the failure of all his expectations. Dr. Jonathan Edwards was chosen
President in April, 1799, and died in office in 1801. In 110
September, of that year, Dr. Jonathan Maxcy was elected President, and having struggled against the embarrassments of the college, arising from its want of pecuniary means, resigned in 1804.

The condition of the college now seemed desperate. An edifice to accommodate the students had been commenced, but its progress was suspended by the utter want
of means to advance in its erection. There were about 111
thirty students lodged in the city of Schenectady, among its inhabitants, occupying such rooms as could be found, and reciting in the academy building. Nine years had elapsed without any perceptible improvement in the condition or prospects of the college; on the contrary, its pecuniary resources had been expended; it possessed no means, except an edifice partly completed, and a few books.
Of the pecuniary appropriations by the Legislature, there 112
remained nothing.

In this emergency, the attention of the trustees was directed to the Rev. Eliphalet Nott, then occupying the position of pastor of the First Presbyterian church in the city of Albany. His activity and devotion to the duties of his station, had collected a congregation altogether the largest in the city, and which could scarcely find accom-
modations within one of its capacious churches. The fame 113
of his talents, particularly of his surpassing eloquence, had overspread the land. He seemed to be the man destined by Providence, to build up a seminary of learning of the highest grade, in the northern part of the State, which was entirely destitute of any such institution, there being but one college then in the whole State, at its most remote eastern and southern extremity, namely, Columbia college
in the city of New-York. 114

When the Presidency of Union College was tendered to
Mr. Nott, in July, 1804, he was occupied in a sphere of
duty for which his great success had shown his peculiar
fitness. Beloved, not to say adored by a congregation composed of the most intellectual, as well as the most refined
and respectable men in the State, exercising an unbounded
influence in the promotion of religious and charitable ob-
115 jects, with a salary beyond his moderate wants, happy in
his family, happy in his associates, and surrounded by
everything to gratify his taste or his ambition, if he possessed any, no position could be more enviable. The call
to abandon this position of usefulness and happiness, and
to undertake a task in which so many able and accomplished men had been baffled, to encounter certain poverty,
at least for a while, to create the materials for a college
116 out of absolutely nothing, to court expense, difficulty,
toil and labor, was a severe trial of the christian principles which he professed. But he thought he beheld a path
of duty evidently indicated to him, and he made the sacrifice of his position. He accepted the offer, relinquished
a station around which all his affections clustered, and
entered at once upon the perilous undertaking.

This event, with its attending circumstances, has been
117 thus fully stated, because it furnishes the key to all the
movements of his subsequent life. It was a sacrifice—a
mighty sacrifice of present enjoyment and a future of hope
and happiness to the cause of education, at a time and in
a region of country when the demands of that cause were
most vehement and importunate. As his devotion to it
began in sacrifice, so the history of Union College will
show that it was constantly accompanied by continued
118 sacrifice of time, labor, and even exposure to obloquy, and
by a noble disinterestedness which consecrated all the
fruits of industry the most untiring, of a profound and
far-reaching sagacity, and of a wonderful capacity to make
everything available, to a cause which he well knew to be
essential to the formation of the character of the rising
generation.

One of his first efforts was to obtain a legislative endow-
119 ment of the college. The State treasury was quite low, the

value of public lands had not been developed, and without
some extraneous resource, no endowment could be granted.
Lotteries had in Europe and our own sister States, been
used to raise money for public, benevolent, and educational
purposes. Their evils had not been experienced, and the
morality of the age was not shocked by their being authorized. Academies, churches, colleges, hospitals, had been 120
endowed by their means. It was quite certain they would
be granted for some purposes, for such was the fashion of
the day, and no resistance of a moral character could have
prevented them. It was better to turn them into a chan-
nel where their beneficial results would to some extent
compensate for their evil consequences. Accordingly a
lottery was granted, although not solicited by the college,
which asked for money. By an act passed March 30, 1805, 121
(Chap. 62 of Session Laws of that year) four lotteries were
authorised to be drawn, to produce eighty thousand dollars, of which thirty-five thousand dollars was to be applied to the erection of additional edifices.

The necessity of a building for the accommodation of
students was most pressing and urgent. Indeed, without
it, there could be no control of the conduct of the pupils,
and the college was likely to become more a nursery of 122
vice than of virtue. In full reliance upon the avails of
these lotteries, and in the exigency of the case, the Trustees made loans of money to complete the edifice already
commenced, to organize a corps of professors, and to commence a classical library for the use of students in indigent
circumstances. Indeed, so strong was the conviction of
the Legislature of the necessity for prompt relief, that by
an act passed April 7, 1806, (Chap. 176, § 21) the Comp- 123
troller was directed to borrow $15,000 on the credit of the
State, and loan it to Union College, to be repaid out of the
avails of the lottery authorized the previous year. But
unfortunately the drawing of the four lotteries was not
completed until the year 1814. In consequence of this
great delay, the interest had accumulated on the loans so
much, that after paying the principal and interest on them,
the net avails of the lotteries amounted to only $76,138.01. 124

(See Report of Wm. James and Silas Wright, July 26, 1831, Doc. XXI.) This sum was applied according to the directions of the Legislature in the grant.

The Trustees and the President of the college struggled with these inadequate means, and although the number of pupils constantly augmented, yet this very increase caused additional expenses. Another application to the favor of
125 the Legislature therefore became necessary, and the President, Dr. Nott, was again obliged to put forth all his energies, and to invoke a further endowment.

The condition of the Treasury was, if possible, worse than before. A foreign war had imposed heavy burdens on the State, and another lottery was considered by the Legislature as affording the only means of relief. The college was then indebted $35,000. Accordingly, by an act passed
126 April 13, 1814, Chap. 120, lotteries were authorized to raise the following sums, which, by the act, were granted as follows:

To Union College, two hundred thousand dollars.

To Hamilton College, forty thousand dollars.

To the Asbury African Church in New-York, four thousand dollars.

To the College of Physicians and Surgeons, thirty thou-
127 sand dollars; with simple interest on these sums for not more than six years after the passing of the act.

At the end of the act, in the Session Laws of that year, the following note is published:

"*Note.*—No bill before the Legislature excited greater interest and attention than this act. Much credit is due to the unwearied exertions of the able and eloquent President of Union College in promoting its passage."

128 By the 51st section of chap. 200 of the laws of the same session, (1814) the managers of the lotteries, authorised by the former act, were directed, after the payment of the sums granted by it, to raise the additional sum of twelve thousand dollars, to be paid to the Historical Society in the city of New-York, but it contained no provision for the payment of interest.

The managers of these lotteries, appointed under the act,
129 were remiss in their duties, and heavy losses were sus-

tained in the sale of tickets. As their compensation was fixed and certain, their interest would be promoted by delay and procrastination rather than by diligence and expedition.

Nothing was realised from 1814 to 1822, to pay a dollar of the *principal sums* granted, and not even sufficient to
satisfy the interest. 130

Another vigorous effort became necessary to retrieve the errors of the past, and to render the Legislative grants of some avail. Again, the President of Union College put his shoulder to the wheel, and on the 5th of April, 1822, an act was passed (chapter 163,) entitled "An act to limit the continuance of lotteries," (Doc. II) The preamble of this act recites that the institutions to which grants were
made in the lottery, authorised by the act of 1814, "have 131
already suffered materially by delay in drawing the same," as a motive for the passage of the act. It authorised those institutions conjointly to assume, or to appoint one of their number to assume, the entire direction and supervision of the lottery, to appoint and remove the managers, to make such contracts in relation to the same as they should deem proper, to direct the time and manner of drawing,
and to recieve the avails and hazard the losses, and be re- 132
sponsible for the payment of the prizes. By section six, the avails of the lottery, *after deducting the expense of managing the same*, were to be paid to the institutions interested in the original grant, *until those grants were satisfied;* and by section seven, the grant of $12,000 to the Historical Society, was also to be paid.

The conditions in this act, by which the State was to be
absolved from all responsibility, and the whole hazard 133
was to be assumed by the institutions interested, naturally excited alarm and apprehension among the officers of those institutions who had witnessed the losses and utter failure of the proceedings of the managers for the preceding eight years. Hamilton College, the Asbury African church, and the College of Physicians and Surgeons, the original grantees with Union College could not be induced
to assume or to participate in those responsibilities. 134

Here was a new difficulty that seemed insuperable.
The wise provisions of the act of 1822, would prove abor-
tive, and the benefit of the grants would be lost, probably
forever, in consequence of the feeling which pervaded the
whole community, against the system of lotteries, and
which had compelled the insertion in the new constitution,
of an express prohibition of them, unless Union College
135 came to the rescue. Again, the President of that college
interposed to extricate it from this complication of difficulties. He proposed to the trustees of Union College, to
purchase the interest in the lottery of all the other institutions, and this being accomplished, to assume all the
hazards and responsibilities imposed by the act, to defray
all the expenses of the management, drawing and conduct
136 of the lottery.

The Trustees of Union College at a meeting on the 24th
of July 1822, concurred in this proposition, by authorizing
the Treasurer with the consent of the President, to accept
the provisions of the act of 1822, and to make such contracts relative to the said lottery as the President should
approve, and committing to the president the supervision
of the lottery, with authority to exercise in behalf of the
137 College *all the powers* vesting in it, by the provisions of the
act of 1822. (Doc. III, folio 13.)

If the contract of purchase from the other institutions,
could be perfected as proposed by the President and assented to by the Trustees, then Union College, would be "appointed" to assume the supervision and direction of the
lottery, within the express terms of the act of 1822, and
would be vested with all the powers conferred by that act.
138 By the resolution quoted, these powers were transferred to
the President.

The President immediately commenced operations to
purchase the interests of the other institutions in the lottery. This was effected with monies borrowed on the individual responsibility of the President, in connection with
that of the College, at the cost of $74,725.94 as stated by
139 the accountant (page 173, 174,) irrespective of interest, and

with a contingent obligation to Hamilton College, which will be hereafter noticed.

The act of 1822 provided that the several institutions should be limited in the drawing of the lottery, to such a time as should be determined by the Comptroller, which should be less at all events, than the time in which the
State could raise the amount, at the rate that monies had 140
hitherto been raised by lottery; and also, that the annual average amount of tickets to be drawn, should not exceed the annual average amount of tickets, according to their scheme price, which had been drawn in lotteries within five years previous to January 1, 1822, to be ascertained by the Comptroller; and that the time in which the lotteries were to be drawn, when so determined, and the annual
average of the whole when so ascertained should be certi- 141
fied by the Comptroller.

Accordingly, John Savage, then Comptroller, on the 9th of April 1822, certified that the amount then due to the several institutions, by virtue of the aforesaid grants, was three hundred and twenty two thousand, two hundred and fifty six dollars and eighty one cents, and that the same could be raised and paid in eleven years. And the Deputy
Comptroller, Ephraim Starr, certified that the amount of 142
tickets at their scheme price during the five years preceding the 1st of January, 1822, had been 1,679,000 dollars, and that to this should be added the further amount of the Oswego lottery, which was afterwards found to be 300,000 dollars, making the whole amount 1,979,000 dollars. (Doc. IV, folio 15 to 22, and folio 23 to 27.)

Calculating the annual average of tickets at the rate 143
thus certified by the Deputy Comptroller, the whole amount of tickets at their scheme price, to be drawn in 11 years, (the time fixed by the Comptroller,) would be $4,353,800

adding to this for the five months of time for drawing the amount subsequently granted to the Historical Society, which would be required according to the same rate.................. $139,000 144 made the total amount of tickets at their scheme price which might be drawn................ $4,492,800

The mode of raising money by the drawing of lotteries, authorized by the acts of the legislature previous to 1822, was by deducting from the amount of the prizes drawn in any lottery, fifteen per cent thereof, so that a nominal
145 prize of 10,000 dollars would be really 7,500 dollars; and in order to raise any given sum, the amount of the tickets to be sold and drawn in any lottery, was fixed at such a sum that fifteen per cent on the prizes therein would produce the amount required. (See Yates and McIntyre's bill in Chancery, produced by the accountant, p. 6 and 7.)

The compensation for supervision and management had
146 been fixed by sec. 25 of chap. 106 of the laws of 1819, at fifteen per cent. *on the sum raised* by each lottery, for all services and expenses in conducting and drawing the same. A short calculation will show that fifteen per cent. on the sum raised is equal to two and one-fourth of one per cent. upon the whole amount of tickets at their scheme price, drawn in any lottery. This system and these calculations were well known and understood at the time.

147 As the manager of a lottery could not be expected to undertake personally the sale of tickets, and encounter the hazards of having on hand any part of them when the drawing should close, it was expedient to enter into a contract with dealers to take the whole amount of tickets in a lottery, and dispose of them, and risk the contingency of effecting sales, as well as the hazard of loss from sales on credit to retail dealers. To compensate for this risk and
148 some expenses attending the drawings, an allowance must be made to the contractors out of the fifteen per cent. deducted from prizes. In the contract with Yates and McIntyre hereafter mentioned, this allowance was fixed at four per cent., part of the fifteen. The compensation for supervision and management, as already mentioned, was two and one-quarter per cent. Deducting these sums
149 would leave eight and three-quarters per cent. out of the

fifteen, for the purposes of the grant. Applying these principles to the whole amount of tickets to be sold and drawn at their scheme price, as above mentioned, $4,492,800,
eleven per cent. thereon would be.............. 494,208
deducting for management $2\frac{1}{4}$ per cent.,......... 101,088

would leave for the purpose of the grants $8\frac{3}{4}$,..$393,120
The remaining four per cent would be the allowance to 150
the contractors. But this sum of $393,120 was to be
raised in eleven years, according to the certificate of the
Comptroller. The present value of that sum, payable in
that time, was $276,090.14.

Having thus ascertained the present value of the grants
to all the institutions, and having acquired the interests of
the others, or having made arrangements for that purpose, 151
Dr. Nott, in pursuance of the authority given by the resolution of the trustees of Union College, of the 24th July,
1822, before quoted, approved a contract made under his
direction by the treasurer of Union College with John B.
Yates and Archibald McIntyre, dated July 29th, 1822, by
which, in consideration of $276,090.14, (the sum ascer-
tained as above mentioned,) for which Yates and McIntyre
gave their note, with interest annually, Union College 152
agreed to transfer to Yates and McIntyre "all the right
and title of the said party of the first part, in their own
right, and as legally representing the aforesaid institutions,
in and to the whole amount of tickets, *at their scheme
price*, authorised to be sold by virtue of the aforesaid act."

The allowance of two and a quarter per cent. on the
amount of prizes drawn, made by law for expenses and
services in the supervision and management of the lotte- 153
ries, remained to be provided for. This was done by a supplemental contract, made under the direction of the president, and approved by him, at the same time, between
the same parties, by which Yates and McIntyre agreed
"to pay for supervision and management, the same per
centum on each class, immediately after the drawing thereof, as has heretofore been paid to managers appointed by 154

the State," which was to be deposited in a bank to the credit of the president. (Doc. VI, folio 39.)

The same agreement contained a stipulation that Yates and McIntyre might elect to pay their note of $276,090.14 in annual instalments of $39,312, which were to be deposited, and they might anticipate such instalments, in which
155 case a rebate of interest was to be allowed them.

These contracts having been made, and Yates and McIntyre having completed their arrangements, they commenced the selling of tickets in the beginning of the month of April, 1823. (See their bill, p. 8.) They proceeded with apparent success for a year or two, when they became environed with difficulties and embarrassments from the want of funds, caused, as is believed, by their
156 adventuring in other speculations, and by a deficiency of prudence and economy. In their emergency they applied to Dr. Nott for assistance. The college could render them none, for it was much indebted, and its corporate responsibility could be of no avail under such circumstances. Yet it was evident that the fruits of so many years of toil and risk would be utterly lost, unless the contractors were enabled to proceed in the sale and drawing of tickets.
157 Dr. Nott came forward, by pledging his own and his wife's property, and by indefatigable personal exertions, he obtained credits and means to relieve Messrs. Yates and McIntyre. A reference to the particular evidence of these facts is reserved to another place in this discussion.

But Dr. Nott justly considered that the profits accruing from the use of the capital he had furnished, should not be exclusively appropriated to themselves by the contrac-
158 tors, and they were of the same opinion. There was also some disagreement between them and Dr. Nott, respecting the construction of their first agreement, relating to the rebate of interest.

Under these circumstances Messrs. Yates & McIntyre, on the 4th of January, 1826, addressed a proposition to Dr. Nott, (folio 88, Doc. IX,) wherein they recite that they have given their note for $276,090, and state that "such
159 have been our losses, that we have no reasonable prospect

of being able to pay the sum stipulated, or even to pay the prizes in the lottery now pending, unless we can procure immediate pecuniary assistance to a large amount." They therefore propose that Dr. Nott and the treasurer should raise for their immediate relief $100,000 and such further sum as should be necessary to sustain their credit. And, they say, "In consideration thereof, we are willing to pay 160
you such additional sum as shall, *together with* the $276,-090.14, for which we admit we are now holden, amount to eleven per cent on the whole amount of tickets sold, or to be sold by us; the same to be paid, estimating the per centum on the tickets sold, at their scheme price in each class, and in all the classes hitherto drawn, as well as those hereafter to be drawn under said act, immediately after the drawing thereof." This proposition having been ac- 161
ceded to, was reduced to a formal stipulation on the 24th of January, 1826. (Folio 106, Doc. XIII.)

The required assistance was furnished, and the contractors proceeded in the selling of tickets and drawing the classes of the lottery.

They had, however, become interested in the Fever Hospital lottery and in the Albany Land lottery, but which could not be drawn until the Literature lotteries were 162
finished, without the assent of Dr. Nott, nor could the tickets be sold and the drawings completed without his personal aid and credit. New propositions were made by them to him on this subject, and new stipulations entered into between them and Dr. Nott. But as it is universally conceded that the profits arising from these stipulations belonged exclusively to Dr. Nott personally, and that the college had no interest whatever in them, and the ac- 163
countant even can find no ground for claiming them for the college, it is not necessary to extend this narrative by particular notice of them. The claim which the accountant has interposed for the college after the completion of his labors, and nearly the close of the sittings of the committee, for some compensation out of these profits on account of a supposed delay in the drawing of the Literature lottery, by mixing a portion of the tickets with those of the 164

other lotteries, is so wholly unsupported by any evidence either of delay or injury, is so unlikely to have escaped the vigilance of such men as Wm. James, Silas Wright, A. C. Flagg, J. A. Dix, and others, and is so obviously an afterthought, that it is not deemed worthy of examination.

The drawings of the lottery were finished in Novem-
165 ber, 1827. (See last item on Cr. side of settlement of 1828, p. 33 of documents.)

Thus in four years and seven months from the time when the sales of tickets commenced, as before stated, in the beginning of April, 1823, and in five years and seven months from the passage of the act of 1822, these drawings, which it had been estimated by the Comptroller would require eleven years, were completed. Under whose agency and
166 by whose powerful aid this was accomplished, the correspondence of Yates & McIntyre abundantly shows.

In December, 1828, a settlement was made with Yates & McIntyre, of their liabilities and payments under their contracts and stipulations. The settlement bears date and is made as of August 1, 1828. A copy of it is given at pages 32, 33 documents, and in the accountant's report p. 176, &c.; although there is an error in the latter, in stating
167 the interest on the balance due at $12,506.16, which should be $21,506.16.

In this settlement Yates & McIntyre are charged, not with their note for $276,090.14 originally given, nor with annual instalments which they had at one time elected to pay, but with eight and three-quarters per cent. on each scheme of the different classes of lotteries as they were drawn, for the college, and two and a quarter per
168 cent on each of the said schemes, for the President's Fund, making eleven per cent, in strict conformity with the stipulations of January 4th and 24th of 1826.

On this settlement, Yates & McIntyre charged themselves, on account of the above mentioned eight and three-quarters per cent. on the scheme price of tickets in the different classes, a principal sum of, ... $433,002 23
And for interest, ... 79,231 39

169 Making, ... $512,233 62

The amount of Yates & McIntyre's original note was, ... $276,090 14

The int. thereon from April 1, 1823, (when interest commenced) to August 1, 1828, 5 years 4 months,.. 103,073 60

379,163 74 170

Leaving, as the profits derived from the stipulations of 4th and 24th January, 1826, $133,069 88 which were realized over and beyond the original note.

The balance owing by Yates and McIntyre upon their admitted liability as above, was $115,877.73 for principal, and $21,506.16, for interest, making $137,283 89
there was deducted from this, as belonging to the original agreement,.................. 4,214 01 171

which leaves the same balance before stated, $133,069 88

This sum was put into 24 notes, payable at different times, ending 1st December, 1831, with the interest included, and making in the whole,............ $162,713 78
Of this sum, there was appropriated to Union College,......................... $95,165 09 172
of which there belonged to it on acc't of the original agreement, the above sum of 4,214 01

so that there was apportioned to the college as its share of the profits resulting from the stipulations of January 4th and 24th, 1826,............................... 90,951 08
There was apportioned to Dr. Nott as his share of the same profits,.............. 71,691 70 173

making very nearly the above amount to be divided............................... $162,642 78
The difference being owing probably to some miscalculation.

This sum of $71,690.70, is claimed by the accountant as having been erroneously allowed to Dr. Nott, and is charged against him with interest. This is the second of 174 the principal matters in dispute, which will hereafter be separately discussed.

Yates and McIntyre proceeded with the Albany land lottery and the Fever hospital lottery, under their stipulations with Dr. Nott, and made considerable payments, until some dispute arose between them.

175 On the 26th of May, 1834, Dr. Nott filed a bill in chancery in his own name and in that of the trustees, against John B. Yates, A. McIntyre, Henry Yates, James McIntyre and John Ely, Junr., founded upon the stipulations respecting the Albany land lottery and the Fever hospital lottery, claiming large balances to be due. As a reason for making the trustees of the college, co-plaintiffs, the bill stated that he had often expressed his determination
176 to appropriate his share of the profits arising from the said stipulations, after providing for expenses, reverses and hazards incurred, to the use of Union College or some kindred institution connected therewith, reserving to himself only the right of determining the objects to which the same should be applied, and the time and manner of making the application; and that in reports to the trustees in 1831 and 1832, he had stated this purpose, and had in-
177 vited the requisite measures to be taken to give it effect, p. 26 of bill. The name of the Trustees of the college was thus used as equitable cestui-que-trusts of the fund sought to be recovered, but as it appears without their knowledge or consent.

To this bill the defendants demurred, and the first and principal ground assigned was, that it did not appear by the bill that the Trustees of the college had any interest
178 in or title to the relief sought, or any equity entitling them to a recovery; and it was urged that the matter stated in the bill, did not show any assignment by Dr. Nott of his interest in the fund to the college, and that the whole interest in those stipulations was originally vested in him, and had not been divested. (P. 6, 27, 28, 29, &c., of Mr. Butler's agreement.) There were other grounds of a technical character.

179 On the 4th of August, 1834, Yates & McIntyre filed their

bill in Chancery against the Trustees of Union College and
Dr. Nott, alleging mistakes in the settlement of 1828, and
particularly alleging that errors had been committed in the
estimates of the Deputy Comptroller, of the amount of
tickets at their scheme price, authorised to be drawn
under the act of 1822, amounting as they alleged to 456,391
dollars worth of tickets; that they had paid to the college 180
the eight and three-quarters per cent on that sum in error
and mistake, and praying that the amount thus paid, might
be refunded to them. (P. 20, 21, of their bill.)

The Trustees and Dr. Nott answered this bill, admitted
the payment of sundry sums by Yates & McIntyre on their
original contracts and subsequent stipulations, but denied
that the alleged error in the amount of tickets at their
scheme price, existed. 181

While these suits were pending, and before any decision
either upon the demurrer or upon the bill and answer, at
the suggestion of either Mr. McIntyre or Mr. Yates, as
testified by Mr. Flagg, who were desirous of a settlement,
a meeting was had, and the terms verbally agreed on.
They were afterwards reduced to writing, and signed by
these parties, Yates, McIntyre & Co., of the first part,
Dr. Nott, of the second part, and the committee of the 182
trustees of Union College, of the third part, on the 27th
July, 1837, and reported to the trustees, November 15,
1838. Folio 205, &c., documents XXVII, XXVIII,
XXIX, and particularly XIII, which is a copy of the agreement in full.

The payments made under this bond, amounting to a
very large sum, were completed on the 7th of March,
1849. It is claimed by the accountant, that these payments, (except $29,430.92) belonged to Union College; 183
but that sitting as a Vice Chancellor, he awarded the above
excepted sum to Dr. Nott, because it clearly did not belong either to Union College, or to Yates & McIntyre; and
that he was disposed to be generous to Dr. Nott.

As the narrative of the transactions with Yates & McIntyre, and their successors, here closes, and as this item is
altogether the most important one in controversy, and its 184

disposition will control much of the case, I propose to discuss it here, as being more convenient in connexion with the narrative just given, and while that is fresh in the mind.

The accountant, Mr. Vanderheyden, in his testimony as a witness, states, what is, perhaps, substantially set forth
185 in his statement, at page 126, that the consideration paid by Union College for this bond of $150,000, consisted in the agreement of the college;

1. To give up to the makers of the bonds, the successors of Yates & McIntyre, the bond and mortgage of J. B. Yates, for $55,000:

Amounting with the interest then accrued, to	$73,237 50
2. To release the assumption of Yates & 186 McIntyre, to pay the Comptroller's bonds to A. H. Lawrence, for the College of Physicians and Surgeons, amounting with interest then accrued, to..............	24,056 71
3. To deliver up to the obligors, 19 notes of Yates & McIntyre, taken at the settlement of 1828, and amounting with interest then accrued, to........................	22,674 87
187 Making in the whole,.............	$120,569 08
To which the accountant adds the balance which he has credited Dr. Nott,........	29,430 92
Which makes the sum of.............	$150,000 00

And he says that the bond was taken for these items. On
188 the face of this statement, what can be more absurd than to suppose that the makers of the bond would execute it to secure the payment of $29,430.92, more than was due, and more than the amount of the securities that were surrendered for it? The witness testifies, expressly, that this sum did not belong to the college. There could be no earthly reason for including it in the bond, therefore, which he claims belonged to the college. There was no
189 more reason for crediting it to Dr. Nott, than to any other

person. What kind of settlement was that by Yates &
McIntyre? According to Mr. Vanderheyden, they gave
up clear and undoubted claims to a repayment of moneys
erroneously received, claims sustained by the opinion of
the Attorney-General, submitted to pay their own costs of
two suits,(as no provision was made for them in the agreement,) and gave nearly $30,000 more for a settlement!
In no other part of their history have they exhibited such 190
fatuity.

The accountant had great difficulty in making up the
account at p. 186, so as to correspond with his strange
theory.

It will be seen by referring to it, that heavy payments
were made by the obligors; in the year 1837, $20,000; in
the year 1838, $10,000; in the year 1844, $55,793.83, and 191
so on until March 7, 1849. The whole interest on these
payments up to the time of balancing the account, amounting to $58,342.32, he charges the college in his account of
receipts and disbursements (No. 3) with having received.
And yet he does not credit a dollar of it in the bond
account at p. 186. Had he kept an interest account on the
$120,569.08, the amount of the securities surrendered, and
also upon the payments made by the makers of the bond, 192
the bond would have appeared to be overpaid some $20,-
000. Adding this to the $29,430.92 which he had the
generosity to give to Dr. Nott, would have swelled the
balance so enormously as to utterly destroy the whole fa-
bric he had raised. He therefore gives the makers of the
bond no credit whatever for any balance of interest in their
favor, but cunningly transfers his troublesome balance to
the Doctor's side of the college account. 193

Can this mode of making up the bond account be accounted for otherwise than by attributing a settled design
to pervert a plain transaction, and to distort and suppress
facts in order to accomplish some foregone purpose?

Is it to be wondered at, that one of the most accomplished accountants in our State, (Edward James, Esq.) in his
testimony before you, should pronounce it incomprehensi- 194
ble.

The narrative already given of the pleadings in the suits between the parties, and the testimony of A. C. Flagg and John A. Dix, show this to be one of the most plain transactions in ordinary life.

Yates & McIntyre claimed that by reason of an error in the estimate of the whole amount of tickets at their scheme
195 price that might be drawn, they had overpaid Union College. Dr. Nott claimed that there was a large sum due him from Y. & McI. on stipulations in which the college had no legal interest. A settlement is proposed by Yates or McIntyre. They consent to relinquish their claims for overpayment, on having surrendered to them securities and liabilities to the amount of $94,448.47. In this, says Mr. Flagg, who was one of the committee, the trustees
196 agree, being convinced that there was such an error. It was conceded, he says. Here the controversy between the college and Yates & McIntyre, is terminated. But the latter desire a final settlement of the whole matter; and there is a suit pending against them by Dr. Nott to recover large sums agreed to be paid to him individually, and which they have by their own pleading insisted, did belong to him individually and that the college had no interest
197 in them. These claims they wish to extinguish. Dr. Nott, says Mr. Flagg and Gen. Dix, was very unwilling to compromise his claims, but finally, at their earnest request, consents to do so. And they testify that these claims were liquidated at $150,000, and that the successors of Yates & McIntyre agreed to secure that sum by this bond.

According to Mr. Beekman's statement of the amount of
198 tickets drawn at their scheme price in the Albany Land lottery and in the Fever Hospital lottery, (to which the stipulations refer, out of which Dr. Nott's claims arose,) which he made some six or eight millions, the per cent due Dr. Nott would have amounted to $300,000 or $400,000.

His reluctance to yield the one half of this large amount to the demands of men already enriched by his labors and
199 talents, as stated by Messrs. Flagg and Dix, is not surpri

sing. His generosity in doing so for the benefit of Union College, meets with a poor reward in the denial to him by strangers of even the moiety which was the price of his forbearance.

This bond, says Mr. Flagg, was given to settle the suit of Dr. Nott against Yates and McIntyre, brought to recover
the percentage they had agreed to give him, and which the 200
College conceded belonged to him. Gen. Dix says he was also a member of the Committee, and that the amount agreed by Yates and McIntyre's successors, to be paid to Dr. Nott, was $150,000, and that this was to be paid on one of the special agreements entered into, after the College had received the amount it was entitled to by law. He remembers Dr. Nott thought they ought to pay him double
that sum. He says the remainder of the bond and mort- 201
gage of J. B. Yates and of the notes of Yates & McIntyre, and the release of their assumption to pay the bonds given for the College of Physicians, were in consequence of an alleged overpayment by Yates & McIntyre, which the College admitted. I know, he says that Dr. Nott assented to the arrangement with great reluctance, and that in doing so, he surrendered his judgement to the earnest wish expressed by Mr. Flagg, Gov. Marcy, Mr. Wright and my- 202
self.

Mr. Flagg says, Dr. Nott was decidedly averse to the settlement, and he thought he would recover a larger amount than the $150,000. Yates & McIntyre's successors were anxious for the settlement. Mr. Wright was decidedly of opinion, Dr. Nott could recover and the Dr. obstinately insisted on it that he could recover.

The same account of the terms of this settlement, is 203
given by Messrs Marcy and Flagg, two of the Committee who effected it, in their report to the Trustees of November 15, 1838, (Doc. XXVII, folio 214,) that the amount to be received on the bond should be considered as received on the suit between Dr. Nott and Yates, McIntyre, Ely & Co. That report speaks of a settlement to be made between Dr.
Nott and the College, in respect to the amounts received 204

on the bond. Until such settlement be made and Dr. Nott
shall relinquish any portion of them, they belong to him.

The original agreement, containing the terms of the settlement which has now been produced, and is printed in
the accompanying case, (Doc. XLII, folio 375) is conclusive
on the subject. It recites the filing of the bill by Dr. Nott
205 in his own name and that of the Trustees, against Yates &
McIntyre, as stated in the preceding narrative, and the
claim of the College to $31,004.00 for money borrowed by
Yates & McIntyre, and also to "a large amount under
certain agreements and stipulations as in said bill set
forth" (and which I have in the narrative particularly recited,) and that the bill prays for a decree to compel the
payment of such amount. It also recites the cross bill of
206 Yates & McIntyre. At folio 383, the agreement says,
"which said bond is given for the claims set up by the
said parties of the second part (Union College) as well as
the third part, (E. Nott,) against the said parties of the first
part." This puts at rest forever, the absurd pretence that
the bond was given for the surrender of the securities, &c.,
as claimed by the accountant.

Two circumstances have been made the ground of a
207 frivolous cavil. One is, that the securities agreed to be
surrendered, are to be retained by the College until the
bond should be paid. This is untrue in point of fact, they
were to be given up on receiving the bond. folio 387, 388.

The other circumstance is, that the bond was made payable to Union College. Dr. Nott had repeatedly declared
his intention of appropriating to the College, the profits of
all his labors, services, advances and risks in the lottery
208 business, and the Trustees had by resolution authorized
the Treasurer to receive any monies or securities that Dr.
Nott might deposit with him. There was great propriety in
allowing his intended cestui-que-trust, to be his trustee also,
and to receive and hold monies he destined for its benefit, so
that in the event of his death or of any accident to him, the
money would be safe and protected by his repeated reports,
and declarations of his having bestowed it on the College.
209 A trust was thus created, by which the College became

trustee for Dr. Nott, to receive these payments and account
to him for them. The agreement itself as already shown,
declares this trust. But if there was any doubt on the face
of the papers, parol evidence is perfectly competent to
establish a resulting trust, such as this is. Mr. Green-
leaf in his work on evidence, vol. 3, p. 70, has stated the result of the law on this subject; he says, "and irrespective of
any allegation of fraud, it has been settled on great consid- 210
eration, that parol evidence is admissible to prove the
purchase money for an estate was paid by a third person,
other than the grantee named in the deed, in order to establish a trust in favor of him who paid the money." See
also Boyd vs. McLean, 1 John. ch. 582, where the question
is considered at much length by Ch. Kent. And he holds
that such testimony is admissible and sufficient in the face
of the deed. This has been recognised by the Supreme 211
Court and Court of Errors, repeatedly; 11 John. 91; 13
John. 462; 16 John. 197, and in the other states, as well
as in England. See Story's Eq., § 1201 n.

Our statute relating to resulting trusts in land, of course
has no application to such trusts of personal property.
The law remains the same as it always was, in respect to
that species of property.

It is idle to say, as has been intimated by Mr. Vander- 212
heyden, while acting as counsel, that if there was any error
in the estimate of the scheme amount of tickets, the profits
arising from the excess belonged to the State, and not to
Yates & McIntyre. The question is not whether the college was legally bound to repay the excess to Yates & Mc-
Intyre, but it is, what in fact did they agree to do? For
if they agreed to repay it by the surrender of the securi- 213
ties specified, and the release of the assumption in respect
to the bonds for the College of Physicians, then that surrender and release formed no part of the consideration for
the bond of $150,000

But in truth, Yates and McIntyre claimed in their bill
that they were entitled to this excess under other laws.
If they are not, they and their representatives are respon- 214

sible to the State for the excess: Union College has none of it.

It is alleged by the accountant, acting as counsel, that in several reports of the treasurer to the trustees of Union College, he states the balance due on this $150,000 bond among the productive funds of the college. He does so,
215 but it is to be remarked, that while all the other bonds are reported in mass, stating merely their amount, this bond is always entered separately and specially, as if it did not belong to the general mass.

In other reports it is included among the funds, but with a special reference to its character. Thus, in the report of 1845, as I have shown the committee, in the original minutes of the trustees, it is entered thus: "To
216 balance on Yates, McIntyre, Ely and McIntyre's bond, subject to future settlement with Dr. Nott, as per stipulation of finance committee, $31,246.44." Surely, the omission to make such a special entry in all the reports, when the facts were so well known, amounts to nothing. At all events, this entry nullifies preceding entries of a different character.

The accountant has also referred to one or two of the
217 annual reports of the treasurer in behalf of the trustees to the Legislature, wherein the balance due on this bond appears to be included in the total amount of the property of the college. The treasurer might well make this statement while he regarded this bond and its proceeds as equitably belonging to the college, in virtue of the repeated declarations in the reports of the president, of his having destined it for the college, and with the knowledge that
218 it had been received and was held by him (the Treasurer), under resolutions of the board, authorising him to receive payments on it. The including the balance due on the bond among the property of the college, in his report, deceived no one and could injure no one. It told the substantial truth, and the occasion did not require an explanation of the trust.

The accountant has also called attention to the circum-
219 stances, that in his answer to a question of the Assembly

committee in 1850, Mr. Holland said that a settlement had
been made with Dr. Nott, and the college owed him $41,-
340.57. Mr. Holland answered that he had been for some
time under an erroneous impression, that the basis of the
settlement made by the treasurer, and sanctioned by the
finance committee, (detailed in doc. XXV, fol. 200,) made
July 26, 1837, was applicable to the bond of $150,000, 220
and he had apportioned the payments received on the bond,
according to that basis, and had stated a balance accordingly. But he says he was mistaken; that the resolutions
directing the basis referred to, to be ascertained, were passed
before the bond for $150,000 was given, and before the
arrangement on which it was predicated had been perfected,
and could have no reference to that bond. And this mistake accounts also for his having stated in his reports, as 221
treasurer, the balance due on the bond, as the property of
the college, supposing that balance to have been its proportion.

But what is the proper and legal effect of any statements in reports made by their treasurer to the trustees,
or in their name to the Legislature? They cannot have
the effect of rescinding formal and solemn agreements,
especially when they contain different versions, and are 222
made under the circumstances mentioned. They can be
used only as admissions by the parties of a state of facts,
which originally entitled the trustees to the fund in question. But the statements import no such thing; their silence, in some instances, to specify the trust, would not
prove that there was none, while the explicit declaration
of the trust in one of them, proves the fact. How can
such after statements be permitted to override and defeat 223
the formal instruments and reports made at the time, declaring the trust?

But it is in vain thus to assail the conclusive evidence of
the original transaction. It does not help a single step to
establish the position of the accountant that the $150,000
bond was a substitute for the securities surrendered by
the college to Yates & McIntyre. And that position utterly failing, there was no consideration whatever for 224

this bond, moving from the college, and as it must belong
to the trustees or to Dr. Nott, it was the property of the
latter, who did yield an abundant consideration as already
shown.

The accountant, as I understand him, contends that the
college was entitled to the benefits arising from the stipulations of May 26, or 30th, 1826, and of July 15, 1830,
225 (Doc. XVIII, and part of XVIII, p. 29, 31,) out of which it
is conceded on all sides, the claims arose, for the satisfaction
of which the $150,000 bond was given, and he founds this
upon certain statements in the answer of the trustees and
of Dr. Nott, to the bill in chancery of Yates & McIntyre.
I do not propose to analyse the answers, and show how
mistaken the accountant is. It would require a comparison
with the charges in the bill, to know precisely what the
226 answer referred to, which would be too tedious and out of
place here. There is a complete and decisive reply to
this pretence, in the accountant's printed statements and
in his testimony before you. From page 168 to 172, of
his printed report, is a statement of the moneys paid on
the stipulations in question, amounting to $192,190.94.
This sum, the accountant has repeatedly sworn, belonged
to Dr. Nott, individually, and that the college had no claim
227 upon it, except for some contingent and indefinite amount
of supposed injury arising from the delay in drawing the
Literature lottery, in consequence of mixing it with the
Fever hospital and Albany land lotteries. This sum of
$192,190.94 is only a portion of the claims of Dr. Nott
upon those stipulations; and if it belongs to him, the residue of the claim must be of the same character. And it
was this residue that constituted the consideration for the
228 $150,000 bond. It is wholly immaterial, therefore, what
statements are made in the answer. They cannot overcome what is conceded on all sides and ever has been.

I may not leave this subject without calling the attention of the committee to the perverseness of the accountant in so entirely changing the character and consideration
of this bond, in the face of the plainest evidence that was
229 in his possession, and to the trickery exhibited in making

up the fabulous account at page 186, of his book, to his
suppression of the interest received on the bond, because
it would overturn his account, to the absurdity of his giving Dr. Nott credit for a part of it, when he denied his
right to any portion of it; and to the obstinacy with which
he has adhered to his fabrication, down to the very last
moment. And I ask whether his whole conduct in this
matter, does not betray a settled design to make up a start- 230
ling balance against Dr. Nott, at all events, by withholding
from undoubted credits to the amount of $342,748.72?

I will now proceed to discuss the charge made by the
accountant against Dr. Nott, for the avails of the 2¼ per
cent fund, called the President's Fund; a charge of his
own original making, and which the Trustees of the college
had never preferred. This 2¼ per cent is the amount of
compensation to the managers of lotteries for supervision 231
and management, provided by §25 of "an act concerning
lotteries," passed April 13, 1819, chap. 206, as follows:
"That on the final settlement of the accounts of the several lotteries hereafter to be drawn in this State, the Comptroller shall allow fifteen per cent on the sum raised by
such lottery *to the said managers*, in lieu of all compensation for services and expenses, in conducting and drawing
the same." 232

This compensation had varied from time to time, having
been originally ten per cent, then fourteen, and afterwards
fifteen per cent; and it was the only compensation allowed
the managers for their services and expenses.

This fifteen per cent on the sum raised is equal to 2¼ per
cent on the amount of tickets drawn at their scheme price,
as previously remarked.

Of course the amount was a charge upon the lottery, and 233
must be first deducted from the amount raised.

It thus appears that there were two distinct sums or
amounts to be raised by this lottery.

1st. The amount of the grants directed to the several
institutions, with interest for six years, except that to the
Historical Society, which was without interest.

234

2d. The expenses of management and supervision, fixed at fifteen per cent "on the sum raised."

The latter being in items for *expenses* and *services* in the management and supervision, necessarily appertained to the person or persons who rendered the services and incurred the expenses. It was in lieu of the sums that had
235 theretofore been paid to the managers of lotteries for their compensation, which had always been raised out of the lotteries, over and above, and in addition to, the principal sums granted, had been received by the managers for their personal benefit, and had never been paid to or pretended to be claimed by the persons or institutions for whose benefit the lotteries were authorized. And so in the present case. Union College and the other institutions named in
236 the act, could derive no other or greater sum or benefit from it, than that which the act expressly granted. The State managers were entitled to the compensation for services and expenses. The institutions themselves had no more claim to it than any stranger.

This principle was not only recognized but reiterated and enforced by the act of 1822, chap. 163.

By the preamble to the 5th section it is declared: "Whereas the object of this act is not to increase the grants
237 made to the said institutions, but to contract with them for assuming the responsibility and running the hazard and taking the management of the Literature lottery," &c.

The 6th section provides, "that said institutions shall apply the avails of said lottery (after deducting the expenses of managing the same) *pro rata*, according to the provisions of the original act in which said grants were
238 made," &c. The division is not to be in proportion to the respectives sums granted, but simply "according to the provisions of the original acts, to carry out its provisions," and the expense of managing the lottery, was thus expressly excluded from the distribution *pro rata* among the institutions. That expense (fixed at 15 per cent as already mentioned) then, did not and could not belong, legally, to the institutions.

239 Yet there was a mode by which the colleges could derive

the benefit of any savings from the fund, by prudence
and economy. That was, that some person should assume
the management and supervision of the lottery under their
appointment, who, while he would be legally and strictly
entitled to the compensation absolutely fixed by law, would
apply whatever surplus could be realized after an econo-
mical management, to the benefit of Union and Ham- 240
ilton Colleges. Hence Dr. Nott offered to take into
his own hands the entire management and supervision of
the lottery, declaring then, and repeatedly afterwards,
verbally and in writing, that he should derive no personal benefit from the amount so realized, but should
devote it to the use of Union and Hamilton colleges. The
rights and interests of the other institutions had been acquired absolutely, and they had no equitable claim upon 241
the fund.

It was with this view and for this purpose that the resolution of the Trustees of Union College was passed on the 24th of July, 1822, conferring on Dr. Nott the sole and exclusive supervision and management of the lottery. (See folio 13, Doc. III.)

And it was for this purpose that the supplemental contract of July 29th, 1822, was made with Yates & McIntyre, 242
(Doc. V, folio 29) by which they agreed to pay "for supervision and management the same per centum on each
class, immediately after the drawing thereof, as has heretofore been paid to managers appointed by the State," by
depositing the same to the credit of the President. The
amount of the principal grant ($276,090.14) was, by the
original agreement, to be paid to the *Treasurer* of Union
College. Thus the funds were to be kept distinct, as they 243
ever have been. The Treasurer has never received any
moneys arising from this fund—has kept no account of it,
and never made a report on it to the trustees.

It was with the same view and purpose that in the contract between Union College and Hamilton College, (Doc.
VII. folio 62,) dated October 12th, 1822, subsequent to the
foregoing proceedings, it was provided that "the whole remainder which should be received by the Trustees of Union 244

7*

College from the supervision and management of the said lottery, over and above expenses, and after meeting losses, should any occur, should be divided between the said colleges *pro rata* or according to their respective interests in the lottery."

This agreement, on the part of Union College, was pros-
245 pective and in anticipation of what they might *receive* in any way, whether by gift or otherwise.

As the trustees of Union College must be presumed to have known that they could not legally and directly be entitled to this fund, the above agreement is in itself evidence of there having been an understanding with Dr. Nott in respect to its ultimate disposal by him.

He thus became the voluntary trustee of a gift to those
246 colleges, consisting of the surplus that should be saved by his personal exertions and responsibilities, but which legally belonged to him.

That the Board of Trustees so understood the transaction is manifest from all their subsequent resolutions and acts.

The report of William James and Silas Wright, to the trustees, July 26, 1831, (Doc. XXI, folio 182) shows an
247 excess of means in the treasury of the college, after having met expenditures and losses, of more than $100,000. "This amount is aggregated, they say, partly by the relinquishment of salaries from principal officers; $8,500 of it appears to have been a fortuitous result of a speculation in chances which had been *generously* added to the funds many years ago. The residue is composed of the net gains on various speculations and contracts made on indi-
248 vidual account (or names) and responsibility in the course of years, all of which had been applied to the sole use and benefit of the college. A sum of $42,000 out of the *last mentioned* sources, has been added to the fund since the last meeting of the board."

The $42,000 had been deposited October 6, 1830, (see Accountant's statement No. 20, p. 132) and it is the only item of that account in the books of the college. This,

249

therefore, is the sum referred to by Messrs. James and Wright.

Now it appears from the original entries in the cash book of the college from 1806 to 1833, under date of October 12, 1830, that this same sum is entered as having been received from "the President's fund."

Of course Messrs. James and Wright saw this entry ; it 250
was the only evidence of the fact of the deposit.

When they say then, that this sum "out of the last mentioned sources" had been added to the funds of the college, they say that this sum was derived from the net gains on various speculations and *contracts* made on individual account and responsibility.

They knew of the two original contracts made with
Yates & McIntyre, for they refer to the sums received from 251
them.

They therefore say explicitly and unequivocally, that the 42,000 dollars were given on a contract, made on individual account and responsibility.

But further, in their report, under the head of funds
which had been received by the college, " either by individuals and corporate donations, or by public appropriations," (folio 145,)they put down as having been real- 252
ized from the lotteries under the acts of 1814 and 1822,
$200,000. In reference to that sum, they say, (folio
154,) " that principal has been liquidated, together
with the six years of interest due thereon, and is now
held by the Trustees in obligations against the managers of the lotteries, and in securities taken from them,"
&c. Those gentlemen then knew what obligations and securities had been taken from Yates & McIntyre, and they 253
claim, in behalf of the college, that $200,000 of them, and
six years interest, belonged to the college. Could such
men have made such a statement, with the knowledge that
obligations for the balance due on the President's fund,
had also been given by Yates & McIntyre, beyond the
$200,000 and interest, without including those obligations,
if they had not regarded them as the nett gains before
mentioned, belonging to Dr. Nott? 254

On the 15th of November, 1838, a report was made by
Messrs. Marcy and Flagg, (folio 205, Doc. XXVII,) in
which they say, "That by the indenture entered into on
the 29th of July, 1822, between Union College and Yates
& McIntyre, as modified by certain subsequent stipulations,
the said Yates & McIntyre covenanted to pay the Treasurer
255 of Union College for *its entire* right, title and interest in
the Literature lottery, 8¾ per cent; and to pay to the
President of the college for the supervision and management
thereof, 2¼ per cent on $4,948,597 worth of tickets,
reckoned at the scheme price, which was the amount computed
to have been authorised to be drawn under the act,
&c.

Here again, is a distinct and unqualified assertion by a
256 committee of the Trustees, that the college sold its entire
right, title and interest in the lottery to Yates and McIntyre
for 8¾ per cent on the scheme price of the tickets, which
was the $276,090.14 already stated by previous committees
as the consideration, and of course, this consideration was
all the college was entitled to.

On the 23d of January, 1840, Messrs. J. P. Cushman
and A. C. Paige, as a committee of Union College, ad-
257 dressed a letter to a committee of Hamilton College, in
answer to an application of the latter, among other things,
for one-seventh of the President's fund.

Further, in their statement of the funds of the college,
(fol. 160 of doc's,) they have a head of securities taken on
settlement of the amount due, under the act of 1814, with
the items of bonds and mortgages taken in payment, and a
note; then bonds and mortgages guaranteed, $36,350, and
258 finally *notes for balance due*, $57,475.39. This expression
for balance due, can mean nothing else but the balance due
under the act of 1814. They thus acknowledge that all
the college could claim under that act had been paid. Of
course it had no further claim upon the president's fund,
or any other. I do not know what stronger or more satisfactory evidence could be adduced of the extent of the
college claim, than is furnished by this report. This re-
259 port was adopted by the board of trustees. The presi-

dent had expressed his intention of giving to the college the whole of the nett gains spoken of by Messrs. Wright and James, and would naturally be desirous for his own protection, that the balance not yet paid in, should be ascertained by an officer of the college, by an examination of the vouchers. To enable this to be done, on the coming
in and acceptance of the report of Messrs. Wright and 260
James, in which the subject had been introduced as already mentioned, the trustees passed a resolution, (doc. XXII, fol. 185,) authorising the treasurer to make a final settlement *whenever desired by the president*, and to receive such *balance*. This is not the language of a creditor, but of a party receiving a favor; and the special authority to receive the balance could hardly have been necessary to
authorise the receipt of a debt to the college. In this re- 261
solution therefor, the trustees themselves recognised and sanctioned the view that had been presented by Messrs. Wright and James of these "net gains on contracts on individual account," of which I have shown they regarded the president's fund as a part.

On the 24th November, 1834, William L. Marcy, Silas Wright, jr., and John P. Cushman, a committee to which
an application of Yates and McIntyre had been referred, 262
made a report, (fol. 186, doc. XXIII.) Reciting the transactions, they say, "on the 29th July, 1822, a contract was signed between J. B. Yates and A. McIntyre and the trustees of Union College, by which contract Yates and McIntyre were, (*in addition* to 2¼ per centage on the gross amount of schemes, to be deposited to the credit of the president of Union College, being the legal per centage
allowed for the management of the lotteries,) to pay to 263
the treasurer of the college *for the lottery*, the sum of $276,090.14. This is an indirect recognition, that the above sum was to be paid for all the interest of the *college* in the lottery.

In a letter of J. P. Cushman and A. C. Paige to a committee of the trustees of Hamilton College, (fol. 80, 81 of documents,) they say "that the interests of Union College
had been *gratuitously* promoted by hazards, assumed by Dr. 264

Nott, in securing from the lottery, after paying all expenses, a considerable surplus to be divided between the colleges," (Union and Hamilton,) thus disclaiming all idea of legal right.

Senator Beekman, after his own examination of the books, minutes, &c., of Union College, says, in his report
265 to the Assembly, April 8, 1850, Assembly doc. No. 190, "the fund denominated the president's fund, is not claimed by the college."

The testimony of the Hon. John A. Dix, and of the Hon. A. C. Flagg, (fol. 289, 292, 293, 308, Doc. XXXVIII,) is explicit, emphatic, and I submit, entirely conclusive on this point. These gentlemen were State officers and State trustees, and could have no object or motive other than the
266 interests of the college, and the faithful application of the public grants. They both declare that this fund was uniformly and continually regarded and conceded by all the trustees, except Mr. Henry Yates, (the partner of Yates & McIntyre,) during their whole term of service in the board, to belong to Dr. Nott. Mr. Flagg was a member of the board nineteen years. Proof on this point might be multiplied, but it is deemed unnecessary.

267 In his reports to the trustees of 1831 and 1832, (doc's XXXI, XXXII,) the president had expressed his design of bestowing the profits of the lotteries on the college; he had paid in a portion of the fund $42,000, which had been reported by a committee of the board as a gift. They had accepted it as such, and so represented it to Hamilton College, and had provided a mode for ascertaining the balance when it should suit his convenience; they have
268 never claimed it, although its existence was well known to them, and acquiesced in his written and practical assertion of his right to it, for twenty-five years and more. Would not any individual, in his transactions with another, be irrevocably and conclusively bound and estopped, both at law and equity, by such a course of conduct? The law, in regard to corporations, is in no wise different, in this respect, than in relation to individuals. They are
269 equally bound, not only by the acts, but by the mere ac-

quiescence of their trustees and agents. (2. Sanford's Sup. Court, Rep. 52.)

Had he appointed himself, or been appointed sole *manager*, no question could ever have arisen. His position as a clergyman, and as the head of a literary institution, forbade his thus publicly assuming the character of a manager of lotteries. Resort was therefore had to other names,
"and he appointed as managers Henry Yates, jun., to whom 270
$1,300 per annum, was allowed; Jonas Holland, to whom $1,000 per annum, was allowed; and Joseph Horsfall, to whom $800 per annum was allowed." (Quoted from the report of Messrs. Marcy, Wright and Cushman, Nov. 24, 1834.) But the devising and arranging the scheme, and the plan of drawing, adopted after Vannini's system, and the execution of all the details of the management, its
correspondence and the collection of the sums due from 271
the contractors, together with the responsibility of providing the means of paying prizes in the inability of the contractors, devolved on Dr. Nott. He was, in fact, and to all intents and purposes, the manager of the lotteries. All this is abundantly shown by the correspondence of Yates and McIntyre, the reports of committees, and the testimony of Messrs. Dix and Flagg. The nominal managers, would, in fact, have the *prima facie* title to the su- 272
pervision fund. But in his arrangements with them, Dr. Nott took care to provide against any such claim, by giving them salaries, which they consented to receive, and thus precluded themselves from all other claims.

It has been supposed that we regarded this as a gift *by the college* to Dr. Nott. The evidence would, undoubtedly,
fully support such a view. Being a right in action, per- 273
sonal property, it required no formal instrument for its transfer; like all gifts of that kind of property, delivery or possession, with the knowledge of the owner, under a claim of title, and accompanied by engagements to bestow it on the owner, accepted and recognised by him, would, as between individuals, be conclusive evidence of the donation originally. (10 John. Rep. 293; 22 Wend. 526.) And I
know of no law that prevents a corporation from giving 274

its property to any person, much less from making a remuneration for labor and responsibility. As between it
and its creditors, a question might arise on the validity of
a naked gift, when it was insolvent. But strangers, among
whom I include the State, have no right to enquire into or
disturb even such a gift. Corporations have the absolute
right of disposing of their own property. Kent's Com-
275 mentaries, section 33, vol. 2, p. 281. 2 John. Ch. Rep.
384, Angel & Ames on corporations, chap. 5, sec. 9, 1 Kyd.
108. In Colchester vs. Lowten, 1 Vesey & Beames, 226,
quoted and approved by Chancellor Kent, it was decided
that neither a court of law or of equity will set aside or
control an alienation of its property by a corporation, unless it be made for an illegal purpose. The statute of
276 charitable uses is not in force in this State; so that no
such authority can be exercised in that class of cases, in
this State. And it cannot be pretended that here was any
alienation of property, *contrary* to any provisions of law,
for there was no law forbidding it; or for purposes foreign
to the lawful business and objects of the corporation. It
was not made to carry on banking or insurance, or any foreign or unlawful business.

277 As between Dr. Nott and the college then, whether regarded as a remuneration for services, or as a mere gift,
the bestowal of this fund on him would be legal, valid and
irrevocable. For an executed gift is as irrevocable as a
transfer for consideration.

While therefore, it might be claimed on either of these
grounds, yet the one on which it has been placed, and which
we regard as the true one, is that this fund never belonged
278 to the College to give. This, it is thought, the previous
remarks abundantly establish.

The papers and books to which the accountant has had
access, show that managers of the lotteries were appointed
by Dr. Nott, that they were allowed salaries, and that other
expenses were incurred in the supervision and management;
and that yet not an entry was to be found on the books of
the College, of its Treasurer having paid a cent towards those
279 expenses. It seems not to have occurred to him, that these

expenses must have been defrayed out of the fund; for he charges the whole amount, without deducting a dollar, to Dr. Nott. In his argument as Counsel, the accountant seems to admit that there should be some deduction from the fund and from his charge against Dr. Nott for the whole balance and interest, on account of these expenses. But he quib-
bles about the salaries of the managers being *allowed*, and 280
its not being said that they were *paid*. The criticism is characteristic, inconsistent as it is, with the course of one who has allowed himself such latitude in contradicting the very words of entries. Had he done what he promised, submitted his accounts growing out of the lottery transactions to Dr. Nott for explanation, before submitting them to the commission, he would have been furnished with the
details of this President's fund and the vouchers for the 281
expenditures on its account, as they were furnished to the Treasurer.

The very paper which he has produced and made evidence, the joint answer of the trustees and President to the bill of Yates & McIntyre, and from which he has quoted so freely, contains the distinct averment at p. 24, 25, that the salaries mentioned in the report of Messrs. Marcy,
Wright and Cushman, quoted at folio 270 *ante*, were *paid* 282
to the several managers, Yates, Holland and Horsfall, from the 6th of January, 1823, to the 1st of April, 1828, besides the traveling expenses of Henry Yates. These salaries amounted to some $17,000, besides the traveling expenses of Henry Yates. Here was the evidence in his own possession, of the same character precisely with that which he had used for making charges against the college and Dr.
Nott, which he utterly disregarded; and which he now 283
disregards in his attempt to show that a trifling deduction only should be made for these expenses. There must necessarily have been others, in the employment of clerks, in the actual expenses of visiting New-York and in the various duties of such a position.

But he says Henry Yates was the only manager who really rendered any service, or received compensation.
How he can tell who was paid his salary, without an exa- 284

mination of the vouchers, will be for him to explain. Henry Yates was indeed paid by the President for his services as manager, during a term of years when, as it afterwards appeared, he was a secret co-partner of his brother John B. Yates and A. McIntyre, in the very business he was sent to New-York, as the agent of the college, to watch
285 and guard on its behalf. And he thus pocketed his share of the profits of the lottery as a partner, and received pay for watching himself and his co-partners.

The proof of these facts is furnished by the very bill in chancery produced by the accountant (p. 8). They were known to him, as he says he referred to this bill for some of his charges. The directions of the Senate to the commission were explicit, that they should enquire "whether the
286 President or *any other officer*, while in the employment of the college, participated individually in the profits of any lotteries which were appropriated by the acts granting such lotteries to Union College." (See resolution quoted at folio 90, ante.) With the knowledge of such participation by Henry Yates, the Treasurer, and with this direction before him, the accountant has not made the slightest allusion to the subject in his report. Whether he brought the subject to the notice of the commission, does not ap-
287 pear. Such has been his impartiality!

From this same Mr. Yates has the accountant obtained papers, pleadings, arguments of counsel, extracts from their books, and every other aid and assistance that could be rendered. Indeed it is notorious that Mr. Yates and his connexions have been active in what I do not hesitate to call a vindictive persecution of Dr. Nott. It is well known that one of those connexions, from the commence-
288 ment of your enquiries, has filled the columns of the filthiest and most abandoned newspaper in the State, with garbled and partial statements of facts in the case, with wholesale misrepresentations, with abuse of me for undertaking the defence of Dr. Nott, and with one continued stream, black with malignity, of the most outrageous calumny against that old man. What portions of this scandalous attempt to prejudice your minds and the pub-

289

lic judgment, previous to your report, you may have seen, I know not. But I do know, that with this exposition of the source of the attempt, you will not mistake its object, and that you will treat it with the scorn and contempt which every man having the least regard to justice or decency, will feel for it and its authors and abettors.

You are too intelligent gentlemen, to be misled by the 290
singular effort of the accountant, in his capacity of counsel, to give such a construction to the act of 1822, to limit the continuance of the lotteries, as shall vest in the institutions the $2\frac{1}{4}$ per cent allowed the managers for their personal services and expenses. He is obliged to make the statute contradict itself, and to reject the clause which directs the distribution of the proceeds of the lotteries among the institutions, after deducting the expenses of
management and supervision, according to the original 291
grants. You are too well acquainted with the principles of the construction of laws to be thus mislead.

The accountant has referred to and read two passages in the joint answer of the Trustees and President of Union College, to the bill of Yates & McIntyre; one of them at p. 4, and the other at p. 24.

In the first of these, at p. 4, the defendants are answering an allegation in the bill, that the $2\frac{1}{4}$ per cent was in- 292
tended to provide for contingent losses, and was to be kept private, &c. And the answer says that the said fund was received by Dr. Nott, solely as the president and agent of Union College, conformably to a clause in their agreement with Hamilton College, (hereinbefore quoted and contained in full in Doc. VII, folio 62) that the remainder of what should be *received* by Union College from that fund, should
be divided between the colleges *pro rata*, &c. 293

In the second passage of the answer, at p. 24, the defendants are answering a charge in the bill, that they pretended the $2\frac{1}{4}$ per cent was for *actual* expenses incurred in the supervision and management of the lotteries, and they deny that they have made any such pretence, but aver that the same, irrespective of expenses incurred, belonged of
right to the institutions, and that by virtue of this right, 294

and in reference to Hamilton College, the fund in question was kept separate.

You have a perfect and consistent explanation of these passages, by referring to the reports of Dr. Nott in 1831, 1832 and 1833, and to the other evidence already quoted, of his having bestowed the proceeds of this fund, after de-
295 ducting expenses, on Union College, and of the college having accepted the gift, and promised Hamilton College its proportion. This fund, therefore, did belong, "of right" to Union College and Hamilton College, and was kept disdinct, as stated in the answer. To understand a part of an answer, it is necessary to see what the point in dispute was, and then to give the answer an application to that point, and that only. General words and expressions are
296 to be restrained by the occasion, the *subject* and the *parties* or *persons* in reference to whom they are used. Here the answer was meeting the charge that *actual expenses* only of supervision and management were claimed by the defendants, so as to lay a foundation for the plaintiffs' claiming the surplus. The answer asserts that *the whole* belonged to the two colleges of right; in other words, denying the right of the plaintiffs to any portion of it. The
297 defendants were not called upon to say anything in relation to the respective rights of the colleges and Dr. Nott, and they did not profess to speak on that point. To strain their language to include matter not in their minds when answering, would be as unjust as it is absurd. There was no occasion for their saying *how* the right was acquired. I have already shown that it could be acquired only through Dr. Nott, or some one assuming the management,
298 who would bestow this surplus, above expenses, on them. It is this surplus that they are claiming, through this donation of Dr. Nott.

In truth the answer, so far from contradicting the ground we have taken, illustrates and confirms the view I have presented at the early part of these remarks upon the subject of this fund.

The whole point of the reference to the answer, is to
299 show that the college claimed this fund as an *original* right

under the acts. I have shown the answer does not assert
this, and that such is not a fair implication from its language. But when you consider that this answer was made
by Dr. Nott, you will see the downright absurdity of supposing that in it he intended to contradict his own reports
to the Trustees, the uniform view he and they had taken,
and their whole course of conduct on the subject; especial- 300
ly when he was not called on to speak at all on the point.
No aid is therefore to be derived by the accountant from
the answers, to overthrow the positions, we have taken in
respect to this fund.

As Dr. Nott has actually given the whole amount of the
surplus of this fund, after deducting expenses, to the college, the questions whether it originally belonged to him
or to the college, or whether it became his by the acts of 301
the Trustees as a remuneration for services, or as a donation, become mere abstract speculations, without any practical consequence whatever. Still, it was due to his character to show that he acted in good faith, and with a
constant regard for the interests of the college.

Another claim advanced by the accountant in behalf of
Union College, and which the trustees have never asserted,
relates to the amount of 22 notes a part of 24, received 302
from Yates & McIntyre, on the settlement of their accounts
in 1828. This is stated in the accountant's report, at page
130, (statement No. 19) as amounting with interest to
$180,547.28, the principal being $71,691.20, and the balance being interest for more than twenty years.

For the history of the circumstances under which, and
the considerations for which these notes were given, I
would refer to the preceding narrative, folio 155 to folio 303
175.

This principal of these 22 notes is said by the accountant in the caption of the account, to have been received
by Dr. Nott on account of the fund known by way of dis-
tinction, as the $8\frac{3}{4}$ per cent college lottery fund.

This statement is contradicted on the face of the receipt
given to Yates & McIntyre by Dr. Nott, and printed in the 304

accountant's report, at p. 177. (See a copy Doc. XX, p.
32, 33.) That receipt states expressly that the notes are
received not only on account of the contract of July 29,
1822, but also on account of a special stipulation respecting class No. 3, for 1825, of Literature lottery, and in
consideration of the personal responsibilities of the President and treasurer *to be assumed* to sustain the contrac-
305 tors. This receipt can refer to nothing else but the stipulations of January 4th, and 24th, of 1826. By referring
to the settlement of 1828, (Doc. XX, p. 32, of Doc's) it
will be seen that class No. 3, for 1825, of Literature lottery, is charged as having been drawn January 19, 1826,
upon which was due to the college $49,665.00. It will
also be seen by the opposite column, that during the whole
year 1826, there was paid by Yates & McIntyre to the col-
306 lege, only 3,000, which was made May 8, and that they
had made no payment since April 13, 1825, although they
were then indebted $57,000. These facts show how much
they were embarrassed at that time. In their letter of Jan.
4th, 1826, just preceding the close of the drawing of the class
No. 3, for 1825, they say: "It has become necessary that
we should inform you, that such have been our losses, that
we have no reasonable prospect of being able to pay the
307 sum stipulated, *or even to pay the prizes in the lottery*
now pending, unless we can procure immediate pecuniary
assistance to a large amount." They, therefore, propose
the terms to which they will accede, if they can be relieved.
(Doc. IX, folio 88.) This proposition was consummated
by Doc. XIII, folio 105. In an instrument like this, which
might come before the public, it was not deemed proper
308 to state all the inducements, particularly one which would
betray the financial embarrassments of Yates and McIntyre. Now the receipt given on the settlement for the 24
notes, says "that they are received in full of all demands
against Yates & McIntyre, arising out of the original contract; and also out of a special stipulation by them made
to provide for the payment of prizes in the class No. 3, for
1826, of Literature lottery, drawn January 19, 1826."
309 The notes were taken then to satisfy demands arising

out of the stipulations of January 4, and 24, 1826, and "in consideration of the personal responsibility to be assumed by the President and Treasurer of Union College, in order to sustain the contractors in the further performance of their contracts." These are the words of the receipt. That such responsibilities were assumed by the President, is abundantly shown by the letters of Yates & McIntyre, 310 and other proofs that will be presently stated. But whether they were or not, here was a new consideration, entirely independent of the original agreement with Yates & McIntyre for $276,090.14, and the receipt says the 24 notes were received in part, on that consideration.

In addition to the explicit language of the receipt, the caption and items of the account, show on their face that it was not a settlement predicated upon the original contract 311 to pay $276.090.14, or on the notes given to pay that sum with interest in eleven years. Had it been, the account would have stated on the credit side the note and interest, or the several notes and the times they became due, and the interest on them. Instead of that, the heading of the first column of figures on the credit side is, "8¾ per cent on *each scheme.*" Then the items are "literature lottery 1st class, 2d class and so on, and the amount of 8¾ per cent 312 on the scheme price of each class is carried out, exactly in conformity to the stipulations of January 4th and 20th of 1826," "the same (the per centage) to be paid, estimating the per centum on the tickets sold at their scheme price in each class, and in all the classes hitherto drawn, as well as those hereafter to be drawn under said act, immediately after the drawing thereof." (Doc. IX.)

This is the exact principle on which the account is 313 stated, and the interest on the percentage upon each scheme is calculated from the time of drawing. Nothing can be more different in results than the two modes of stating the account.

Had it been stated in the form of crediting the College (equivalent, to *charging* Yates & McIntyre,) the amount of the note for $276,090.14 with interest, and then crediting the College (equivalent to crediting Yates & McIntyre) 314

with the payments on the Dr. side of the account as they
stand, by thus stopping interest, the total amount due the
College would not have been $300,000; or, if it had been
stated in the form of crediting the College (or charging
Yates & McIntyre) with the ten notes of $39,312 each, ac-
cording to the election given by the supplemental contract,
315 then the total would have been $393,120, and indeed much
less, because the interest on the last four notes would have
stopped, they being paid before they became due; whereas
it is now $433,002.23, a result that could not possibly have
been attained in either of the other modes of stating the
account. There is therefor on the face of the account
conclusive evidence that it was not made and settled, upon
the original contract for $276,090.14

316 But it affords in itself affirmative and conclusive evidence, from the fact of crediting the College the percentage on the scheme price of the tickets in each class, that
it proceeded on the terms of the stipulations of January 4,
and 24 of 1826, thereby recognizing those terms. There
was no agreement or stipulation other than those, then
in force, which provided for any percentage on any scheme
price.

317 It is evident on the face of the proposition, that it was
made to induce great pecuniary advances to be made, personal responsibilities to be incurred, and individual effort
to find and procure the desired relief. In its terms it required personal services, which, of course, the college
could not render, and which were not within any legitimate duties of its president. Yates and McIntyre were
then greatly indebted to the college, as already shown;
318 the college was itself borrowing large sums of money, as
appears by the accounts, and had neither means nor credit to afford the desired relief. That Yates and McIntyre
looked to and availed themselves of the personal services
and personal responsibility of the president, is abundantly established by their correspondence, of which a small
portion only is printed in the accompanying documents.

In their letter of May 30, 1826, written soon after the
319 stipulation was accepted, (doc. XVIII, fol. 119,) they made

a new proposition in relation to other lotteries, in respect
to which they say they have made a contract, "which contract they cannot execute without your content and co-
operation, as it will require a *further continuance* of the
heavy *personal* responsibilities assumed by you on our behalf," thus acknowledging that such responsibilities had
been assumed. 320

In a letter of A. McIntyre, of January 23, 1826, (doc.
XI, fol. 95,) he expressed "a grateful sense of our obligations to you for the prompt relief you have afforded us
in the hour of our difficulty and distress. We were, it
cannot be doubted, on the very verge of ruin." In a letter
of the same person, May 15, 1830, (doc. XIX, fol. 125,)
he says, "it gives me sincere pleasure, that we have been
able at length, to get released your property, which you 321
kindly hypothecated to raise funds for us in 1826, to save
us at a critical moment from ruin."

The pamphlet called chancery documents, which Mr.
Beekman made part of his testimony, abounds with ac-
knowledgments by Yates and McIntyre of monies, drafts
and securities sent to them by Dr. Nott, many of them
previous to their operations under the subsequent stipulations.

But there is one decisive piece of evidence on the sub- 322
ject, that disposes of this point. Jonas Holland, the treasurer, was directed to ascertain the amounts of their responsibilities and hazards, incurred respectively by the college and Dr. Nott. He did ascertain and state them, (see
doc. XXV, fol. 200,) and he says the responsibilities assumed
by Dr. Nott in behalf of Yates and McIntyre, amounted to
$338,000, while those of the college were $140,000. The 323
amount of their responsibilities was to be ascertained from
numerous papers and letters, many of them, doubtless, of
a confidential character. Mr. Holland never could have
discharged his duty without examining them, and the character we have had of him from all sides, forbids the idea
of any collusion. He was the chosen agent of the college;
his acts were communicated to its finance committee, who
approved them, and the trustees were satisfied. Better 324

evidence than this of transactions that occurred more than twenty years since, cannot well be furnished.

Some of the particular responsibilities assumed by him, that to Wm. James for his note of $100,000, and pledging his own and his wife's property to the amount of $40,000, for the relief of Yates & McIntyre, are stated in the re-
325 port of Messrs. Marcy and Cushman, of November 20, 1834. (Doc. XXIII, folio 185, beginning of the report.)

And that the trustees themselves, understood and acknowledged that these stipulations of January 4 and 24, 1826, were made with Dr. Nott individually, and not with the college, appears from the report of Messrs. Cushman and Dix, of July 25, 1837, (Doc. XXIV, folio 193,) where they say: "Whereas Yates & McIntyre *in addition* to the, *entire amount* due to Union College under their contract of
326 July 29, 1822, have stipulated to pay to Eliphalet Nott certain additional amounts in consideration of subsequent services rendered, monies advanced, and responsibilities assumed in behalf of Yates & McIntyre, either singly by himself, or jointly by himself and the college," &c.

These advances were made and these responsibilities were incurred, on the faith of, and in consideration for the *additional* sum stipulated to be paid by Yates & McIntyre,
327 so as to make their entire payments equal to eleven per cent on the amount of tickets sold at their scheme price, and to be paid immediately on the drawing of each class. (Doc. IX and XIII.)

These propositions were not in themselves contracts, from the want of mutuality; there was no promise or engagement by Dr. Nott, or any other party to it but Yates & McIntyre. It was the compliance with the request they
328 contained, that made them contracts, and of course they were contracts with the parties who thus complied. They were consummated by the settlement of August 1, 1828, and they then became contracts, and their conditions were then fulfilled. I have already shown that that settlement was based on the terms of these propositions.

If Mr. Henry Yates had any rights under them, he relinquished them by being a party to that settlement, and
329 assenting to the application of the profits arising out of the

contracts; but certainly, after an acquiescence of twenty-five years, he is forever precluded from setting up any claim under them; and in the tripartite agreement before mentioned, he released all present and future claims. This remark is made to dispel any apprehensions of any claim by Mr. Yates.

On this settlement of August 1, 1828, there was found a 330
balance due from Yates and McIntyre, of.. $137,383 89

For which 24 notes were given, payable at different times with interest. (P. 177 accountant's report.)		
There was due to the college, on the $8\frac{3}{4}$ per cent, upon the scheme price,...........		4,314 06
Leaving as profit, over and above the amount agreed to be paid by the original contracts,...........................		$133,068 23
Adding the interest to the times of payment,		33,788 56
Made the sum to be divided between the college and Dr. Nott, ...		$166,856 79
All the notes were made payable to E. Nott, and were delivered to him, and carrying out the spirit of the propositions in relation to the respective responsibilities of the college and himself, he divided to Union College, ...	$95,165 09	
To E. Nott,...............	71,691 70	
		166,856 79

331 332

And in this he did himself great injustice. The proportions of responsibilities assumed by the parties respectively, as stated by the treasurer, and above quoted, would have 333
given Dr. Nott a much larger sum. But in this, as in every instance, he evinced his devotion to the interests of the college.

And even the amount retained by him, has not been applied to any personal purpose, but spent in the improvement of the property purchased and held for the college.

The college is entirely concluded by its own acts on the 334

subject. The Trustees, by an express resolution, (Doc.
XLI) adopted the recommendation in the report of Messrs.
Cushman and Dix, (Doc. XXIV, folio 195,) that a settlement should be made with Dr. Nott, "based *on a division*
between him and the college of the said additional amounts
so received under such several stipulations, *pro rata*, ac-
335 cording to services rendered, moneys advanced, and responsibilities assumed by each," and that the Treasurer,
with the approbation of the other members of the finance
committee, be directed to consummate such settlement."

In pursuance of this authority, the treasurer stated the *pro rata* on which the settlement should be made, and this was approved by the other members of the finance committee, Messrs. Cushman and Flagg. (Doc. XXV.) Mr. Flagg's testimony, folio 310 of Doc's.

336 Being thus empowered, the treasurer and Dr. Nott made the settlement and distribution of the 24 notes, and the portion taken by the college was duly entered on its books, and used and applied to the purposes of the college. How can a settlement thus deliberately made under the authority of the Trustees, and fully executed by their officers, and of the fruits of which it has availed itself—how can it be disturbed, especially after such a lapse of time?

337 There never has been, and there cannot be, any allegation of fraud, misrepresentation, or even ignorance, on the part of the Trustees. They must have known, and were bound to know, that the money was in their treasury, and how it came there.

The Trustees never did question it, or express the least
dissatisfaction with it. Mr. Flagg says in his testimony,
(folios 309, 310, Doc's.) that this percentage was conceded
338 by the Trustees to belong to Dr. Nott, and was never
claimed by them; and this is confirmed by Gen. Dix, at
folio 292, Doc's.

This argument of the college being precluded by its own
acts from now advancing any claim for these 22 notes, is
not a mere technical one. It is founded in the purest justice and the highest morality. The condition of the par-
339 ties is changed, in consequence of the settlement. The

money retained, has been expended on the identical property bestowed on the college, so that if the charge were
made against Dr. Nott for these notes, common justice
would require that the amount so charged should be deducted and retained out of the property whose value has
been enhanced by the application of the amount charged.

I maintain, however, that if the question were entirely 340
open, no impartial tribunal on a consideration of the terms
of the propositions of January 4, and 24, of 1826, and of
the consideration actually rendered by Dr. Nott, would
hesitate to award him much more than the amount of the
22 notes.

One of the grounds on which the accountant places his
charge of these notes against Dr. Nott, is that by the bill
in Chancery, filed by Yates & McIntyre, against Union Col- 341
lege and Dr. Nott; they allege that all the notes given by
them (with certain exceptions that do not affect these
notes) were paid by them to Union College, and that this
is admitted by the answer. The averments in the bill
are simply that the notes have been paid; (see folio 29 to
31.) And the answer admits that they have been paid *at
the times* stated in the bill, but says nothing in respect to
the parties or persons to whom the payments were made. 342

It was not a point of controversy in that suit, *to which*
of the defendants the notes had been paid. The trustees
of the college and Dr. Nott were joined as defendants and
confederates, and the bill prayed relief against both. A
payment to one was a payment to both; and in no way determined their rights as between each other. With these
Yates & McIntyre had nothing to do, nor had the suit any
bearing upon them; and the answer was not intended to 343
embrace that question. But conceding, for the sake of the
argument, that the payments were made to the treasurer
of Union College, and are so admitted in the answer, it
has not the least bearing upon their accounts as between
themselves. It was a joint fund, and either might receive
it, subject to an account and settlement. And payments
to the treasurer were equally available to Dr. Nott, as if 344

made to himself; or if made to Dr. Nott, they would come
into his account with the college.

The accountant declares that he utterly rejects the books
of the college and their entries, in respect to the settlement of 1828, and depends wholly on the bill in chancery
of Yates & McIntyre, and the admissions in the answers.
345 This is a strange proceeding for one who has made a voluntary oath at the end of his statements, that "the foregoing accounts have been carefully prepared by him from
the books of account and fund books of the said college
as they were when delivered to him, and from vouchers
therein referred to." (Page 190, of his report.) The bill
and answer to which he refers, are no where referred to in
the books of the college, as vouchers or otherwise.

346 But he does not adhere to his own rule. Thus, in the
bill, Yates and McIntyre claim that the bond and mortgage of J. B. Yates, for $55,000, included in that settle-
ment of 1828, was not a payment, but was collateral security for their notes, (folio 26, p. 9, of bill.) Of course,
it should be deducted from the amount then paid.

They allege (folio 89, p. 21,) that the settlement of
1828 was entirely erroneous, and did not conform to the
347 agreements between the parties; and yet the accountant
makes this settlement the basis of his charge.

They allege (at folio 32, p. 4,) that the payments they
have made under the agreements in relation to the lottery,
exceed $534,000, exclusive of interest; and yet the ac-
countant takes the sum of $433,000.

Numerous other instances might be pointed out, but
these are sufficient.

348 Another ground of the accountant is the most extraordinary presented in this investigation. He labors to overturn the official decision of Comptroller Savage, the allegations in the bill of Yates & McIntyre, and their settlement with Union College, in respect to the amount authorised to be drawn by the Literature lottery, and having, as
he supposes, made this amount unlimited and indefinite, he
claims that the 22 notes were a part of it, and therefore
belong to the college. To accomplish this herculean task,
349 he begins by asserting that the $12,000 granted to the His-

torical Society, was not included in Comptroller Savage's decision of the amount of $322,256.81 to be raised for all the institutions. The production of the detailed statement of the amounts authorised to be raised by the lottery, in schedule E. annexed to Yates & McIntyre's bill, in which the grant to the Historical Society is included, and making
the total less than that fixed by the Comptroller, seemed 350
to put this assumption at rest, and to silence the accountant on this point.

He then seeks to give a construction to the fifth section of the act of 1822, (folio 10, 11, of Doc's) by which he says the amount to be raised, was indefinitely extended. That section relates exclusively to the average amount of tickets at their scheme price, that may be sold and drawn
annually, and has nothing to do with the *gross* amount. 351
That was provided for in the first section of the act, directing the Comptroller to ascertain and certify a limited time within which the lottery should be drawn and closed, which time was to be less than that within which monies had theretofore been raised by lottery by the State managers. This *time* could not be ascertained without first determining the whole amount to be raised, because it was a proportional question of time and amount. This the Comptroller did. I need not say to you that it is contrary to 352
all rule and all reason to strain one section of a statute so as to make it contradict a previous one, especially where the subject matters of the two are entirely different.

It is not the least of the accountant's difficulties, that his construction of the act is directly contrary to that of the Attorney General Bronson, in his report to the Assembly in 1833. (See Doc. XXVI). He overrules both the
Comptroller and the Attorney General. This assumption 353
is so preposterous, that there can be no occasion for further remark upon it.

The accountant, in his argument as counsel, refers to passages in the joint answer of the Trustees and Dr. Nott, to the amended bill of Yates & McIntyre, which he thinks are inconsistent with the idea that any part of the 24 notes
taken on the settlement on account of the stipulations of 354

January 4 and 24, 1826, belonged to Dr. Nott. Thus at
p. 26 of that answer, it is said that Dr. Nott had ample
authority to enter into those stipulations, under the original resolution, committing the whole control of the lottery
to him; and the accountant therefore infers that Dr. Nott
acted only as an agent of the college. The bill had al-
355 leged (p. 14) that those agreements were not obligatory,
because they had not been made under any authority derived from the Trustees, &c. The passage quoted from the
answer, is in answer to that charge, and merely affirms the
authority, and points to its source. A portion of these
agreements was undoubtedly made solely as agent, namely,
that portion which related to the mixing of the tickets of
the Literature lottery with the Albany and Fever Hospital
356 lotteries. But there was another portion of them that related to the procuring of pecuniary aid for Yates & McIntyre by Dr. Nott. In respect to this he acted individually,
and the promise of Y. & McI. was made to him personally,
and so acknowledged by them in the settlement of 1828, as
already shown. The passage quoted from the answer had
no reference to the respective interests of the college and
Dr. Nott, but related exclusively to his authority to act
357 in the premises at all.

The accountant also refers to a passage at p. 27 of the
answer, where it is said: "And these defendants further
answering, admit that they have pretended and still insist
that they became entitled to the eleven per centum on the
diferences between the two sums in that behalf stated, on
account of a stipulation between them and Y. & McI., as
hereinbefore stated." The accountant overlooked the cir-
358 cumstance that this was a joint answer by the Trustees
and Dr. Nott, and that when the answer says "these defendants" it means both. This, therefore, so far from being evidence of an admission that the college alone was
entitled to this eleven per centum, is evidence that it was
claimed as belonging to both, it and Dr. Nott, as we have
always maintained, and as the proceeds were ultimately
divided.

359 The accountant also refers to passages in the upper part

of p. 26 of the answer, as containing admissions that the
Trustees were parties to the agreement of January, 1826,
and that the Trustees had a legal and valid right to the
eleven per centum. Here the accountant has entirely
mistaken the subject of that part of the answer. Y. &
McI. had in their bill (pp. 19, 20,) alleged that the sum of
$2,004,099 of tickets which was stated in the agreement of 360
1826 as being the amount yet to be drawn for Union College, was erroneous, and that the expression in reference
to it in the agreement was "incorrect and unfounded in
fact."

The answer, beginning at the foot of page 35, answers
this allegation, and all that follows and to which the accountant refers, relates exclusively to the *amount* on which
the eleven per centum was to be calculated; affirming that 361
the sum was correctly stated in the agreement, and had no
relation whatever to the eleven per centum itself.

It is very probable that in such a long answer, loose and
general expressions may be found, which do not always
discriminate the respective rights of the two sets of defendants. But this answer, like every other paper, is to be
read as a whole, and where discriminations are once made
or a fact is once stated with precision, the omission to re- 362
peat it exactly in other parts, is not to be regarded either
as a contradiction or as an admission contrary to the more
precise statement.

The idea has been thrown out, that all these contracts
and arrangements were made by Dr. Nott in his official
character, as president and as agent for Union College,
and that therefore the profits and benefits accruing from
them, resulted to his principal, the college. 363

In the first place, the fact is otherwise. It has already
been abundantly shown that a consideration and moving
cause in each case was the personal services, the hazards
encountered, and the responsibilities assumed, and advances made personally and individually by him, and that
the college in its corporate capacity was not in a condition
to render any effectual service or aid, without collateral 364
guarantees of Dr. Nott.

In the second place, the rule which gives to the principal the profits of an agent, applies only to the cases where
the agent deals with the property of the principal, and by
using it makes a profit. It would be absurd to say that
Union College was entitled to any advantages one of its
officers might gain by dealing with his own property, or
365 rendering his own personal services, or his personal
responsibilities. It has been shown that Union College had
not and could not have any legal interest in the fund for
management and supervision, other than that given by Dr.
Nott. And it has also been shown that the profits made
under the stipulation of January 4, 1826, were at least in
part for the personal services and responsibilities of Dr.
Nott. And accordingly, the college has treated with the
366 supposed agent, as acting for himself, and not as agent, in
respect to that part. There is no principle which requires
a man receiving a salary to account to the party paying it,
for the profits of any other business in which he may engage. The remedy for a waste of time is to dismiss the
officer, or to deduct from his salary a rateable sum for the
time lost.

It will hardly be alleged that the pecuniary interests of
367 the college suffered by any appropriation of the time of
its president to the supervision of the lottery, and to the
sustaining the credit of the contractors, by which the latter were enabled to fulfil their obligations to the college,
and which they never could have done without such aid.
On the contrary, it must be gratifying to the trustees and
friends of the college, to find, after so much labor and
hazard and censure, that while the literature lottery, un-
368 der the management of officers appointed by the State, had
not, at the expiration of nine years, produced enough even
to pay the interest on the grants for which it was authorised, and which, in the judgment of the sagacious Comptroller, Savage, was not likely to fulfil its purpose in less
than eleven years more, it has, under private management
in five years satisfied all the grants it was created to raise,
and been finally closed. It would really seem as if some-
369 thing beside obloquy and reproach in private, and in pub-

lic legislative enquiries and reports, instigated and made
by strangers to the institution; it would seem as if something beside these was due to the individual whose energy,
perseverance and ability had saved the contractors from
ruin, and enabled them to pay their obligations to the
college. That the reputation of the college, as a seminary
of learning, has not suffered by any misapplication of the
time of the president to its pecuniary affairs, is quite evi- 370
dent from the regular and constant increase of the pupils
during the period of the president's being thus employed,
and since.

I think you will be satisfied that the three principal
items which have been discussed, the $150,000 bond, the
president's fund, and the twenty-two notes of Yates and Mc-
Intyre, (part of the twenty-four given by them,) did belong to Dr. Nott individually; and that the corporation of 371
Union College never can assert, as it never has asserted,
any claim to them or either of them. I say nothing about
the bar of the statute of limitations, which would indeed
be sufficient, but I rely on the facts and circumstances exhibiting the equity of Dr. Nott's claim, and on the formal
and deliberate settlements and acts of the trustees with
him, and their acquiescence in and confirmation of those
acts. 372

How can strangers, the State, or any one else, set up
claims thus extinguished, and demand an incredible
amount as being due to the college on account of them?
Is it not preposterous on its face?

The accountant has utterly misconceived his duty. He
was to examine the books of the college for ascertained
facts, and to state the results. He had no authority to go
beyond those books, and to fabricate claims and accounts 373
which the trustees never made.

And how, gentlemen, can you entertain jurisdiction of
these claims? For what purpose, to what end? You
cannot award the amounts of them to Union College.

It would seem indeed, that the addition made to the resolution for your appointment on the motion of Mr.
Beekman, and to which the Senate assented probably to 374

terminate his importunities and a long discussion, provides for your reporting to the Attorney-General. That officer is an ex-officio trustee of the college, and one would suppose could make his own enquiries, without a committee of the Senate becoming his scavengers. When the report comes to him, what is he to do? As to disturbing
375 the arrangements made with Dr. Nott in good faith, and overturning the conclusive acts of the parties, he can no more accomplish it than the trustees themselves. As to proceeding against the present trustees for the acts of their predecessors, even if they had been fraudulent, which no one pretends, it is too absurd to be attempted.

The only practical effect of the enquiry, is, therefore, to ascertain whether the funds granted by the State have
376 been faithfully applied, and whether the permanent funds are safely invested. Beyond these objects, the result of your enquiries can only affect the personal character of Dr. Nott.

The fourth enquiry contemplated by the resolution for your appointment is whether any losses have occurred in the management of the college, and the causes of such losses?

377 The accountant in schedule No. 6, p. 67, gives a list of losses amounting to $44,727.14, as having occurred during a period of 56 years! in the concerns of an institution, whose receipts have amounted to $4,469,915.34, as exhibited by him, page 56; about one dollar on a hundred. And of this amount, losses of $40,197 were upon stocks in banks to which the college had been invited to subscribe by acts of the legislature. Considering the great induce-
378 ments to such investments by institutions that do not desire to speculate on their sale, and the great revolutions in trade, commerce, and all money transactions, particularly banking operations, during the last fifty years, the wonder is, not that there should have been such losses, but that they were not of greater magnitude.

Under the head of losses, may be classed the investments which the accountant has so strangely charged to
379 the account of Dr. Nott.

At pages 83, 84, the accountant charges to Dr. Nott
$55,641.92, the amount with interest of certain investments
there specified. He finds no such charges in the books of
the college, but undertakes arbitrarily upon his own discretion to make them. And he seeks to justify his unau-
thorized decision, by appending a resolution of the Board of
Trustees of the college in 1831, directing on what security 380
loans shall be made, and that they should be sanctioned by
the finance committee. He does not question the fact that
they were so sanctioned; but he assumes the office of a
judge, and undertakes to decide that at the several times
when the loans were made, they were not upon unincum-
bered real estate worth double the value of the moneys
loaned, exclusive of buildings. He had no evidence except the *present* value of the property mortgaged, and that 381
the investments have proved to be losses! He assumes
that the finance committee abused the discretion vested in
them, and thereupon charges the losses, not to the members
of the committee who participted in the loans, but to one
of them!

It is scarcely necessary to say to this committee, that the
circumstances which shall render a private trustee responsible for a breach of trust, and the extent of that responsi- 382
bility, present questions of great difficulty and delicacy to
courts of equity, and require a very thorough examination
and a recurrence to principles of considerable complexity;
and yet here is a man who assumes all these functions of a
court, and in the absence of the party charged, and without
a particle of evidence, except the mere fact of the investments turning out to be bad or questionable, at once charges
honorable and distinguished men with culpable neglect, 383
and proposes to punish them by holding one of them responsible for the result! You know very well that such
responsibility cannot be incurred by a trustee or director
of a public corporation, without *culpable* neglect or intentional fraud, one or the other of which is therefore imputed
by the very fact of charging the supposed loss. 2 John.
Ch. 389; 3 Paige 231; 5 Paige 612.

All that is necessary to say on this subject is, that the 384 presumption that these investments were made in good faith, and in the exercise of a sound discretion upon an honest estimate of the value of the property mortgaged, exists and is conclusive until the contrary is shown. No evidence of the kind has been or can be adduced.

The accountant, has, as usual, a strange theory on this
385 subject. He says, as counsel, that Dr. Nott is chargeable personally, because he received the avails of these investments! A man who assigns securities to another, without fraud, and without any guaranty of the value of the securities, or the responsibility of the parties to them, is, according to this new law, to be charged with the amount of them, if at any time they prove worthless! And this, without any enquiry as to the diligence of the assignees,
386 or as to notice to him. I think you will regard this law, as of the same quality with that we have so often had expounded from the same quarter.

With respect to one of these investments, that in the bond and mortgage of Edward James, for $14,000; it is proved, beyond all question, by Mr. James himself, (see folio 339 to 340, and 344 of Doc.'s,) that they were given to secure his debt to H. Nott & Co., who authorised them
397 to be made directly to E. Nott, and guaranteed the payment, as was just and proper; and that it was provided for by their assignment, and paid by their assignees, and its receipt acknowledged by the Treasurer. This testimony was fully corroborated by B. Nott, one of the firm of H. Nott & Co. It is impossible for the accountant to make Dr. Nott chargeable with the amount of this security, and the enormous amount of $15,383.03 interest on it, as he
388 does at p. 113 and 83, as a bad investment, by assuming that Dr. Nott is responsible for certain notes of Stratton and Seymour, delivered to him. When such a distinct charge is made, in a tangible shape, it will be time to attend to it. But it can not destroy the fact, that the bond and mortgage are paid, and are not chargeable to any one. How they have been retained by the college, and considered a part of their assets, may be explained by the con-
389 fusion arising from the death of Jonas Holland, the Treasu-

rer, and by the fact that they were regarded as worthless,
and not of sufficient importance to inquire about. But it
is not seen how this course of the college officers can revive or make them chargeable to Dr. Nott.

The note of John A. Yates, which the accountant regards
as a loss, and also charges to Dr. Nott, was given for an
advance made to him while he was a professor, to enable 390
him to visit Europe, and having been made by Dr. Nott, in
behalf of the college, the note was endorsed by him to vest
the title to it in the college. The Trustees assumed it, in
the hope of securing its payment out of the salary of the
professor. A payment in that way of $168.05 seems to
have been made on it, (accountant's report, p. 129.) The
college never charged Dr. Nott as endorser, and the treasurer testifies that he did not charge him, because, under 391
the circumstances, it ought not to be done. The accountant, however, in his argument, admitted that this charge
ought not to be made against Dr. Nott; and he also admitted that the bond of B. Nott ought not to be charged as it
had been, because he could not trace any agency of Dr.
Nott in the exchange of another security for it.

These are all the items that can be called *losses*. The
first set, at p. 67 of accountant's statement, 392

amount to..............................	$44,727 14
The second set of bad investments, (pp. 83, 84,) amount to,....	55,641 92
Making a total of,......................	$100,369 06

It appears from the report of the treasurer, January 1,
1853, and by the report of the auditing committee, (Doc's.
XXXV, XXXVI,) that the college has gained, in the pur- 393
chase of property by Dr. Nott, out of his own means, and
which was charged by him at cost, $118,930.45. Besides
this large gain, it appears from the testimony of the treasurer (Doc. XLVI, folio 426,) that the college has derived
large pecuniary profits from the purchase of the rights of
the other institutions in the lottery, which was accomplished by the advance of Dr. Nott's private means; and 394

that he had expended considerable sums, gratuitously, on the improvements of the college grounds and buildings; so that, as the treasurer testifies, if all the losses on loans and bad debts, debited to Dr. Nott by the accountant, were charged to him, and he were credited with the gains that have enured to the college from the use of his private
395 funds, he would, on a final settlement, be found a creditor of the college to a large amount.

In the broad, equitable view, which I am persuaded you will take, of the dealings between the college and its President, it is most apparent that a cruel injustice would be committed in charging the losses and bad debts to Dr. Nott individually, whatever may have been his relations to any of them.

396 The 5th inquiry directed by the resolution is, whether the President or any other officer has, while in the employment of the college, participated individually in the profits of any lotteries which were appropriated to Union College?

So far as the President is concerned in this inquiry, it has already been answered in relation to the only matters that Mr. Vanderheyden has ventured to specify, viz, the President's fund and the 22 notes of Yates & McIntyre.
397 It has been shown that these were not profits of lotteries appropriated to Union College by the acts granting lotteries; that the President's fund and the profits arising from the proposition of January 4, 1826, were wholly independent of the grants to the institutions; that it was not entitled by the act of 1822 to the President's fund, and that the second item arose from a personal contract with Dr. Nott.

398 Having now finished the answers to the specific enquiries, I propose to consider the account stated at p. 81 of the accountant's report, between Union College and Dr. Nott, wherein he is made a debtor to the college in the enormous sum of $885, 789.62.

That such a debt should exist without the knowledge or suspicion of the Trustees, very many of whom were familiar with the affairs of the college, is one of the marvels
399 in book-keeping, calculated to astonish every one. That

this is a fabricated, forced and utterly unfounded account,
I now proceed to show.

It commences with what he calls *loans* to Dr. Nott,
a misnomer which a member of the committee has noticed.
The accountant gives that name to any charge or series of
charges he has been able to rake up out of the rubbish of
years, for what he considers mis-payments or over-pay- 400
ments, and to temporary transactions where the President,
in order to save for the college the greatest amount of interest, took any considerable sum that was in the Treasurer's hands, for which he gave his own obligations, and
then deposited it with houses of the first character, to
be repaid at call or on demand, at 7 per cent interest, until
they could be permanently invested, always leaving collateral security. What is called loan No. 1, $1.564.42 401
principal, is for cash paid Dr. Nott July 18, 1807, very nearly
50 years ago! Of course an explanation of such a charge
is next to impossible. Common experience, as well as the
law, assumes that an individual or a corporation, who will
omit to make a claim until all evidence on the subject is
presumed to be lost, has no right to the claim. This is a
sufficient answer to the charge. But we think we have
shown you that the President had claims for allowances 402
for fuel, lights, repairs, &c., and that he made advances to
the college on general account from time to time. The
present Treasurer says, that it is evident from the books
that the college had no money to lend on a long credit,
and that if an account was opened for the different advances made by Dr. Nott, and this and other items of a
like character were charged to him, he would be a creditor
of the college to a large amount. (Folio 429.) All these 403
considerations show the impropriety of this charge.

The next, called loan No. 2, is a principal sum of $15,-
006.01, consisting of payments made to Dr. Nott between
July 1, 1826, and August 31, 1829, as entered on the
books of the college, *as payments* for "interest on money
borrowed," and for "interest;" on their face, they are payments of debts due. But the accountant denied that there
was any interest due by the college on any loans made to 404

it, which was not paid otherwise and so entered on the college books. On the contrary, we have shown from the copies of accounts in the Mohawk Bank produced by the accountant, that there *was* interest due from the college to that bank, on the balances of accounts against the college, stated every six months, *part only* of which was paid by
405 the college; and that the residue unpaid, amounted in all the cases but one or two, to the precise sums entered as having been paid to Dr. Nott for interest. (See Mr. Pearson's testimony, Doc. XLVII, and his statement.) We maintain that neither the college, nor any one for them, can at this day be permitted to contradict their own entries; and that if permitted, the burthen is on them, not on us, to establish a clear and manifest error. And we say, that so far
406 from establishing any error in the payment of this interest, the evidence strongly corroborates the entries.

Loans 3 and 4 are paid and balanced, and nothing is claimed for them by the accountant.

On loan No. 5, the interest only is claimed.

The items of the account, as stated at p. 197, comprise various advances at different times; some of them to Dr. Nott, as chairman of the finance committee in 1835, 1836,
407 1837, and 1838, but no interest appears to have been charged on either side. Dr. Nott is unable to explain why it was not charged, otherwise than that the nature of the transactions was such, that in the opinion of Jonas Holland, the Treasurer, who was a faithful and vigilant officer, no interest should be charged, or it certainly would have been. Where so many sums of money have been received and paid by the parties, it depends on the selection of the items,
408 whether the payments are cotemporaneous or nearly so, with the receipts. It has been difficult to discover the rule adopted by the accountant, and we are unable to say whether a different classification ought to be made, or whether it would produce a different result as to the interest. But we suppose it a sufficient answer to the charge, that after such a lapse of time as 15 years, the just as well as legal presumption is, that it ought not to have
409 been charged. The rule of law, as well as of equity is,

that where the principal debt is satisfied, interest cannot be claimed, unless there is an express agreement to pay it. 13 Wend. 639; 15 do. 76; 11 Paige, 42.

The 6th, is also a claim for $1,160.79 of interest upon a very long account, commencing at p. 102, and occupying four pages, and part of another. The same remarks are aplicable to this, as to the last preceding one. 410

What are called loans 7 and 8, are balanced, and nothing is claimed.

Loan No. 9, was an apparent balance of $12,000 principal, and $1,343.80 interest. A mortgage had been placed in the Treasurer's hands, as Mr. Pearson testifies, to the amount, but was withdrawn, on account of some objections as to the property being free from incumbrances, in order to substitute another, for which purpose the account was left 411
open. The acting Treasurer says, the security has been replaced, and the interest paid.

The next is loan No. 10, or the special loan, p. 112, principal $6,720, and interest $433.78. The acting treasurer testified that this was an open and running account, that fluctuated from time to time, the balances varying on each side, and on the 1st of January, 1853, happened to be as stated; but that since that time, to which the ac- 412
countant's report was made up, the balance has been paid, and that it was in Dr. Nott's favor when he testified.

The next item, the amount of the 22 notes of Yates & McIntyre, amounting with interest to $180,547,28, has already been fully discussed, and the injustice of charging Dr. Nott, with those notes, has been fully exposed.

The next item is the balance of the principal of the President's fund, after crediting the $42,000 paid, but not 413
crediting any expenses arising from the supervision and management of the lotteries, amounting to $80,798.84, and the interest, $151,740.63, making a grand total of $232,-539.47. This, also, has already been disposed of.

The next item, is a charge for 305 shares of Albany Commercial Bank stock, principal $6,786.25, and amounting with interest to $16,601.37.

The documentary proof herewith presented, (Doc, 414

XXVII, folio 265,) and the testimony of Edward James, and
Benjamin Nott, establish, beyond question, that this stock
was loaned to Howard Nott, & Co., that it was assigned as
collateral security, for a debt that was afterwards paid,
and surrendered to H. Nott, & Co., and they sold it in
parcels to several persons. That on their failure they
415 executed an assignment of their property, specially
providing for the payment of their liabilities to Union
College, and for the liabilities of E. Nott, on their
account; and that the assignees paid to the treasurer
of Union College, $78,214.27, in full, of all claims and
demands of the college against Howard Nott, & Co.,
and the treasurer gave a full and general receipt and
discharge of the claims of the college against them, and
416 against E. Nott, for advances to them through him. Mr.
James is positive that the price of this stock was included
in the sum paid by the assignees, and Benjamin Nott corroborated him. It stood in Dr. Nott's name, and was transferred by him directly to the company that loaned money
upon it, instead of passing through H. Nott, & Co. The
accountant seemed to have had great difficulty in understanding how the stock could belong to the college, or af-
417 terwards to H. Nott, & Co, without a regular transfer of it
appearing on the books of the bank. Few will entertain
the same difficulty; at all events, it is certain the college
has received the price of this stock; and if it did not own
it, it should account to Dr. Nott for it, instead of his being
charged for it.

The attempt of the accountant to revive this charge, after it had thus been effectually disposed of, evinces both
418 his tenacity and his perverseness. He admits it was paid,
as proved, but claims that inasmuch as certain notes of
Stratton and Seymour, were returned to Dr. Nott, to an
amount much more than the price of this stock, and which
notes he says are not accounted for, therefore he ought
still to be charged with the stock. Now, we suppose, that
if the stock is paid for, there is an end of this charge at
least. And when any charge for the notes is made, we
419 will meet it.

The next item consists of the bad investments which the accountant in the exercise of the plenary powers of a court of equity, has charged to one of the officers of the corporation who made them. These have already been discussed, and I hope satisfactorily disposed of.

The next item is the charge of $8,657.91 for Hallet Cove and Williamsburgh Turnpike stock. 420

This stock was subscribed for by the college in 1839 and 1840, while the property to be benefited by the turnpike belonged to the college. (See p. 134 accountant's report.) The authority for the subscription, by the trustees of the college, was produced before the committee in the original minutes of the board. How Dr. Nott is to be responsible for this purchase of stock by the Trustees, more than any other member of the board, surpasses comprehension. The 421
accountant himself is so convinced of the injustice of this charge, that he abandons it.

The next items are the charges for the Hunter Point land and the Stuyvesant Cove property. Here, too, the accountant has assumed judicial powers, and undertaken to set aside transactions deliberately made and sanctioned by the board. (Doc. XXX, folio 223.)

The accountant seems, from his statement, (p. 133) to 422
consider the re-conveyance of the half of the Hunter farm by Union College to Dr. Nott, in 1845, after having purchased it from him in 1838, seven years previous, as restoring the parties to their original condition, and therefore charges the interest on the consideration from 1838, instead of charging it from the time of the conveyance by the college. And for the same reason, he charges interest on the original consideration paid by the college for the half of 423
the Stuyvesant Cove property, $58,632.15 from 1838, when the college bought it.

Now, it is not denied that Dr. Nott is accountable for the consideration money for the purchase of these tracts; but we contend that interest should be charged only from the time the title vested in him. And in relation to the Stuyvesant Cove property we say, that he should be charged 424

the consideration for the whole, which was actually conveyed to him, not for the half only, with interest from the time of the conveyance. This makes the amount chargeable to Dr. Nott, for both the tracts, $348,447.78, while the accountant's charges amount to $306,034.81 for the same lands, a difference of $42,412.97 against Dr. Nott.
But it is submitted that this is the only legal and correct
425 mode.

An issue has been got up in relation to these tracts, which is entirely collateral to the accounts, and will therefore be postponed for the present; with the single remark, that these lands were paid for by Dr. Nott, by offsetting the price of them against the same amount of monies in the treasurer's hands belonging to him; and that as those monies were always intended as donations to the college, and
426 the lands are given to it, it was merely a change of the
form of the donations, converting the money into land, and that therefore it is quite immaterial what price was allowed the college, so long as it did not exceed the amount of monies deposited with the treasurer.

The last item is a charge for mortgages, taxes, assessments and rents on the Cove property, $25,623.92, and interest to Jan'y 1, 1853, $27,637.47, the particulars of which
427 are given at p. 135, 136, &c., of the accountant's state-
ment.

These rents, taxes and assessments, were charges on the property while it belonged to the college. See the dates of them in the statement 23, p. 135, &c.

It is inconceivable why they should be charged to Dr. Nott. He purchased the property subsequent to the accruing of these charges.

428 When was it ever before heard of, that the vendor of
land charged the purchaser with the taxes and assessments on it, which he had paid previous to the sale?

With regard to the mortgage on this property, at the foot of p. 137, and top of 138, is the following entry: "Cash paid on a mortgage on the Stuyvesant Cove property, sold to Dr. Nott, *on condition that said mortgage be paid.* The amount now due, *given* to Dr. Nott, and the
429 college released from their obligation to cancel said mort-

gage," $6,058.02. This entry is contradictory and unintelligible, unless it means that the college was in some way originally under obligations to pay this mortgage, and having paid the balance of the principal due, $6,000 and the interest, it was released from that obligation. Of course, Dr. Nott is not chargeable with it.

At p. 138, he enters as a credit, 23 shares of stock in the 430
Poudrette company, received on account of rent, $2,300. But he says as it was valueless, its credit is withheld. Of course, the withholding it, increases just so much the charge against Dr. Nott.

By what authority does he withhold this credit, and thus charge Dr. Nott a loss occasioned by the college receiving in payment of its debts, a worthless stock? It is
evidently erroneous. 431

Having thus examined each item on the Dr. side of this account, it will be seen, that with the exception of the Hunter farm and Stuyvesant Cove, and the loans 9 and 10, there is not a single correct charge; and these loans, 9 and 10, have been paid since the report was made. It is apparent, therefore, that of this monstrous account of 855,000 dollars there is nothing really chargeable to Dr. Nott, except
the Hunter farm and Stuyvesant Cove. 432

Let us now turn to the *credit* side of this account, and notice the remarkable omissions of credits that should be there, and which the accountant has arbitrarily rejected.

1st. Neziah Bliss' bond and mortgage, $75,225.32 on interest, received from Dr. Nott, July 1, 1834.

This is stated by the accountant, in statement No. 24, p. 139. But on the Dr. side, the same sum is charged to Dr.
Nott; immediately under the charge is a note by the Trea- 433
surer, Jonas Holland, " that in reality, there was no money paid by the Trustees for the said land, but the record was made in a way that would not increase the Treasurer's responsibility."

The reason given by Mr. Vanderheyden, on his examination as a witness, for not crediting this bond and mortgage to Dr. Nott, was, that the Treasurer, Jonas Holland,
was an honest man, and would not have charged it to Dr. 434

Nott, unless he thought he ought to be charged; and that
the fact of the charge being made, is evidence that the
bond and mortgage were at the same time returned to Dr.
Nott, and thus the account was balanced by the debit
charge.

The memorandum attached by Mr. Holland, not only
435 imports no such thing, but shows the reverse. It does not
intimate that the securities were returned to Dr. Nott,
which would have been untrue, as will presently appear,
but it is made to record the fact, that no consideration was
paid by the college for them. The Treasurer seems to
have supposed it necessary to debit the amount, in an account *between him and the college*, to avoid a charge against
himself of $75,225.32, which would have been the case,
436 if not debited. The account made out by Mr. Vanderheyden, at p. 139, is between Dr. Nott and the college, and
gives to this entry a different character from what it possesses in the college books, as an account between the college and the Treasurer; it is made in the Treasurer's cash
book, he first debiting himself with the bond and mortgage, and then crediting himself with it; and to explain
this credit to himself, he makes the above memorandum.
437 He makes no charge against Dr. Nott.

This bond and mortgage were received under a resolution
of the Trustees of July 25, 1837, directing them to be
taken. (See folio 196, Doc's.) The college received a
release by Bliss of his equity of redemption in the mortgaged premises, and discharged his bond; (See Bliss' testimony and the records,) and the college subsequently
conveyed the premises to Dr. Nott, for which it is credited
438 by him $75,225, in the consideration for the whole proper-
ty. It is impossible that any theory of book-keeping can
exonerate the college from accountability for the value of
this bond and mortgage, and the perverseness of the accountant in thus making Mr. Holland's entry mean just
the reverse of what it was made to express, is not a little remarkable.

2d. There is a credit of $29,430.92, given to Dr. Nott as
439 principal, and $31,606.67 for interest on it, as the balance

of the $150,000 bond of Yates, McIntyre & Ely, after ap-
propriating the great bulk of it, $120,569.08, to Union
College. This matter has been so fully discussed, that it
is unnecessary to dwell on it here. This credit should be
for the whole amount of the payments made by Yates,
McIntyre & Ely, on their bond to the treasurer of Union
College, and by him received in trust for Dr. Nott.

I have prepared, and submit herewith, a statement of 440
the transactions between the college and Dr. Nott, on the
above principles. It shows a balance in favor of Dr. Nott,
more than sufficient to cover the supposed interest due on
loans 5 and 6, the only items in Mr. Vanderheyden's account, which there is the least pretence, unfounded as
it is, for charging to Dr. Nott, except the Hunter farm and
Stuyvesant cove property. But there is an item which
should be charged against Dr. Nott, of $46,649.85, paid 441
him September 21, 1848, and the interest, with which he
has always charged himself, with some difference in interest, but which the accountant has discovered to be chargeable, only since he made out his report.

Thus, it will be seen, that the indebtedness made out
by the accountant against Dr. Nott, of $885,789.69, is in
fact, not only imaginary, but that the college is indebted
to him, regarding it as a mere money account between him 442
and the college.

But although in the form of one, it is not a money account.
It is a condensed view of the donations of Dr. Nott to the
college, and of the changes of form which they assumed
when converted into other property. Thus the amount of
the Bliss bond, and a large portion of the payments on the
$150,000 bond, are changed into the half of the Hunter 443
farm and Stuyvesant cove property, which have taken, and
are to take the same destination as the moneys and security they represent were to take; that is, they belong in
fact to the college. The title was taken merely for convenience in the management of the property. The $46,-
649.85, received and credited by Dr. Nott, has been expended, with much more, in the improvements of the real
estate given to the college. Dr. Nott has never claimed 444

payment from the college for any balance of this nominal account, but has always considered it the property of the college.

In his report to the trustees for 1833, (Doc. XXXIII, folio 241,) he states that the moneys received from Yates & McIntyre, under his personal contract with them, al-
445 though appropriated as he mentioned to the college, had been invested in lands in New-York and on Long Island, and in good securities, with the approbation of the finance committee. He thus, at that early day, indicated that whatever form of investment these profits he destined for the college, might take, they were to be and were held as the ultimate property of the college.

It is, therefore, an entirely erroneous view, to regard
446 these transactions of Dr. Nott with the college, as between debtor and creditor. They were, as already said, mere changes in the forms of his donations, of which a memorandum was kept, for the sole purpose of being able to trace the funds through their different shapes, and to see that they were kept entire; and such is the character of the account I now lay before you.

In the account thus made up by the accountant, are items
447 of interest amounting to $541,630.59, and after deducting the interest allowed Dr. Nott on the $29,430.92, balance of the $150,000 bond, and amounting to $31,606.67, he makes a balance of interest against Dr. Nott, of $510,-023.92. This balance he carries into the revenue account of No. 4, p. 60, as part of the assets of the college. It is hardly necessary to observe, that as this balance of interest is predicated upon principal items which have no existence
448 but in the brain of the accountant, it is wholly incorrect, and that there is no such sum due the college; and thus the revenue account has no such balance as he states, $432,-095.61, or any other balance to carry to the summary No. 1, p. 6, where he has placed it.

The accountant has stated that other charges than those contained in his report, should be made against Dr. Nott. The first is the $46,649.85 already mentioned, and with

449

which Dr. Nott has always charged himself with some difference of interest.

The next is $1,500 premium on Farmers' Bank stock,
which Dr. Nott took at par. All that can be said on this, is
that the Treasurer testifies (Doc. XLVI, folio 439,) that he
sold it for the best price he could get, after making inquiries
respecting its market value, and that its value fluctuated. 450
Mr. Vanderheyden offers himself as a witness on this point,
and testifies that the stock was, *in reality*, worth as much in
1842, as in 1834!

He claims, also, an indefinite sum of about $7,000, for
excess in payments of salary, of which a statement is given
at p. 141 to 149. Our answer is, that Dr. Nott had other
charges against the college for allowances, for fuel, light,
repairs of dwellings, &c., amounting to more than the 451
balance claimed, as testified by the Treasurer (Doc. XLVI,
folio 429). The charge is brought forward at the last moment of the sitting of the committee to take testimony, and
can only be answered as generally as it is made.

The differences between us and the accountant, respecting most of the principles of his account, have thus been
presented. But there is an important principle adopted by
him, which swells the apparent amount of the property of 452
the college, as we conceive, most unwarrantably. In his
revenue account, he has charged for interest received, of
all kinds, $358,744.62, while the only credits for interest,
are those paid on loans, $232,500.68.

The difference, $126,243.94, is thus made an accumula-
tion of income, when it is notorious, and is shown by the
accountant himself, that the current expenses exceeded the 453
income. The history of the college shows, that it is impossible that there should have been such an accumulation.
The difference of interest, or large portions of it, must,
from the history we have of the embarrassments of the
college, have been applied to the payment of interest on
ordinary expenses previously incurred, contained in accounts and contracts, the payments of which would be en- 454
tered in gross, without separating the interest.

There does not appear to be any account of interest received or paid previous to 1826, except a single item of
$3,861.99, paid the State, April 14, 1806, p. 58. The de-
tailed statement, furnished by the accountant, commences
in the year 1826. It is in proof that the college was
much embarrassed previous to that time, and borrowed
455 money, besides running in debt otherwise. Much interest
must have been paid before the account commences. The
interest account is therefore imperfect.

It is submitted, that as it is evident from the accountant's own exhibit in No. 4, that the current expenses exceeded the income, including interest, the balance of that item ought not to be brought into the account as capital.

Various instances have been presented during the inves-
456 tigation, in which interest and rents received have been
charged as capital. Many of these are pointed out in a
paper submitted by me, and prepared for the convenience
of the committee, containing our objections, in the most
brief form, to the items in the accountant's summary No. 1.
These objections are now submitted as a part of this argument, and are printed in the documents annexed as Doc.
XLIX, together with the accountant's summary. The trea-
457 surer has also prepared a summary of the financial condition
of the college on the 1st of January last, according to our
view of the facts, and the principles on which it should be
made, which is also printed as Doc. L. This has been read
to you. It contains the substance and essence of this whole
inquiry.

We have prepared and now submit an account of receipts
and disbursements in the only mode which was now practi-
458 cable. We have adopted the statement No. 3 of the accountant, except where any item is struck out or amended
by us; and we have shown the results of the debits and
credits where the account is so reformed.

It seemed idle to copy some 40 or 50 pages of items to
which no objection was made; and it seems to us that the
mode we have adopted is far more convenient for compa-
459 rison.

The results of our account are exhibited in the following

RECAPITULATION:

To be added to the debit side of accountant's statement No. 3, ...	$3,750 00		
To be deducted from the debit side, ...	861,768 19		
To be added to the credit side,	....		460
To be deducted from credit side, ...	828,255 64		
Debit side of accountant's statement No. 3, total, ...	$4,469,015 34		
Additions as above, ...	3,750 00		
	$4,472,765 34		
Deductions as above, ...	861,768 19		461
Remaining, ...	$3,610,997 15		
Credit side of accountant's statement, total,		$4,469,015 34	
Additions as above, ...		....	
		$4,469,015 34	
Deductions as above, ...		828,255 64	
Remaining, ...		$3,640,759 70	462

And now it becomes my duty to notice some charges that have been brought before you against Dr. Nott by James W. Beekman. This gentleman, who has been so conspicuous in the persecution of Dr. Nott, appeared before you, and was examined as a witness. My client and I rejoiced in the opportunity thus at last afforded, of meeting this prime mover of the inquisitions against Dr. Nott,
face to face, where his statements could be met by proofs, 463
and overthrown by the plainest evidence. He has given us a re-hash of the matter of his long and violent phillipics in the Senate, where there was no information or evidence to confute him. If he shall present a different appearance at the close of this discussion, from that which he exhibited when marching out of the Senate Chamber,
triumphing in his unanswered calumnies of a defence- 464

less old man and a venerable clergyman, the consequence will be of his own producing.

He commenced his testimony before you by producing a pamphlet called Chancery Documents, which he testified had been handed to him by the officers of the college during his examination of its affairs in 1849 by the commit-
465 tee of the Assembly, of which he was a member; and referred to a copy of a bill in chancery, which it contained, filed by Yates and McIntyre against the trustees and Dr. Nott. And he also produced a printed copy of a bill filed by those persons against the same parties, both purporting to have been sworn to on the fourth of August, 1834. He read from the last bill numerous passages and whole pages that were not contained in the bill printed in the Chancery
466 Documents, handed him by the officers of the college. And he pointed out how material were many of the passages thus omitted. I saw your astonishment at this apparent evidence of deliberate deception and fraud, an impression which it was Mr. Beekman's design to make, and which he had made in the Senate by a similar exhibition. But your astonishment was still greater, when I demonstrated that this foul charge was the coinage of Mr.
467 Beekman's malevolence, by calling your attention to the first page of the pamphlet thus produced by Mr. Beekman, and to the letter there printed, of Jonas Holland, dated November 22, 1834, stating that he had then *printed* that pamphlet; and when your chairman, at my request, produced the printed office copy of the bill in chancery, identical with that which Mr. Beekman had produced and compared with the pamphlet copy,
468 and read the clerk's indorsement thereon, that it was filed on the 16th of May, 1835, *six months after the pamphlet was printed!* and into which, of course, it could not be copied. Mr. Beekman himself produced the joint answer of the trustees and Dr. Nott, to this amended bill, which answer was filed September 8, 1835, so that he must have known, as his testimony showed he had read that answer, that there had been another and different bill than that in
469 the pamphlet. I then produced the original bill of Yates

and McIntyre, sworn to August 4, 1834, and compared it with the copy of the bill contained in the pamphlet produced by Mr. Beekman, and showed that they were identical. Thus, this charge of deliberate fraud on the part of the officers of the college, and upon which so many changes had been rung in the Senate, was exploded.

The next effort of Mr. Beekman, was to show that the 470
$192,000 received by Dr. Nott, out of the stipulations made
by Yates & McIntyre, in relation to the Albany lottery, &c.,
belonged to Union College; and he had two ways to establish the position. First, he maintained that the $2,004,099
worth of tickets in the *mixed* lottery, mentioned in the
stipulations of May 31, 1826, (Doc. XIV, folio 110) had
produced the $192,000 of profits. This was soon exposed,
by recurring to the settlement of 1828, (p. 32, 33, Doc's) 471
where it appeared that all the proceeds of the mixed lotteries had been paid to Union College, and were included
in the sum of $433,102.23, the total of Y. & McI.'s liabili-
ties. This was too absurd, even for Mr. Vanderheyden's
endorsement, and he promptly admitted the blunder of Mr.
Beekman.

Second, he endeavored to make out that, by chap. 186,
of the laws of 1826, Union College became responsible for 472
the payment of *all* the prizes in the mixed lottery. This
depended upon an entire misconstruction of the 3d section
of that act, which required the *managers* to give the same
bond to the people of the State, for the payment of prizes,
that had been required by the act of 1822. The responsibility of the college to the extent of the $2,004,099.00
worth of tickets which it had in that lottery, out of which
it received the avails, created by the act of 1822, of course 473
continued whatever change of lotteries might be made.
But Mr. Beekman sought to extend that responsibility to
all the prizes in the mixed lottery, so as to entitle the college to the profits arising from the whole. And to accomplish this, he gravely makes a clause of the act of
1826, relating to the bonds of the managers, applicable to
and creating a responsibility of the college. It is only
necessary to state the proposition, to ensure its condemna- 474

tion. It is but justice to Mr. Vanderheyden, to remark, that he utterly disclaimed these views of Mr. Beekman. It was upon this frail basis that he sought to justify his charge originally made in his report, and repeated, day after day, in the Senate, that the college had received from Y. & McI. $850,000, very nearly the sum which the ac-
475 countant has brought out in another way, seeming to have his eye fixed on his patron's orignal statement. With the fall of the foundation falls the superstructure. Mr. Beekman further made a great display of figures, to show that some ten or twelve millions worth of tickets had been drawn by Yates & McIntyre, under their different purchases of the rights granted for the Literature lottery, the Albany Land lottery and the Fever Hospital lottery. The ap-
476 plication of this to Dr. Nott or Union College, was not discoverable. The question was, what the college was entitled to receive.

Thus terminated the pompous exhibition of Mr. Beekman, in the total overthrow of every one of his positions. The enquiry of one of the committee, how a man of Mr. Beekman's intelligence could have committed such mistakes, was answered by me, that to a mind diseased, black
477 would appear white, and white would appear black.

The reason and meaning of the remark was, that Mr. Beekman's mind was strongly imbued with violent prejudices, amounting to personal hostility against Dr. Nott. This had been evinced by the over-zealous and pertinacious zeal with which he had made, and caused to be made, statements and reports assailing the integrity of the President and the condition of the college, and with which
478 he had caused them to be printed and circulated through the United States, among localities that could have no possible interest in the questions. His near connexion, J. G. Sanders, has done little else for three years, but to busy himself in these matters, and circulate the calumnious reports against Dr. Nott.

He even ordered an edition of 1000 copies of the report of the majority of the commission to be printed in a
479 mutilated form, so as to omit the minority report of Messrs.

Buel and Van Rensselaer, and the memorials of the Trustees and President of Union College to the Senate, and which that body had ordered to be attached to the report. He has been hovering around this capitol during your sittings, advising the accountant, and stimulating him in his efforts to ruin Dr. Nott.

The origin of this animosity of the whole family is to be 480
ascribed, I am informed, to an old difficulty with the President about the purchase of some land of the college, and by a steady refusal of Dr. Nott to minister to the ambition of one of the family to be a Trustee of the college. But whatever its source, there is no man that knows them, who does not also know, that for many years no terms of vituperation against the President of Union College have been spared by the members of that family. 481

In this feeling, Mr. Beekman has evidently participated largely. Nothing but some such powerful motive could have induced him to neglect the vast and varied interests of his own constituents, in the city of New-York, and the corruptions, frauds and public evils that have, and still do so much abound there, in order to devote so much time, labor, zeal and expense, in the affairs of Union College.

The impartiality of Mr. Beekman, his anxiety to serve the 482
public, his deep interest in the concerns of the college, which prompted his efforts to expose and punish the depredators of its funds, are exemplified in his forbearance to Mr. Henry Yates. The very bill in chancery from which he quoted so largely, contained evidence of the fact that Mr. Yates had been employed as the agent of the college, with a salary, to superintend and watch the movements of the contractors, his brother J. B. Yates and A. McIntyre, 483
and their associates in New-York; and that instead of performing that duty, he became their co-partner in the profits of the lotteries! His forbearance towards that gentleman was doubtless occasioned by their fellow feeling of animosity against Dr. Nott. The Doctor's steady resistance against the schemes of spoliation by Y. and McI, his defeat of their efforts to evade and violate their engagements, and the consequent disputes between them, kindled a feel- 484

ing of revenge, which even the immense fortunes they realised from the exertion of his talents and sagacity, his
hazards, his advances, and his labors, could not assuage.
Hence Mr. Yates and Mr. Beekman had a common object
and common sympathies.

I have now to notice some collateral charges, the off-
485 spring of the joint labors of James W. Beekman and Levinus Vanderheyden. The latter now drops his character
of accountant, and comes forth as the public accuser of
Dr. Nott. After the termination of all his duties as accountant, by the transmission of his report to the Senate,
he addressed a communication to that body on the 19th of
March, 1853, praying that it would order to be printed
and attached to the report of the commissioners, his own
486 affidavit, and those of Neziah Bliss and Joseph D. Monell.
And Mr. Beekman, on the coming in of this application,
introduced a long resolution, studiously embodying the
venomous points of the communication, and reasoning
upon the alleged facts, directing it to be printed and attached as desired. This evidence on its face, establishes
the joint work of these chivalric, impartial and just citizens. The paper was thrown in, after an application by
487 the President and Trustees of Union College for some opportunity to meet the charges against them, and with a
view of defeating that application; for Mr. Beekman
strenuously resisted it, and compared the proceeding to
the impeachment of Warren Hastings, and the efforts of
Hastings to delay and procrastinate. The falsity of this
charge against the Trustees and President, was palpable,
as they were then pressing for an investigation by an im-
488 partial committee. It has been rendered still more palpable by the readiness with which they have appeared before
you. Mr. Vanderheyden's part in this drama was to furnish Mr. Beekman with the materials for his speeches and
his efforts. As they have thus yoked themselves together,
I propose to keep them in that mutually agreeable relation.

The first object of this communication to the Senate was
to establish by the letter of Neziah Bliss, to which he had
489 appended a worthless and illegal affidavit, that Dr. Nott

had paid a very trifling consideration for the half of the
Stuyvesant Cove property, and none whatever for his (Bliss,)
bond and mortgage for $75,225.32, which he had assigned
to the college for its nominal amount. A comparison between Mr. Bliss' letter in the Senate Doc. No. 68, of 1853,
and his own testimony taken under an obligatory oath before you, contained in the accompanying documents (Doc. 490
XXXVIII, folio 323) will show such discrepancies, as to
shake the credit of any man. But when you regard the
testimony of Edward James, (Doc. XXXIX, folio 346) and
see the plump contradictions of Mr. Bliss, by a disinterested and impartial witness, corroborated as they are by the
testimony of B. Nott, you will come to the same conclusion
that Mr. Bliss did, "that his mind at that time was
in such a state, that he knew very little what he did," 491
(folio 334) and that if he had added that his mind continued in such a state now, that he did not know what he said,
he would not be much out of the way. Mr. James proves
that Bliss' bond and mortgage were given to secure the
payment of money actually advanced to him by Dr. Nott,
and ascertained and agreed to on a settlement of the accounts; he specifies the consideration and gives full details
of the transaction. B. Nott corroborates him, from the de- 492
clarations of Bliss. How much more consistent is Mr.
James' account of the transaction than Bliss'. The latter
says that Dr. Nott wished the mortgage to enable him to
raise money upon it, (folio 327.) And yet he says, "Dr.
Nott said it (the mortgage) should never be recorded."
"Did not suppose the mortgage would be transferred or
recorded, but would come back," (folio 331.) He does not
explain how a man is to raise money upon a mortgage, with- 493
out recording or transferring it! His testimony is a tissue of
inconsistencies. Mr. James swears that the mortgage was
given for an amount actually due, and admitted by Bliss to
be due, and upon property that Bliss considered worth much
more than the debt. This is established also by a memorandum endorsed on the mortgage, and forming part of it, by
which Bliss was allowed to sell any part of the premises
mortgaged, and on paying an amount proportioned to the 494

comparative value of the part sold, in reference to the whole,
he should be entitled to a release of the part so sold. (See
the copy of the memorandum furnished by Bliss, at p. 13
of the document No. 68, got up by Messrs. Beekman and
Vanderheyden.)

This memorandum demonstrates Bliss' estimation of the
495 value of the property, and his belief that he could receive
some considerable sum from it, after paying the debt, and
in itself utterly disproves his story about the mortgage being given without any consideration.

Bliss says he considered this Stuyvesant cove property
worth $500,000 in 1842, if properly managed, (folio 333.)
After this declaration of their own witness, the gentlemen
who relied on him to prove that, when Dr. Nott transferred
496 his one-half for $58,632.15, he swindled the college, for this
is the classic language they use in reference to this subject;
and after this same witness had declared the other half of the
same property, good security for $75,225, (see folio 349,)
after such evidence, these gentlemen, probably, will not
repeat their calumny, or if they do, they will be silenced
by an indignant community.

Another point these associates sought to establish by
497 Bliss, was, that the transfer of one-half of the Hunter farm, was for a sum which was the value of the
whole (p. 213, 214, appendix to accountant's report). This
purchase was made in 1835, for the sum of $104,800,
(Bliss' testimony, folio 323.) Gen. Jeremiah Johnson,
who was the agent in effecting the purchases, and
lived near the property, and was well acquainted with
it, was of opinion that it was a very advantageous pur-
498 chase, and that the property could be sold the next day,
for $50,000 advance, and so told Bliss, (folio 335.) Bliss,
himself, represents it as extremely valuable, and that a
great deal of money could be made by selling it to any
one. During the ensuing three years after its purchase,
extensive improvements were made in its vicinity, and it
is notorious, that real estate in and about the city of New-
York, within that time, advanced beyond all precedent.
499 When these circumstances are considered, and the interest

that had accrued, and the expenses that must have been
incurred in protecting the property, it will not appear
strange that it should have been considered worth nearly
double its original cost. Gen. Dix who visited and examined it, deemed it very valuable, and certain, if retained, to enrich the proprietors. (Folio 298, of his testimony.) 500

This real estate was afterwards conveyed by the college
to Dr. Nott. And one of the allegations of the associates
is, that the college lost by this re-conveyance, the interest,
the taxes, assessments, rents, and the amount of a mortgage on a part of the property, which the college had paid
while the property was in its hands; and again a charge of
"plundering" the college (as Mr. Vanderheyden expressed
it) is brought, founded on this allegation. 501

But it is an entirely erroneous view, to regard these purchases at all as money transactions. It was a mere change
in the form of a donation. The college had, in the hands
of its Treasurer, monies deposited by Dr. Nott, intended as
gifts. It had the legal title to the above mentioned prop-
erties. They could not be improved and brought into
market, unless the title and power of absolute disposition
rested elsewhere than in a Board of Trustees. Dr. Nott, 502
therefore, exchanged the monies and securities in deposit,
for these tracts of lands; which, when brought in proper
condition, would take the place of the monies and securities he applied in procuring the title to them. Dr. Nott
informed Bliss at the time, (see folio 324,) that he wished
to invest college funds in the purchase of the Hunter farm.
In his report to the Trustees in 1833, (folio 241,) he informed them that he had invested a portion of the funds 503
received by him on his personal contracts, though to be appropriated to the college, in real estate, situated in New-
York and on Long Island.

Viewing these transactions as a whole, it will be seen
that any consideration that might be stated for the transfer
of the title of the college to these tracts, to Dr. Nott, would
be entirely nominal, and that any idea of profit or loss on
either side, would be out of the question. 504

The apparent delay in giving legal effect to his often and
public declared intentions of bestowing this property for
the use of the college, is abundantly explained in the testimony of Chancellor Walworth and Judge Paige, (Doc.
XXXIV, folio 245). By them he was advised, that in the
then state of the law, the property could not be conveyed
505 for the trusts he had designed. After the necessary
statutes were passed, the condition of the bond of Yates,
McIntyre & Ely, for $150,000, heavy payments on
which were becoming due, and the last of which was
not completed until May 5, 1849, prevented a final
settlement of the lottery transactions, without which the
amounts could not be ascertained, so as to be embraced in
any conveyance, and the condition of the real property
506 above mentioned, which was constantly and necessarily
changing, prevented the final execution of his designs.
He, however, as soon as practicable, executed a deed of
trust, prepared under the best legal advice, and delivered
it to the Treasurer. This deed was the best that could be
devised under the circumstances, and, although, as the
property had changed, it became necessary to make corresponding alterations, yet it has been re-acknowledged when-
507 ever such alterations were made; and the acting Treasurer,
who produced it before you, testified that it had been re-
acknowledged several times, and the last time so late as in
the month of October, of the present year. What is intended to be done now, to render the title of the college
perfect, will be hereafter stated.

Any one who can perceive in the transactions, relating to this real estate, any other than the purest integ-
508 rity, and the most generous liberality, must have all the
prejudices and hostility of Messrs. Beekman and Vanderheyden.

The next charge of the associates, relates to the sale of
the stock in the Bank of Hudson. At p. 15 of Vanderheyden's communication to the Senate, Doc. 68, he gives the
affidavit of J. D. Monell, that he was a director of that
bank, and that it failed and ceased to do business in the
509 early part of June, 1819. To this Vanderheyden appends

this note: "The above stock of $5,000, bought from E. Nott by college, by *resolution* of Trustees, July 28, 1819." The venom of this sting is in the date of the supposed purchase, a month after the bank had failed, and in the word "bought," and the imputation is thus sought to be cast on Dr. Nott, that he knowingly palmed upon the college the worthless stock of a broken bank, with knowl- 510
edge of its worthlessness.

Now the plain history of the transaction, which ordinary care would have discovered, and ordinary honesty would have represented truly, is this. In chap. 98, of the Laws of 1813, pp. 104, 105, was a reservation of a right to certain institutions to subscribe to the stock of the Bank of Hudson; among them, Union College is enumerated to subscribe $5,000. This was a kind of *bonus* exacted by 511
the legislature when bank stock was considered very valuable property.

The subscription was made by Dr. Nott, in behalf of the college. But it would seem that it had no funds on hand at the time to pay the subscription, and it was advanced by Dr. Nott, who held the stock in his own name as security for the advance. On the 28th of July, 1819, the Trustees passed a resolution, which has been read to you 512
from their minutes, directing the treasurer to pay Dr. Nott the amount of that stock held in his name, on his transferring it to the college. It was so transferred, but the amount remained unpaid for some time, and the college paid interest on it to Dr. Nott. The stock has ever since been entered and reported among the assets of the college. The very fact which Mr. Vanderheyden seeks to establish, namely, that the bank had broken one month previous, 513
rendered it the duty of the Trustees to relieve Dr. Nott from the burden of the advance, since the stock was no longer any security to him; and the resolution of the Trustees was, on its face, evidence that the college had *not* "bought" the stock as alleged by Mr. Vanderheyden, but recognized its ownership of it. And yet he refers, as shown above, to this very resolution to sustain his charge!

This charge furnished Mr. Beekman a rich theme for 514
vituperation in the Senate, and although it was then ex-

plained and disproved by a senator, neither Mr. Beekman
nor the accountant, has withdrawn it. If any further evidence were wanting of the disposition of these gentlemen
towards Dr. Nott, their conduct in this transaction furnishes
it.

The next subject of this veracious communication is,
515 what we have heard so much about at every step in this
investigation, particularly when the accountant indulged in
his bursts of passion; viz., the account in the fund book of
Dr. Nott's deposits with the treasurer, and the credits given
the college. The present inquiry does not relate to the
accuracy of that account, but to the charge which Mr.
Vanderheyden makes in his voluntary and worthless affidavit, which he, like Mr. Bliss, seems to have deemed ne-
516 cessary to inspire confidence in his statements, contained in
the document referred to, (No. 68,) to the effect, that after
the fund book had been returned by him to the acting
treasurer, Mr. Pearson, or as he strangely calls it, loaned
to him, and while it was in the hands of the latter, and
before he returned it to Mr. V., there was inserted in it the
above mentioned account; and this he has a thousand
times denounced as a fraudulent interpolation and mutila-
517 tion of the books of the college.

Now, Mr. Pearson testifies (folio 446) that the books
were put in his hands by Mr. Vanderheyden's request,
that he might bring the accounts down to January 1, 1853.

It was evidently the duty of the treasurer to enter the
account in the fund book, and whether it was done at one
time or another, is of no consequence, provided it was
done in time to bring the items to the notice of the account-
518 ant, that he might investigate them. That was the object
of inserting any accounts in the book at all. The book
belonged to the college, and its officers had a right to
make any entries they pleased in it, at any time. It was
not a book of original entries, but a ledger; and the veri-
ty of its contents depended on other books. It could mislead no one. It would really seem as if this ridiculous
charge had been invented as a set-off to an anticipated at-
519 tack upon the accountant, for his own gross violation of
duty and propriety, in tearing from a book of the college

that had been delivered to him, a most important memorandum, explanatory of an item, and not restoring it when
he returned the book, but keeping it from the officers of
the college until the very close of this investigation.

I have now finished the examination of the charges
made by Messrs. Beekman and Vanderheyden, in this extraordinary communication, and have shown, I trust, to 520
your entire satisfaction, that each and every one of them,
is not only false, but wilful and malignant.

Not satisfied, apparently, with the publicity which the
efforts of Mr. Beekman and his connexions would give to
the communication to the Senate, No. 68, Mr. Vanderheyden, in his libel in the Albany papers of March 24, 1853,
before mentioned, reiterated the most odious charge, that
relating to the Hudson Bank stock, the falsity of which 521
has already been exposed, and dwelt at large on the iniquity
of Dr. Nott's charging the college for the Commercial Bank
stock, without ever having transferred it, merely because
the books of the bank did not exhibit a formal transfer!
This charge too, has been disposed of, and the reference to
this publication is now made, as further proof of the persevering malignity of the accountant and witness, on whom
you must rely, if on anything, for the results of his state- 522
ment.

Mr. Vanderheyden has complained of the irregularities
of Dr. Nott in making or directing entries in the college
books, and has frequently called your attention to them as
evidences of great impropriety. These entries related exclusively to his deposit of moneys with the treasurer under
resolutions of the board of trustees of November, 1834,
and July 1837, adopting the recommendations of two com- 523
mittees, that the monies and securities deposited by Dr.
Nott, arising from his personal contracts, should be received by the treasurer, and accounts thereof kept under Dr.
Nott's directions. (See folios 191, 193, 197, 374.) He had a
right, therefore, to direct the entries referred to, which were
not of sums deposited, but explanatory of the purpose for
which, and the authority under which the deposits were
made. The entry in pencil in a ledger, of the words "Dr. 524

Nott," after the words "President's fund," respecting the
$42,000 deposited by him, was of the same character, and
to designate the person from whom received. The entry
was not in any cash book, but in a ledger, and could mislead
no one, or change the fact as stated in the cash book.

In what he called the "pathetic" part of his closing
525 speech, Mr. Vanderheyden tried to be very severe upon
Dr. Nott, and the officers of the college, for circulating the
pamphlet produced by Mr. Beekman, called Chancery
Documents, and insisted that it was fraudulent and decep-
tive, because it did not state all the sums of money that had
been received by Dr. Nott, from the profits of his stipulations concerning the lotteries. This charge, even he, would
have been ashamed to make, if he had read the book. It
526 not only contained the sums referred to, but Mr. Beekman, in the presence and hearing of Vanderheyden, had
read them from the pamphlet, for his own purposes!

Having, in vain, attempted to brow-beat a most worthy
witness, E. James, Esq., and to irritate him by the most in-
sulting and vulgar epithets, this man Vanderheyden has
had the audacity to hand in to you a memorandum, stating
that he declined to continue Mr. James' cross-examination,
527 because he appeared prejudiced against him, Vanderheyden,
and had exhibited an interest in Dr. Nott. Not being able to
anticipate what disposition the committee will make of this
memorandum, I notice it, merely to pronounce it as false
as it is scurrilous, and to deny that any exhibition of any
prejudice against Vanderheyden, or of any partiality or favor for Dr. Nott was made by Mr. James, other than should
be exhibited by any impartial and honest man.

528 This exploit of the accountant, was doubtless performed
with the hope of thus nullifying the effect of Mr. James'
testimony, in relation to the manner in which the accounts
are presented in the printed report. His evidence on
that subject, (folios 351 to 357, and 359 to 362,) was anything but satisfactory to the pride of the accountant. It
is evidently a just condemnation of the manner in which
the accounts are made up. The character of Mr. James
529 as an accomplished accountant, probably not surpassed in

the State, and his long service in that capacity, amid the successive changes of the board under whom he holds office, are known to one of you, personally, and to the other members of the committee, and the public generally by reputation. He is corroborated fully in his views by another, who has been described, by Mr. Vanderheyden, as an able accountant, Mr. Holland. He tells you (folio 432), 530
that the entire tendency of these accounts is to deceive and mislead, and give an appearance to matters, the very reverse of what was contained in the books delivered to him.

The evidence of Andrew White, Esq., and Powiss L. Green, Esq., to the general skill and ability of Mr. Vanderheyden, as an accountant, and to his success in unravelling complicated accounts, proves, if anything, that he has not successfully exerted his faculties on this occasion. 531
What the cause of his failure was, you will judge.

In addition to the remarks on this subject already made, folio 76, respecting the manner of making up these accounts, and in corroboration of them, I refer to the numerous instances which have been pointed out in the course of this argument, of erroneous statements and combinations; to the inconsistent accounts of the cost of the west college buildings and grounds, stated in the objections 532
to his summary, at folio 472 of Doc. XLIX. And I particularly refer to the extraordinary paper furnished by Mr. Vanderheyden, after long preparation, contained in Doc. XL, attempting to establish his item of interest received from Yates & McIntyre. Let any one read it and judge what reliance can be placed on the man who could make out such an account, so complicated in itself and so directly contradictory of his previous statements on the same sub- 533
ject, as shown by the notes of his testimony appended to that document.

In strong contrast with these accounts, you have the clear, distinct and lucid statement of the condition of the college in 1831, by Messrs. Wm. James and Silas Wright, contained in Doc. XXI, folio 143. The difference between it and Mr. Vanderheyden's exhibits, can not be the result of different degrees of capacity alone. Those gentlemen 534 had no motive or object but the simple truth, and the conscientious discharge of their duty. Their opportunities were ample, and their research appears in the report itself to have been thorough.

William L. Marcy, Azariah C. Flagg, John A. Dix, John
P. Cushman and others of the Trustees, have also made
535 thorough examinations of the condition of the college, as
appears by their reports, some of which are given in the
accompanying documents. All these gentlemen speak in
the highest terms of the ability and integrity with which
the President has managed the concerns of the college, and
they all report its condition sound. Annual committees
of the trustees examined the treasurer's accounts; and
there was a standing finance committee. The treasurer
536 reported each year a summary of the affairs of the college
to the Trustees. None of the members of the special and
standing committees, no treasurer or other officer or Trustee ever discovered any improper loans to the President
for his personal benefit, any misapplication of the college
funds or property by Dr. Nott, or any debt or demand
against him.

In the extraordinary conflict thus presented between
537 these distinguished and very capable gentlemen, acting
under the peculiar responsibilities of their stations, and
having reputations to maintain dearer to them than life,
on the one side, and Mr. Vanderheyden on the other, with
his mystified and unintelligible accounts, his prejudices
and animosities, on which, will you as impartial and experienced men, rely?

Recurring to the nature and importance of the questions
538 involved, with which I commenced this argument, may I
not ask whether you have such strength, force, and clear-
ness of reliable and uncontradicted evidence from Mr. Vanderheyden, as ought to overcome the presumptions arising
from the characters of the parties sought to be implicated?

The accountant, at the close of the very last moment
of this investigation, furnished the last and worst proof
of his bitter hostility to Dr. Nott, by a false and fraudu-
539 lent comparison of the sums respectively received by the

college and Dr. Nott from the proceeds of the lotteries. I use these expressions false and fraudulent, deliberately, as truly characterising his conduct on that occasion. You will remember, gentlemen, that among the sums he put down as having been received by Dr. Nott, was $165,000 of notes of Yates & McIntyre. Now, he knew perfectly
well, for it had been the subject of repeated discussion, 540
and is shown by his own book, in statement No. 19, p. 130, that of these notes Dr. Nott received only $71,691.20, which sum he charges the Doctor at p. 82, as having been received out of these notes. The balance, $95,165.09 was received by the college. (See Holland's statement, Doc. XLV, folio, 417.) Can any thing be more scandalous than this brazen attempt to deceive you?

The sums retained or received by Dr. Nott, are the fol- 541
lowing:

The above 22 notes on the stipulations of January 4, and 24, 1826,.............................. $71,691 20

And this is *all* that he received from any transactions growing out of the Literature lottery.

The sum stated at p. 172, of the accountant's report, of sums received from the 542
Albany land lottery, &c., and with which the college had no connexion and no interest more than I had,................ 192,199 94

He received, or rather the treasurer received for him, the payments made on the bond for $150,000 for principal only. (See Doc. LI, folio 593.)............. .... 203,091 75

543
$466,982 89

The whole of which has been applied to purchases of property, and its improvement for the college, so that in fact, he has not realised a dollar, personally, from these receipts.

He also retained the balance of the Presi-
dent's fund, after deducting expenses,... $115,640 53 544
The whole of which he has transferred to the college;

and from the beginning to the end, he has avowed the design of bestowing all these funds on the college.

Let us next see what the College has received:

By the statement of the treasurer, folio 421, it realised from the lottery (exclusive of other grants,) after deducting
545 the payments to the other institutions
and the repayments to Yates & McIntyre, 277,522 33

It receives the balance of the President's fund, ... 115,640 53

And the amount of the 22 notes of Yates & McIntyre, and the profits of the stipulations in which the college had no interest, the above amount of 466,982 89

546 Making a total of................. $860,145 75

And the college is at this moment worth more than this sum, as will appear by the following:

The property on hand, productive and available, (see treasurer's statement, fol. 482,) is,.... $190,169 50

Its buildings, library and apparatus cost, (see same statement, fol. 484,)........ 333,431 10

547

$523,600 60

Deduct for debts,.......... $18,547 76

Actual and assumed losses, (see fol. 486,)........... 81,332 66

99,880 42

Leaving property on hand,............. $423,720 18

Add to this the property conveyed by Dr.
548 Nott,.............................. 600,000 00

And the college is now worth,.......... $1,023,720 18

What a different view of results does this present from the Flemish statement of the accountant!

In reviewing the history of this college, its struggles and difficulties, and then adverting to its present palmy condition, as now exhibited, no one can avoid perceiving, that it
549 owes *every thing* to the wonderful devotion, the continued

and idefatigable labor, and the sagacity of one man. His whole long life has been devoted to this one object, and all the fruits of his labors and hazards, which he had a right to appropriate to himself, and which almost any other man would have so appropriated—he has bestowed on this child
of his affections and his hopes. The funds and property 560
acquired by the profits on the lotteries, whether President's fund, notes of Yates & McIntyre, or bond of Yates, McIntyre & Ely; whatever stocks or money have come to his hands, other than such as he invested for its benefit, have been applied to the improvement and enhancement of the very valuable property, he has always destined for one sole purpose, the object of all his cares.

For years has he submitted to private suspicion and to
public imputations, by persons who would not understand 561
his purposes and his plans, or who chose not to become acquainted with them. The newspapers have teemed with garbled and one-sided statements; the Senate chamber has rung with the foulest charges, which reporters have transferred to the press; the widest circulation of exparte reports has been caused by the ceaseless activity of the men who have pursued him as if he were a wild beast or a
demon; until a large portion of the community has be- 562
come saturated with prejudice.

Some of those who had a partial knowledge of what he had already done to consummate his designs, have affected to believe, that the conveyance and will executed by him, were invalid or insufficient.

Now that the condition of the property he has secured, is such that an exact description of it can be given, that the har-
rassing and vindictive persecutions against him are lulled, 563
at least for a season, and the inquiries of this committee have closed, the President is able to perfect his long cherished design, of vesting in Union College, the legal title to the rich inheritance he has so long labored to acquire for it, by an instrument confirming and reiterating the existing conveyance, so that all doubts or scruples, real or imaginary, that may have existed, in relation to the validity of that
conveyance, in consequence of subsequent changes in the 564

property, rendered advisable if not indispensible by circumstances, or from any other cause, shall be forever and
effectually removed.

And he has, therefore, instructed me to prepare a full
release to Union College, of all his claims to any pecuniary
balance that may appear to belong to him on the books of
565 the college, or otherwise, on account of deposits made by
him without consideration, with the Treasurer. This will
include the balance of the President's fund or the 2¼ per
cent, not already deposited, and the balance of the Bliss
bond, and of the payments on the $150,000 bond, so often
mentioned. And it will embrace all gains the college has
realised by the sale and re-purchase of the original college
sites and buildings, and the sales of portions of the new
566 college sites, acquired by the private means of Dr. Nott,
and the sums gratuitously expended by him, on the grounds,
gardens, houses, and out houses of the college.

He has also instructed me to prepare a more formal conveyance, confirmatory of that already executed, and vesting
in Union College the immediate title in trust, for the establishment of professorships, scholarships, an observatory, a
cemetery, and other educational purposes, under the acts of
567 1840 and 1841, of specific bonds, mortgages and contracts
arising from the sale of the Stuyvesant Cove property, and
from the sale of lots in the tract consisting of the Hunter
farm, and other lands united therewith, by Dr. Nott, and
by Messrs. Crane & Ely; and of his interest in the said
united tracts remaining unsold, being one-third thereof,
the whole amounting in value, at this time, to at least
$600,000. The lots remaining unsold, are constantly in-
568 creasing in value, which will be greatly augmented, if
the country continues for a few years, in its usual prosperity.

And here is the same KEY, to all the movements of Dr.
Nott's life, with which I presented you in the early part of
this argument, when speaking of the great sacrifice he made
on leaving his church in Albany, in 1804, to occupy the
office of President of Union College. It unlocks and ex-
plains his every act from that time to this. It proclaims
569 the reason and motive for the years of toil he has devoted,

the rigid economy he has practised, and the plans and schemes in which he has been engaged for fifty years. His own personal benefit, and that of his family, have been disregarded. Union College, the idol of his affections, of his hopes, and of his ambition, has been the sole, steady, and unvarying object of his ceaseless labors by day, and of his anxious thoughts at night. 570

And now, I ask, who will dare to stigmatise such designs, and such actions, as systematic plunder and robbery, of this child of love and hope, as deliberate fraud, falsehood and deception?

Dr. Nott is a clergyman, and like his brethren, unacquainted with the modes and forms of business transactions; he is not an accountant; his mind looks to general plans and great results, and like all such minds, is not always 571
attentive to details and strict regularity and precision. His modes of transacting business are different from those of most people. With these characteristics, and under the trying circumstances, in which he has, for so many years, single handed, sustained Union College, amid perils and difficulties that often threatened her existence, it would be wonderful if irregularities had not occurred. What portion of these are attributable to him, and what part to other offi- 572
cers of the college, can not now be determined. But whatever those irregularities have been, and for whatever portion he is responsible, it has been made most manifest, that they have not been the result of any mercenary or selfish motive on his part. On the contrary, you will, I doubt not, bear your testimony to the pervading integrity and honesty of purpose, and the noble disinterestedness, which have marked his whole administration of the affairs of Union 573
College, and which entitle him to the highest credit and honor, and to the lasting gratitude of all friends of education, and of the amelioration of our race.

THE PRINCIPAL

DOCUMENTS, TESTIMONY, AND STATEMENTS

PRODUCED IN BEHALF OF

ELIPHALET NOTT and the Trustees of Union College,

BEFORE THE COMMITTEE OF THE SENATE APPOINTED
MARCH 28, 1853, TO INVESTIGATE CERTAIN
PECUNIARY AFFAIRS OF THAT
COLLEGE:

TOGETHER WITH SOME OF THE TESTIMONY AND STATEMENTS
ON THE PART OF THE PROSECUTION.

CONTENTS.

NOTE.

The documents herein contained are not all that were produced before the committee. The books of account and the minutes of the Trustees were all examined and referred to, during the whole of the investigation. These are quoted, and extracts given in the argument. The most material of the documentary evidence, however, is given in full. They are all derived either from the pleadings in the suits in chancery given in evidence, the pamphlet called Chancery Documents produced by Mr. Beekman, or other authentic publications; and the reports of committees, and of the President to the Trustees, and the resolutions of that board, were verified by the testimony of Mr. Holland, Mr. Pearson, or Mr. Willard.

It was impracticable to give the testimony of Mr. Vanderheyden, as it was desultory, full of repetitions, mingled with remarks as counsel, and occupied at least a fortnight. The other testimony on the part of the prosecution is given, except that which related to Mr. Vanderheyden's character as a man of truth, and for integrity as an accountant, the result of which is stated in the argument at folio 87; and except the testimony in respect to his capacity as an accountant. On the latter subject, Andrew White and Powiss L. Green testified to his capacity and skill, and specified instances of his having regulated intricate accounts and discovered errors and frauds. Hamlet H. Hickox also testified favorably as to the accounts in the report being plain and intelligible, but on cross-examination very much qualified his opinion.

Testimony was also given, tending to show that some of the property in which investments had been made was not good security, and the books of the Commercial Bank were produced, showing that no transfers of the stock of that bank had been made by Union College to H. Nott & Co.; but that they had been transferred by E. Nott to the Farmers' Loan Company, and by that company to H. Nott & Co. Nor is the testimony of Benjamin Nott, in behalf of the defence, given, because it was mainly corroborative of that of Edward James, in respect to conversations with Neziah Bliss, and in respect to the stock of the Commercial Bank, which he testified was obtained by H. Nott & Co., of which firm he was a partner, from Union College through Dr. Nott; that his firm borrowed money on it; that they provided for it in their assignment, and that it was paid for to the college.

The statements of James W. Beekman before the Committee, were not testimony of any fact within his knowledge, except the delivery to him of a pamphlet, by the officers of the College. The residue consisted of comparisons of different statements, and the construction of a statute.

A desire to abbreviate the pamphlet as much as could be, consistent with a fair exhibition of the case, induced the above omissions, which could as well be supplied by this statement of their substance, for all practical purposes.

The documents and testimony are separately numbered, and in the margin the number of each folio is given for convenient reference.

DOCUMENTS, &c.

[Instead of giving at length the early acts of the Legislature appropriating moneys or lands to the benefit of Union College, it is deemed better to save room, to reprint an abstract of those acts, as given by Robert H. Pruyn, Esq., one of the Committee of the Assembly to investigate the affairs of that College, in his report to the House of Assembly, March 30, 1850. Assembly Doc., No. 190, p. 54. The fidelity of the abstract can be tested by comparing it with the acts themselves, given at large in the appendix to Mr. Vanderheyden's report, p. 191, to 197.]

STATEMENT *of all the acts in which grants have been made to Union College.*

1. By the act of April 9, 1795, for the purchase of Library and apparatus, ... $3,750 00 1
2. By the act of April 11, 1796, for the erection of buildings,..................... 10,000 00
3. By the act of March 30, 1797, seven hundred and fifty dollars a year for two years, for the support of a Professor, ... 1,500 00
4. By section 1, of the act of March 7, 1800, for the completion of the College edifice, 10,000 00
5. By section 3 of the same act, ten military lots were granted, of 550 acres each, for the support of the president and professors,.............................
6. By the act of April 8, 1801, and of April 3, 1802, the Garrison lands, by the Regents, ...
7. By the act of March 30, 1805, by lottery,. 80,000 00
8. By the act of April 13, 1814:
    1. For the erection of buildings,................. .. $100,000 2
    2. For paying an existing debt, 30,000
    3. For library and apparatus,. 20,000
    4. For the relief of indigent students, ... 50,000

——— 200,000 00

[Six years' interest on the last,........... 84,000 00]

II.

AN ACT *to limit the continuance of Lotteries.*

Passed April 5, 1822.

3 Whereas the public institutions to which grants were
made originally, in the lottery instituted April 13th, 1814,
for the promotion of literature, have already suffered materially by delay in drawing the same: And whereas it is
believed, that said lottery might be managed with greater
economy and less hazard, by the institutions interested in
its success, than it has hitherto been, or can hereafter be,
by the state: And whereas all that could be thus saved,
by greater economy in the management of said lottery, would
go to diminish the loss of said institutions: And whereas,
by such an arrangement, the state would be relieved from
the hazard of future losses: Therefore,

*BE it enacted by the people of the State of New-York, rep-
resented in Senate and Assembly,* That it shall and may be
lawful for said institutions to assume conjointly, or to appoint one of their number to assume the supervision and
4 direction of said lottery, and from time to time to appoint
such and so many managers thereof, and other agents, for
the conducting the same, as to them may seem proper; and
the said managers and agents, or any of them, from time to
time to remove at their pleasure, and others in their stead
to appoint, and to make such contracts in relation to the
said lottery, and to take such security for the fulfilment of
such contracts, as to them shall from time to time seem
proper and reasonable, and to direct the times and manner
of drawing the said lottery, and the sum to be raised by
each class thereof, and to adopt such schemes as may be
5 proper in relation thereto, and to receive the avails and
hazard the losses, and be responsible for the payment of
the prizes of said lottery for a limited time, in lieu of, and
as an equivalent for, the several specific grants to them
therein made: *Provided,* they will accept thereof for any limited time, less than the time in which the state can raise and
pay said grants, at the rate monies have hitherto been raised
and paid, or can, in the judgment of the comptroller, be calculated, with safety to the state, to be hereafter raised and
paid; which time shall be determined by that officer, from
the facts and information in his possession, and a certificate
6 thereof filed in the office of the secretary of this state immediately after the passing of this act.

And be it further enacted, That whenever said institutions shall have severally accepted in writing of the provision contained in this act, in lieu of, and as equivalent
for, the grants to them severally made in said lottery, and

shall each of them have filed such acceptance in the office
of the secretary of this state, it shall be lawful for them
to assume the management thereof: Provided however,
And be it further enacted, That from the time such acceptance is filed, the state shall be absolved from all respon- 7
sibility to provide for any loss or losses that may occur on
any future class or classes of said lottery, and also from all
obligation to pay any prize ticket or prize tickets drawn
therein, out of any monies belonging to the people of this
state.

And be it further enacted, That the provisions contained
in the act relative to lotteries, passed April 13th, 1819, from
the ninth to the thirty-first sections thereof inclusive, shall
not be considered as applicable to lottery managers or
agents of said institutions, appointed under this act, except so far as the said institutions shall deem it expedient
to adopt and apply the same. 8

And be it further enacted, That before it shall be lawful for
any manager or agent, acting under the authority of said institutions, to offer the tickets of any class of said lottery for
sale, he shall enter into a bond to the amount now required
of lottery managers, with the people of this state, with sureties to the satisfaction of the comptroller, conditioned for
the faithful payment of all prize tickets by him signed,
when duly presented; and in case of failure or refusal, the
comptroller shall, on proof being made to him thereof, deliver such bond to the attorney-general for collection; and
on recovery, shall pay from the avails thereof said prize
tickets, if presented within the time limited by law. 9

And whereas the object of this act is not to increase the
grants made to the said institutions, but to contract with
them for assuming the responsibility and running the hazard, and taking the management of the literature lottery,
and thus to place them in a situation to save in all future
classes of said lottery, by more prudent contracts, and more
careful management, whatever can be saved out of that
indefinite amount that is liable, on the present plan of conducting said lottery, to be raised and absorbed by the recurrence of losses and the payment of managers: Therefore, 10

And be it enacted, That the annual average amount of
tickets, according to their scheme price, in all lotteries hereafter to be drawn under this act, during the term of years
fixed by the comptroller, shall not exceed the annual average amount of tickets, according to their scheme price, in
the lotteries already drawn within this state, during the
five years immediately preceding the first day of January,
one thousand eight hundred twenty-two, which amount of
tickets shall be ascertained by the comptroller, and a cer-

tificate thereof filed in the office of secretary ot this state; and said institutions shall furnish the comptroller a certified copy of the amount of tickets, at their scheme price,
11 in all classes hereafter to be drawn, that the same may be also filed in the office of the secretary of this state; and so soon as the whole amount of tickets, at their scheme price, authorised by this act, shall have been sold and drawn, the authority herein granted to said institutions shall cease, though the time fixed by the comptroller, in his certificate, may not have expired.

And be it further enacted, That said institutions shall apply the avails of said lottery, (after deducting the expense of managing the same,) *pro rata*, according to the provisions of the original act, in which said grants were made,
12 and make report thereof, annually, to the regents of the university, as said act directs.

And be it further enacted, That if said institutions shall accept of the provisions of this act, then in that case it shall be their duty to raise and pay the grant made by lottery to the historical society, in the same proportions as the other grants are raised and paid; and in consideration thereof, the limitation of time contained in the first enacting clause of this act, shall be proportionately extended.

III.

13 *Resolutions of the Trustees of Union College.*

At a meeting of the trustees of Union College, July 24, 1822—*Resolved*, That the treasurer of this board be authorised, by and with the consent of the president of college, to accept, under the seal of this board, of the provisions of the act to limit the continuance of lotteries, passed April 5th, 1822. And that the said treasurer be further authorised, under the seal of this board, to assume such responsibilities, and to give and take such securities, and to make such contracts relative to the lottery instituted for the pro-
14 motion of literature, or any part thereof, and to pledge or alienate such property belonging to this board, in carrying the same into effect as *the president of the college shall approve, to whose supervision the same is hereby committed, with authority to exercise, in behalf of this institution, all those powers vesting in it by virtue of the aforesaid act to limit the the continuance of lotteries.*

IV.

Acceptance by the Trustees of Union College, of the provisions of an act to limit, &c., in which is recited the
15 certificate of the Comptroller and Dep. Comptroller.

Whereas the comptroller of the state of New-York has

filed in the secretary's office, certificates in the words and
figures following, viz:

Whereas by an act of the legislature of the state of
New-York, entitled "An act to limit the continuance of
lotteries," passed April 5th, 1822, it is recited and enacted
as follows:

Whereas the public institutions to which grants were
made originally in the lottery instituted April 13, 1814,
for the promotion of literature, have already suffered materially by delay in drawing the same: and whereas it is
believed that the said lotteries might be managed with
greater economy and less hazard, by the institutions inter- 16
ested in its success, than it has hitherto been or can hereafter be by the state: and whereas all that could be thus
saved by greater economy in the management of said lottery, would go to diminish the loss of said institutions:
and whereas by such an arrangement the state would be
relieved from the hazard of future losses: Therefore,

Be it enacted by the people of the state of New-York,
represented in senate and assembly, That it shall and may
be lawful for the said institutions to assume conjointly, or
to appoint one of their number to assume the supervision
and direction of said lottery, and from time to time to appoint such and so many managers thereof, and other agents 17
for the conducting the same as to them may seem proper;
and the said managers and agents, or any of them, from
time to time, to remove at their pleasure, and others in
their stead to appoint, and to make such contracts in relation to the said lottery, and to take such security for the
fulfilment of such contracts, as to them from time to time
shall seem reasonable, and to direct the times and manner
of drawing the said lottery, and the sum to be raised by
each class thereof, and to adopt such schemes as may be
proper in relation thereto, and to receive the avails, and 18
hazard the losses, and be responsible for the payment of
the prizes of said lottery for a limited time in lieu
of, and as an equivalent for, the several specific grants
to them therein made: Provided they will accept thereof,
for any limited time less than the time in which the state
can raise and pay said grants, at the rate monies have
hitherto been raised and paid, or can in the judgment of
the comptroller be calculated with safety to the state, to
be hereafter raised and paid, which time shall be determined by that officer, from the facts and information in 19
his possession, and a certificate thereof filed in the office
of the secretary of this state, immediately after the passing
of this act.

And whereas a certificate was made on the 9th day of
April, 1822, in the words and figures following, to wit:

In pursuance therefore, of the duty imposed on the
comptroller, I, John Savage, comptroller of the state of
New-York, do hereby certify, that from facts and information in possession of the comptroller, it appears that the
net avails of lotteries drawn in the last twenty-five years,
have produced the annual average of twenty-four thousand
20 five hundred and eighty-four dollars and fifty seven cents.
In the last five years, the annual average has been twenty-
nine thousand nine hundred and fifty six dollars and thir-
teen cents; and in the last three years, the annual average
has been thirty-two thousand eight hundred and nine dollars and ninety-three cents. It is ascertained that the
amount now due to the several institutions, is three hundred and twenty-two thousand two hundred and fifty-six
dollars and eighty-one cents. In the judgment of the
comptroller, therefore, it may be calculated with safety to
21 the state, that the above amount of three hundred and
twenty-two thousand two hundred and fifty-six dollars and
eighty-one cents, can be hereafter raised and paid, in eleven
years.

In witness whereof, I have hereunto subscribed my name, and affixed my official seal, the 9th day of April, 1822.

JOHN SAVAGE.

Which certificate was made without reference to any
22 failure or delay in the payment of the net avails of the 6th
class of the literature lottery, then drawing, which net
avails were estimated at $33,000, any ultimate failure in
the payment of which, must affect the above calculation
to the extent of such failure, and extend proportionally
the time in which it might be calculated with safety to the
state, that the whole amount due the several institutions
could be raised and paid.

And whereas it is further recited and enacted in said act
to limit the continuance of lotteries, as follows, to wit:
23 "And whereas the object of this act is not to increase
the grants made to the said institutions, but to contract
with them for assuming the responsibility, and running the
hazards, and taking the management of the literature lottery, and thus to place them in a situation to save, in all
future classes of said lottery, by more prudent contracts
and more careful management, whatever can be saved out
of that indefinite amount that is liable on the present plan
of conducting said lottery, to be raised and absorbed by
the recurrence of losses and the payment of managers:
24 Therefore,

"Be it enacted, that the annual average amount of tickets, according to their scheme price in all lotteries, hereafter to be drawn under this act, during the term of years fixed by the comptroller, shall not exceed the annual average amount of tickets, according to their scheme price in the lotteries already drawn in this state, within the five years immediately preceding the first day of January, one thousand eight hundred and twenty-two, which amount of tickets shall be ascertained by the comptroller, and a certificate thereof filed in the office of the secretary of this state."

In pursuance, therefore, of the duty imposed on the
comptroller, I, Ephm. [Starr] dep. comptroller of the state 25
of New-York, do hereby certify, that the following several amounts of tickets, reckoned at their scheme price, were drawn in this state during the five years preceding the first of January, one thousand eight hundred and twenty-two, viz:

In Medical Science Lottery,	No. 3,....	$182,000
do	No. 4,....	182,000
do	No. 5,....	400,000
In Literature Lottery,	No. 1,........	200,000
do	No. 2,........	200,000 26
do	No. 3,........	225,000
do	No. 4,........	150,000
do	No. 5,........	140,000
Making,	....	$1,679,000

To which amount of one million six hundred and seventy-nine thousand dollars, there remains to be added the further amount of the Owego Lottery, drawn in New-York
by virtue of an act passed April 21, 1818, the amount of
which said lottery is not found in any documents in this 27
office. EPHM. STARR, *Dep. Comp.*

Comptroller's office, State of New-York, Albany, 4th February, 1823.

To all whom it may concern: Know ye that the trustees of Union College, in the town of Schenectady, in the state of New-York, one of the institutions interested in the said lottery, have for themselves and for the other institutions by whom they are appointed and authorised, accepted and do hereby accept of the provisions of said act of April 5th,
1822, conformably to the above recited certificate of the 28
comptroller, filed in the office of the secretary of this state. In testimony whereof, the said trustees of Union College have caused their common seal to be hereunto (L. S.) affixed, this eighteenth day of April, in the year of our Lord one thousand eight hundred and twenty-three.

HENRY YATES, Jun.,
Treasurer of Union College.

V.

29 *Original Contract with Yates & McIntyre.*

Whereas by an act of the legislature of this state, entitled "An act to limit the continuance of lotteries," passed
April 5, 1822, certain powers were vested in the several
public institutions interested in the lottery, instituted for
the promotion of literature, on their acceptance of said
act; and whereas certain of said institutious have empowered the trustees of Union College to act in their behalf, in
accepting and executing the provisions of said act; and
whereas the other institutions may empower the said trustees of Union College to perform in behalf of said institutions the same acts; now, therefore, in case all the re-
30 quisite powers vesting in said institutions jointly, on their
acceptance of the conditions of said act, shall become vested in the trustees of Union College, so as to enable them
legally to act in the premises, this indenture made the
twenty-ninth day of July, in the year of our Lord one
thousand eight hundred and twenty-two, between the said
trustees of Union College, in their own behalf, and in behalf of the other institutions, for which they are now or
may hereafter be authorized to act, of the first part, and
Archibald McIntyre and John B. Yates, of the second part,
31 WITNESSETH that the party of the first part, for and in consideration of the sum of TWO HUNDRED AND SEVENTY-SIX
THOUSAND AND NINETY DOLLARS AND FOURTEEN CENTS to them
in hand paid, or secured to be paid with interest annually,
and also in consideration of the covenants herein contained,
doth covenant and agree to *transfer* to the party of the
second part, all the right and title of the said party of the
first part, in their own right, and as legally representing
the aforesaid institutions, in and to the whole amount of
tickets at their scheme price, authorized to be sold by virtue of the act aforesaid.

And the said party of the second part, for and in consideration of the covenants herein contained, doth cove-
32 nant and agree, in addition to the amount paid or secured
to be paid as aforesaid, to pay all printing, to provide and
sign all tickets and to furnish a well lighted room for drawing the same; and also to pay, after the drawing of each
class, all the prize tickets that shall have been drawn therein, whenever the same shall be duly presented for payment, pursuant to legal provision and their own contract
with the holders or owners thereof.

And whereas tickets have been sold in preceding lotteries, at an exorbitant profit, the said party of the second part *stipulate not to sell any tickets required by virtue of this contract, at more than twenty-two per centum advance* on the

scheme price, unless by consent of the president of Union College or the board of managers by him appointed, until within four days of the drawing of the class in which such tickets are contained; and whenever tickets have been 33
selling for more than four days at any greater advanc, such class shall be forthwith drawn.

And the said party of the second part further covenant, *not to sell the tickets in any class, unless it be for cash, without the consent of the treasurer of Union College*, to be deposited when received by them, in some bank or banks in a separate account, and not to be redrawn therefrom unless by consent as aforesaid, *except for the purpose of fulfilling this contract*, and till the same is fulfilled so far as relates to each class successively.

And the said party of the second part further covenant, that they will at all times give to the treasurer of Union College an opportunity to examine their lottery accounts, 34
and such other information relative to their situation as shall be deemed necessary, to enable him to form his judgment in relation to the continued responsibility of the said party of the second part, and the sufficiency of their security for fulfilling this contract; and if the security given shall be deemed insufficient after any such examination, other security to the satisfaction of the treasurer of Union College, shall be forthwith given. It is further agreed between the parties aforesaid, in case of the death, disability or *failure in business of either of the persons composing the party of the second part*, that the survivor, in case of the death of either, and in case of disability or failure in busi- 35
ness, the one not so disabled or having so failed in business, shall be solely entitled to all subsequent benefit to be derived from this contract: and *shall be authorized, on performing the requisite covenants herein contained, to go on and complete its fulfillment on his own account*, and for his own benefit in the same manner as if the said contract had been made by himself solely.

And it is further understood and stipulated between the parties, that this contract shall not become obligatory on the party of the first part until the party of the second part shall have executed to the party of the first part, a bond *with sureties to the satisfaction of the treasurer of Union* 36
College in the penal sum of seventy thousand dollars, conditioned for the true and faithful performance of the stipulations contained in this contract, and until the party of the second part shall have executed and delivered to the comptroller, such bonds as are required by the act to limit the continuance of lotteries, passed as aforesaid.

And it is further stipulated that all the classes in said lottery shall be drawn by or under the direction of the

board of managers, or such other persons as they shall appoint or approve. The said board of managers to be appointed by the president of Union College. In witness
37 whereof, Henry Yates, Junior, treasurer of Union College, in virtue of a resolution hath hereto affixed the common seal of the College and signed his name; and the parties of the second part have affixed their seals and signed their names.

(Signed) HENRY YATES, Jun.,
Treasurer of Union College.

Seal of Union College.

(Signed) ARCH'D McINTYRE,
(Signed) J. B. YATES.

Duplicate acknowleged by Archibald McIntyre and John B. Yates, in presence of (Signed)
WILLIAM JAMES.

38 Having examined the within contract, I consent to and approve of the same.

(Signed.) ELIPHALET NOTT.

VI.

Supplement.

Whereas an agreement has this day been executed by the trustees of Union College of the first part, and Archibald McIntyre and John B. Yates of the second part—Now therefore, this agreement made on the twenty-ninth day of July, one thousand eight hundred and twenty-two, be-
39 tween the aforesaid parties, witnesseth that it was understood and agreed between the said parties to the aforesaid agreement, to which this agreement is a supplement, and is to constitute a part as of one instrument, and it is expressly stipulated in this agreement that the said party of the second part shall pay, and the said party of the second part, *do therefore covenant to pay for supervision and management, the same per centum on each class immediately after the drawing thereof, as has heretofore been paid to managers appointed by the State*, which payment shall be made by depositing in the Mohawk Bank, or such other bank as may be designated, to the credit of the President of Union
40 College, such per centum, of which payment the certificate of such bank, shall always be a sufficient voucher.

And it was further understood between the parties, and is herein expressly stipulated, that all the tickets to be sold by virtue of the act to limit the continuance of lotteries, are to *be divided from time to time into classes of a fixed number of tickets at a fixed scheme price*, with a fixed amount of prizes and a fixed time for drawing the same, all which to be done by the consent and approbation of the president of Union College, or the board of managers by

him appointed, which said classes to be denominated class No. 1, No. 2, No. 3, &c., of Literature Lotteries, new series, and immediately after the execution of the bond by
the party of the second part to the party of the first part, 41
as stipulated in the aforesaid agreement, a right shall vest in the party of the second part to dispose of tickets calculated at their scheme price, to an equal amount with the amount of said bond, together with such other and further security as may hereafter be given by the party of the second part, to the party of the first part, to the satisfaction of the treasurer of Union College. And whenever, from time to time, the whole or any part of the tickets, the right to dispose of which, had vested, as aforesaid in the party of the second part, shall have been drawn and the obligations arising therefrom, shall have been satisfactorily cancelled, or put in a train of being so drawn and cancelled, 42
a right shall vest in the party of the second part to dispose of an additional amount of tickets valued at their scheme price equal to the amount of those tickets, the obligations arising from which have been satisfactorily cancelled, or put in a train of being so cancelled, the same arrangement to continue, and the same process to be repeated, until said lotteries shall be completed.

It being, however, understood and expressly stipulated between the parties, that *no right to dispose of any subsequent amount of tickets, shall ever vest in the party of the second part, until the obligations arising out of the antece-
dent amount of tickets to which such amount is consequent,* 43
shall have been satisfactorily cancelled, or put in a train of being so cancelled, of which the treasurer of Union College *shall be the sole and conclusive judge.*

And whereas events may occur that shall prevent the party of the second part from paying their note of two hundred and seventy-six thousand and ninety dollars and fourteen cents, given as one of the considerations of this agreement, at the time the same is stipulated to be paid: *It is, therefore, further agreed*, that if, before the end of the year eighteen hundred and twenty-three, the said party of the second part shall elect to pay said note *in annual installments of thirty-nine thousand three hundred and twelve
dollars*, commencing from the day the interest commenced 44
on said note, and continuing until said note shall be fully paid, said party shall be allowed to do so. IN WHICH EVENT, said party shall immediately after the drawing of each class *deposit to the credit of the treasurer of Union College, for safe keeping in the Manhattan Bank*, or such other bank as may be by him designated, such part of the aforesaid annual payment, as shall bear the same proportion to the whole annual payment, as the amount of tickets in said

class reckoned at their scheme price, shall bear to *four
hundred forty-nine thousand two hundred and eighty dollars,*
a certificate of which deposit shall be sufficient evidence of
the receipt thereof by the treasurer aforesaid, and the
amount of the several receipts, shall on the last day of
45 every year, reckoned as aforesaid, be endorsed; or if not
endorsed, shall have the effect of an endorsement to the
amount thereof on the aforesaid note.

But it is understood between the parties, that if less than
four hundred and forty-nine thousand two hundred and
eighty dollars worth of tickets, reckoned at their scheme
price, shall be drawn in any one year, then less in proportion
may be deposited in the bank to the credit of the said
treasurer. But it is expressly stipulated between the parties,
that if less shall in any one year be deposited than the
sum of thirty-nine thousand three hundred and twelve
dollars, the deficit together with the interest thereon, from
the time when it was payable, shall be added to the installment
of the ensuing year; and if less shall again be
46 deposited than the above sum, together with the deficit of
the preceding year, the balance, with the interest as above,
shall again be added and made up and endorsed as aforesaid.

It being, however, further understood and expressly
stipulated, *that at the end of any year in which there shall
be a deficit in the sum stipulated to be deposited,* or in the
deposit of the per centum, for supervision and management
as aforesaid, the treasurer of Union College shall be
at liberty, previous to the adopting of the scheme for any
subsequent year, to *give notice to the party of the second
part, that this agreement has become forfeited,* and from that
47 time forth, the parties shall no longer be allowed to act
under it, except so far as to close the business already
commenced, and to settle their accounts; and if at the
time such notice is given, any scheme or schemes shall
have already been adopted by consent and approbation as
aforesaid, the same shall be drawn, (except by the consent
of the parties,) within the time specified in such scheme.

And it is further stipulated, that the said party of the
second part, may at any time anticipate the payment of
the stipulated annual payments as aforesaid, by depositing
the same to the credit of the treasurer of Union College, as
aforesaid, on or *before the first day of the year, commencing
48 as aforesaid, in which year such payment would otherwise be
made, in which case, a rebate in the amount shall be made
equal* to the amount of interest that would accrue on such
payment, during the whole time the same is anticipated,
except six months; and though such rebatement be made
in the deposit, the full sum of thirty-nine thousand three

hundred and twelve dollars shall be endorsed therefor, on the aforesaid original note at the close of the year, reckoning as aforesaid, in which the same would otherwise have been fully deposited, or if not so endorsed, the deposit shall have the effect of such endorsement.

And it is further stipulated by the party of the second
part, to sell on the first four days of sale, in each class, at 49
the scheme price to adventurers, and to the several licensed lottery dealers in such proportions as may appear discreet, *and to such amount as may be required*, except that the said party of the second part, may always retain one-third part of each class for their own use, and such other and larger proportion as may from time to time, be consented to either by the president of Union College, or by the board of managers appointed as aforesaid. In witness whereof, Henry Yates, Jun., treasurer of Union College, hath hereto affixed the common seal of Union College, and signed his name in virtue of a resolution; and the parties of the second part have affixed their seals and signed their
names. 50

(Signed) HENRY YATES, Jun.,
Seal of *Treasurer of Union College.*
Union College. (Signed) ARCHIBALD McINTYRE.
(Signed) J. B. YATES.

Interlineations being made before execution, and all acknowledged in my presence by Archibald McIntyre and John B. Yates.

(Signed) Wm. JAMES.

Having examined the above contract, I consent to and approve of the same.

(Signed) ELIPHALET NOTT.

VII. 51

Contract between the Trustees of Hamilton College and the Trustees of Union College.

This indenture, made this twelfth day of October, in the year of our Lord one thousand eight hundred and twenty-two, between the trustees of Hamilton College, of the one part, and the trustees of Union College, in the town of Schenectady and state of New-York, of the other part, *witnesseth* :—

Whereas by an act of the legislature, entitled "An act instituting a lottery for the promotion of literature and for other purposes," passed April 13, 1814, it was enacted, that out of
the avails of the lottery by the said act instituted, the sum of 52
forty thousand dollars should be appropriated to the said trustees of Hamilton College, together with the simple interest accruing thereon, till the same should be raised and paid: provided, that no payment should be made of interest ac-

cruing on said appropriation for more than six years from
the time of passing the said act. *And whereas* by a subsequent act of the legislature, passed April 5, 1822, it was
enacted that it should be lawful for the public institutions,
to which the monies to be raised by the said lottery, by virtue of the act first heretofore mentioned, were appropriated,
53 to assume conjointly, or to appoint one of their number to
assume the supervision and direction of the said lottery,
and to receive the avails and hazard the losses, and be responsible for the payment of the prizes of said lottery, for
a limited time, in lieu thereof, and as an equivalent for,
the several specific grants to them therein made. *And
whereas* it has been agreed between the parties of these
presents, that the trustees of Hamilton College shall transfer all their interest in the said lottery instituted for the
promotion of literature, amounting to forty-four thousand
four hundred and seventy-two dollars, to the trustees of
Union College upon the terms and conditions hereinafter
54 particularly mentioned.

Now therefore, this indenture witnesseth, That for and in
consideration of the sum of fifteen thousand dollars, to
them in hand paid, or secured to be paid to the trustees of
Hamilton College, by the trustees of Union College, and
in consideration of the further covenants hereinafter con-
taiued, they, the said trustees of Hamilton College, have
bargained, sold, assigned, tranferred and set over, and by
these presents do for themselves and their successors, bar-
gain, sell, assign, transfer and set over, unto the said trustees of Union College, all and singular their right, title, interest, property, claim and demand, in and to the said lottery instituted by the said act entitled "An act instituting
55 a lottery for the promotion of literature and for other purposes," passed April 13th, 1814, and in and to the avails
thereof, and any monies to be raised thereby and appropriated to the trustees of Hamilton College, to have, hold,
take, receive, and enjoy the same, with all and singular
the benefits and advantages to be derived therefrom, unto
the said trustees of Union College, their surcessors and assigns, and for their only proper use, benefit and behoof.
And the said trustees of Hamilton College, do hereby make,
constitute and appoint the trustees of Union College aforesaid, their true and lawful agents and attorneys, for them,
and in their name, place, and stead, to accept (in writing)
56 of the conditions and provisions contained in the said act
entitled "An act to limit the continuance of lotteries,"
passed April 5th, 1822, in lieu of, and as an equivalent for,
the grant to them made as aforesaid in the said lottery, and
to file such acceptance in the office of the secretary of this
state, and to do all other acts, and matters, and things,

whatsoever, in relation to the said lottery, as fully, to all
intents and purposes, as the trustees of Hamilton College
might or could do, according to the provisions of the aforesaid act, entitled "An act to limit the continuance of lotteries," or as if the said grant to Hamilton College, contained in the act entitled "An act instituting a lottery for
the promotion of literature and for other purposes," had 57
originally been made to the trustees of Union College.

And the said trustees of Hamilton College, do hereby
for themselves, and their successors, covenant, promise and
agree, to and with the said trustees of Union College, that
they and their successors will, at any time hereafter, on
the reasonable request of the trustees of Union College,
their successors or assigns, execute (to be filed in the office
of the secretary of this state) any certificate which may be
lawfully required of them, to signify their acceptance of
the provisions contained in the said act entitled "An act
to limit the continuance of lotteries," in lieu of, and as an
equivalent for, the grants to them made as aforesaid, in
the said lottery. And further, that they and their succes- 58
sors will, at any time hereafter, on the like reasonable request, duly execute and deliver all, and every such other
and further deeds, conveyances and assurances in the law
whatsoever, as may be lawfully required for the further
and better, and more effectually transferring, assigning or
confirming all their right, title and interest in the said lottery and the avails thereof, to the trustees of Union College, their successors and assigns, according to the true in-
tent and meaning of these presents.

And the trustees of Union College, in consideration of
the aforesaid sale, transfer and assignment by the trustees
of Hamilton College, of their right, interest and claim, to 59
the avails of the said lottery, to the said trustees of Union
College, have agreed, and do agree and covenant to pay to
the said trustees of Hamilton College, the sum of thirty-
three thousand three hundred and fifty-four dollars and
fifty-three cents, with interest from the ninth day of April,
in the year one thousand eight hundred and twenty-two,
which payment is to be made as follows: three thousand
dollars to be deposited in the New-York State Bank, in
Albany, to the credit of Erastus Clark, on or before the
first day of November next, and seven thousand dollars to
be deposited in like manner, at the New-York State Bank,
in sums of not less than one thousand dollars at a time, 60
before the twelfth day of February next, and a certificate
of each such deposite, to be sent said Clark by mail immediately thereafter.

And the sum of eighteen thousand three hundred fifty-
four dollars and fifty-three cents, to be secured said trus-

tees of Hamilton College, by the note of the Rev. Eliphalet
Nott, and Henry Yates, Jun., Esq., guaranteed by William
James, Esq., of Albany, payable within four years from
the date hereof, with interest, from the ninth day of April
last past, payable annually on the twelfth day of October,
in each year: and also to secure the sum of five thousand
dollars, by the joint note of said Eliphalet Nott and William James, to said Erastus Clark or order, payable at the
Mohawk Bank, with interest, in three years from the date
hereof. And to pay the residue of said sum of thirty-
61 three thousand three hundred and fifty-four dollars and
fifty-three cents, with interest, from the ninth day of April
last past, to the said trustees of Hamilton College, in four
years from the date hereof. All the money which shall be
received on the said several notes of Eliphalet Nott and
Henry Yates, and of said Eliphalet Nott and William
James, and also the money to be deposited in the New-
York State Bank, as aforesaid, to be received as part performance of the covenants herein contained, to be performed by the trustees of Union College, and to be allowed and
endorsed upon this agreement.

And the trustees of Union College covenant and agree
with the trustees of Hamilton College, that whatever shall
62 be received by the said trustees of Union College from the
supervision and management of the said lottery, over and
above the expense incurred by them therein, shall be and
remain a contingent fund for the meeting of losses, should
any occur: the whole remainder of the sums so received
for supervision and management, shall be divided between
the said colleges pro rata, or according to the interest they
had respectively at the time of signing this contract, or
may thereafter have acquired. And the trustees of Union
College will indemnify and save harmless the said trustees
of Hamilton College from any loss or damage, by reason
of the conducting or managing said lottery. And the said
63 trustees of Hamilton College, further covenant and agree,
duly and fully to indemnify and save harmless, the trustees of Union College, from all payment or loss to be by
them sustained, on account of any lien or claim, the state
may acquire, or have acquired by virtue of an act entitled
"An act for the relief of Hamilton College," passed March
18th, 1817, on any part of the original appropriation in
said lottery made to Hamilton College, which appropriation has been herein fully and without any reservation,
transferred to the trustees of Union College, as the same
existed on the 9th of April last, after deducting eight hundred and seven dollars, since received from the comptroller
64 by the trustees of Hamilton College.

In testimony whereof, the said trustees of Hamilton College and the said trustees of Union College have caused their respective seals to be hereunto interchangeably set and affixed, the day and year first above written.

[L. S.] By Henry Yates, Junr., Treasurer of Union College.
Approved by Eliphalet Nott.

[L. S.] I certify the above to be a true copy of the original, deposited in the archives of Hamil- 65
ton county.

BENJAMIN W. DWIGHT,
Treasurer of Hamilton College.

CLINTON, *August* 13, 1834.

VIII.

Extracts from the correspondence with Hamilton College.

To B. W. DWIGHT, ESQ., *Treasurer of Hamilton College:*

Dear sir—Yours of the 26th Nov. was received during
the absence of the President of Union College to whom it 66
was addressed. Since his return an earlier meeting of this committee has been prevented by sickness and other unavoidable occurrences.

In reply to your communication we beg leave to make a brief statement of facts.

The amount due to the several institutions from the literature lottery was $322,256.81. Union College borrowed funds, and bought out all the other parties in interest. By the original indenture of Yates and McIntyre, to whom its entire interest was sold, said College was (if paid in advance, and thus protected against loss, as the other in-
stitutions had been) to receive $276,090.14, estimated with 67
interest by Yates and McIntyre in a bill subsequently filed against the trustees at $393,120. In the execution of this indenture, however, they met with losses, and became reduced to the verge of ruin.

To prevent their failure, the President of Union College raised funds for them to a large amount, in consideration of which, Jan. 24th, 1826, they stipulated to vary the terms of their original indenture, so as to require the payment of eleven per cent on $4,492,208 worth of tickets, a supposed contingent residue of $456,389 worth to remain subject to a new contract. Soon after this an act was
passed authorising the mixing of the Albany land lottery 68
with the Literature and Fever Hospital lotteries. To enable Yates and McIntyre to execute a contract under said act, they applied to Dr. Nott for his consent and co-opera-

tion, stipulating May 31st, 1826, in consideration thereof,
after having drawn all the tickets then supposed to belong
to the literature lottery, including the contingent residue,
and after having also drawn a certain amount of tickets in
the Fever Hospital lottery, (the drawing of which was in-
69 hibited by law till the drawing of the literature lottery was
finished) to pay to him a certain per centage on all the
subsequent classes drawn; under this stipulation, however, no classes were ever drawn, or per centage paid.

After the whole of the $4,948,597 worth of tickets as-
sumed to belong to the literature lottery, including the
supposed contingent residue, had been drawn, and the
drawing of the Fever Hospital lottery commenced, a settlement was effected with Yates and McIntyre, to wit: on
the first of August, 1828, under their original indenture,
as modified by their stipulation of Jan. 24, and May 31,
1826, in which Yates and McIntyre agreed not only to pay
70 the per centage due to the College under their original indenture on the whole amount of tickets then supposed to
have belonged to the literature lottery, but also to pay the
additional amount stipulated to be paid Jan. 24, 1826, for
moneys advanced by the president to enable them to meet
the payment of certain prizes.

Yates and McIntyre, after commencing the drawing of
the Fever Hospital lottery still continuing embarrassed,
applied repeatedly to Dr. Nott for pecuniary assistance to
very large amounts, for which they stipulated to pay a
certain per centage on the tickets thereafter to be drawn,
71 which per centage after being paid for some time, was ultimately refused. For the recovery of which Dr. Nott filed
a bill in chancery, in which the trustees of Union College,
without their consent, or even knowledge, were joined as
plaintiffs.

And the trustees of Union College then supposing that
the whole of the $4,948,597 worth of tickets, on which
Yates and McIntyre had stipulated to pay per centage, actually belonged to said lottery, and of course supposing
that there was a contingent residue, as stated in the stipulation of 24th of January, 1826, and that said college had,
72 in consequence, an interest in tickets drawn long after
their treasurer, Henry Yates, became a partner in the said
firm, directed a bill to be filed in chancery for the recovery of his portion of profits arising therefrom.

To the bill filed by Dr. Nott, Yates & McIntyre demurred on the ground that the stipulation was entered into
with him after the literature lottery was closed, and that
the same was for personal advances, services and hazards
only in which the college had no interest, which was, indeed, the case.

And the lottery question having been referred to the At- 73
torney General (See Ass. Doc. Vol. 4, p. 10,) by the Legislature, he reported that the whole amount of tickets contained in the literature lottery, in place of being $4,948,597 worth, as had been supposed, was only $3,693,800 worth, making a difference of $1,254,797 worth of tickets in the lottery, and of $138,027 in the amount of percentage to have been paid by Yates & McIntyre. Whereupon Yates & McIntyre filed a bill in chancery for the recovery of this excess of per centage, claimed to have been paid in error.

After considering the report of the Attorney General, 74
and perceiving if said lotteries contained only $3,693,800 worth of tickets, that there was no contingent residue when the stipulation of the 24th Jan., 1826, was entered into, and of course that the stipulation of May 31, predicated on such residue, must be invalid, and perceiving also that little if anything could be recovered of Henry Yates, as in that case the literature lottery closed soon after the partnership commenced, a negotiation was, by advice of counsel, opened with a view to effect an amicable settlement,
and thus prevent a protracted and expensive litigation, 75
when it was found that Yates & McIntyre would, on their part, agree to cancel their entire claim against Union College for all payments made in error, provided the college would surrender to them certain evidences of debt amounting to $126,037.57, and further, that they would agree to pay $150,000 in ten years, in installments, provided the claim against them for the payment of percentage under their stipulation entered into July 15th, 1830, with Dr. Nott, for personal advances, hazards, &c., was cancelled,
and it was also found that Dr. Nott would, on his part, also 76
agree to cancel said stipulation on said terms:

Whereupon an article of agreement was entered into between the trustees of Union College and the president, setting forth that the $150,000 to be received from Yates & McIntyre, was to be received on account of the stipulation aforesaid entered into with him for personal advances, &c., and for the recovery of which said suit had been commenced, and that the same was to be accounted for to him on a final settlement.

After which a tripartite agreement, on the conditions 77
above set forth, was entered into between Yates & McIntyre, the Trustees of Union College, and the President of Union College, in which the parties severally agreed, not only to discontinue the suits which had been commenced, but also to relinquish all cause of future suits, arising out of said lottery transactions.

Thus the amount realized by Union College from the College fund, up to the present day, *falls short* in place of

exceeding, as you suppose, the amount actually due under the original indenture. Nor will the amount to be realized
78 hereafter, ever exceed the amount so due, even though all the evidences of debt received from Yates & McIntyre, should eventually be paid. And in place of having received from the imaginary contingent residue to which you allude, the sums stated, or any part thereof, Union College has been required to refund, and has actually refunded $126,037.57 of per centage paid on tickets claimed to have been drawn in error, over and above what the law allowed, irrespective of such contingent residue.

In reference to the 2¼ per cent. on the tickets of the litera-
79 ture lottery, set apart by Union College in the contract with Yates & McIntyre, for supervision and management, and set apart in like manner in the subsequent contract with Hamilton College, the same being the compensation previously allowed therefor by law, referred to in your letter, as the President's fund, and estimated at about $122,000, the undersigned remark that according to the aforesaid calculations of the Attorney-General, in accordance with which the aforesaid bill of Yates & McIntyre, was framed, and the aforesaid settlement made, the whole amount of
80 tickets authorised to be drawn in said lottery, and of course the whole amount on which 2¼ per cent. could be lawfully reckoned, was $3,693,800 worth, on which sum said per centage amounts to $83,210.50, and no more.

The president of Union College having by great personal exertion and at great personal peril, (in which no other trustee was found willing to participate, and which all considered in him rash and even presumptuous,) succeeded in sustaining the credit of Yates & McIntyre till the entire literature lottery was drawn, and having also succeeded in
81 securing from said lottery after paying all expenses, a considerable surplus to be divided between the colleges, it was felt that Union College, whose interest had been so gratuitously and greatly promoted by hazards assumed by him in its own behalf, would therefore come forward with an ill grace to claim a share in the avails, if any there should be, of hazards subsequently assumed by him in behalf of others. And however frequently the trustees of Union College may have expressed their sense of the indebtedness of said college to its president for his interference as afore-
82 said, still they deem it proper distinctly to state, that they have neither received, nor claimed to be entitled to receive, the compensation stipulated to be paid, either to the president of said college in the form of per centage for monies advanced or hazards run by him in behalf of Yates & McIntyre, or to be entitled to receive the compensation stipulated to be paid to the late treasurer of Union College

in the form of profit sas co-partner in said firm after the drawing of the Literature lottery had ceased, and that of the Fever Hospital lottery had commenced; and whatever claim said
trustees might have had to the comparative small amount 83
of profits arising previously thereto was relinquished by them on the final settlement aforesaid, in order to put an end to litigation.

Nor can the undersigned even now perceive, particularly since no contingent residue existed as has been supposed, on what grounds of either law or equity Union College could have sustained a claim to compensation received by any individual or individuals, however related to said institution, for personal advances made, hazards run, or services performed, to facilitate the commencement or further 84
the progress, and to be paid out of the avails of a lottery in which said college had no interest, over which it exercised no control, and the commencement of the drawing of which was inhibited by law, till all the tickets in the Literature lottery, in which alone said college was interested, were drawn. Be this however as it may, rather than submit to the evils of a protracted litigation, Union College was willing to secure, even at a sacrifice, the benefits of an immediate and amicable settlement; and the
more so as its own rights were the rights chiefly affected 85
thereby. For of the whole $126,037.57 refunded to Yates & McIntyre, only $20,394.19, or thereabouts, were claimed by Yates & McIntyre to be due from the fund for supervision and management, which was the only fund in the judgment of the undersigned, in which Hamilton College in any event could have had an interest. And this for the obvious reason that such was the original understanding between the two colleges, as appears from previous legal
provisions, from the express terms of the contract itself, 86
and from the documentary evidence in the possession of the undersigned, as well as from the testimony of the living witnesses to that transaction who still remain.

What losses have already occurred or may hereafter occur, in consequence of the change of the times, the failure of individuals, and the depression of real estate, or what the ultimate profits to be realized by either the president, or the late treasurer of Union College, for advances made,
hazards run, or services rendered in behalf of Yates & 86
McIntyre, after the drawing of the literature lottery closed, are questions concerning which the undersigned are not informed, and over which they do not claim to have any control. And they have therefore only to add, that so far as any funds have been already or may ever hereafter be received, in which the colleges are interested, the undersigned are prepared to effect an immediate settlement; and

for that purpose will meet the committee of Hamilton
87 College at such time as may suit its convenience.

In behalf of the finance committee,

Very respectfully, yours, &c.

J. P. CUSHMAN.
A. C. PAIGE.

SCHENECTADY, *Feb.* 23, 1840.
To. B. W. DWIGHT, Esq.,
Treasurer Hamilton College.

IX.

NEW-YORK, *January 4th*, 1826.

88 Rev. E. NOTT, *President of Union College :*

Sir—We have stipulated, as you are aware, to pay to the trustees of Union College, the sum of two hundred and seventy-six thousand dollars, within ten years, with interest annually, for and in consideration of their transferring to us their right in and to the grants made by the act to limit the continuance of lotteries. It has become necessary that we should inform you that, such have been our losses, *that we have no reasonable prospect of being able to pay the sum stipulated, or even to pay the prizes in the lottery*
89 *now pending, unless we can procure immediate pecuniary assistance to a large amount.* If such assistance can be procured, we are confident that we shall be able to fulfil our contract with the college and save ourselves harmless.

In view of these circumstances, we have thought it our duty to propose *that you and the treasurer* SHOULD RAISE FOR OUR IMMEDIATE RELIEF ONE HUNDRED THOUSAND DOLLARS, together with such further sum as may be necessary to sustain our credit, until we can be fully relieved, by converting our property into money, and collecting the amounts
90 due to us, which are still good, but merely delayed in consequence of the general pressure. And *in consideration thereof we are willing to stipulate to pay you such an additional sum as shall, together with the* $276,000, *for which we admit that we are now holden,* amount to eleven per cent. on the whole amount of tickets sold, or to be sold, by us, under said act; the same to be paid estimating the per centum on the tickets sold at their scheme price in each class, and in all the classes hitherto drawn, as well as those hereafter to be drawn, under said act, immediately after the drawing thereof.

With respect, we are,
91 your obedient servants,
YATES & McINTYRE.

X.

J. B. YATES TO E. NOTT.

NEW-YORK, *Jan'y 17th*, 1826.

Dear Sir—Your letter, with the check for the sum of
$345, has been duly received. The package on which you
have thus paid the difference between its selling scheme
price and the least sum it must draw, contains the following Nos.—Com. 1 4 19; reg. 100—com. 2 3 12; reg. 955—
com. 5 9 41 ; r. 3,676—c. 6 14 18 ; r. 4,559—c. 7 15 33 ;
r. 5,307—c. 8 11 16 ; r. 5,830—c. 10 14 20 ; r. 7,155—c.
17 21 30 ; r. 10,623—c. 22 38 39 ; r. 12,392—c. 23 31 40 ;
r. 12,554—24 27 44 ; 12,906—25 32 42 ; 12,969—26 36 37 ; 92
13,177—28 29 43; 13,388—34 35 45; 13,980. No. of the
package, 727.

Our prospects, since our return, have somewhat brightened.
The Washington and Con't. class have turned out well,
and if we should have any luck like it in our New-York
class, we will not need to use the paper; but on that I
build nothing. All the present feeling is, that we have
now no doubt remaining, that, eventually, our friends, and
the institutions, will be safe, *let the worst come that may,*
and if our credit shall be FULLY SUSTAINED, *of which I now* 93
entertain no fears, even if the money should not be obtained on the papers with Mr. James' endorsement. *With re-*
gard to the stipulation and explanation you name, that shall
be done. It is immaterial now whether we want the aid we
asked or not. It has passed from us by promise. It is no
more our right. I looked over the memorandum you gave
my brother, with Mr. McIntyre. We see *nothing in it*
wrong, and will write an agreement pursuant to its directions. We have some thought of not attempting to nego-
tiate the notes of Mr. J's. if it should be requisite, after the 94
drawing until towards the close of the 40 days, in which
the prizes are payable by us.

Yours truly, J. B. YATES.

P. S. I perceive you have inadvertently written your letter on the back of your draft. Of course, it can not be used. We will charge you with the money, and you can, if you wish, hand it to brother Henry, when he returns. The draft I have cancelled by drawing my pen across it, and your name.

XI.

95 A. M'INTYRE TO E. NOTT.

[*Grateful for assistance—presence of H. Yates requested—larger allowance to contractors suggested—sends draft of land bill.*]

NEW-YORK, *Jan'y* 23, 1826.

Rev. and Dear Sir—I cannot omit, on the return of Mr.
H. Yates, to express to you *my very grateful sense of our
obligations to you for the prompt relief you have afforded us
in the hour of our difficulty and distress. We were, it cannot
be denied, on the very verge of ruin*, and I am now, thank
heaven, (if the Union Canal Lottery afford us the least
sum we have calculated on realising from it,) enabled to
96 believe that we are safe, if we pursue a uniform and prudent course, which I think we are fully prepared to do.
We have had a lesson sufficiently appalling and distress-
ing, to keep us in very constant remembrance of it during
life.

As, however, I am, more than ever, sensible of the frail-
ty of human nature, and the uncertainty of all earthly calculations, I am anxious, above all things in this world, to
get through with our present engagements without ruin to
ourselves and our friends; and I have thought that *the
97 presence and advice of Mr. Henry Yates here*, for as much of
his time as he could possibly spare, with us, might be useful. He has consented to come, and we shall provide as
liberally as we can for his sacrifice. Perhaps you too can,
with propriety, make him an allowance on account of the
INCREASED SAFETY TO THE COLLEGE.

The very extraordinary change of times within the last
four months, affecting our business as much, if not more,
than any other, added to recent losses, and the opposition
which has sprung up, can not but alarm us, with the heavy
98 engagements we have on our hands. I am, therefore, on
the constant look out, where something may be saved,
where, by some modification or change of contracts, something may be made, and our ultimate safety be increased.
I have thought, and take, therefore, the liberty of suggest-
ing for your consideration, whether it would not be for the
safety and interest of the college to make us a more liberal
allowance than is now made us. Four per cent on the
schemes, when all the tickets are sold and paid for, affords
a good profit, I acknowledge—but really that allowance is
99 not sufficient to indemnify for the risks that we are compelled to run. *Were you to allow us 6 per cent instead of 4, we
could afford to run off all your schemes in less than two years.*
Would not, then, the saving of interest on the capital to
be produced for the college, and the increased security to
it by the success of our operations, be sufficent inducement
to you, on behalf of the institution, to give a favorable ear

to my suggestions. You are to judge of it, and I only now pray for your serious attention to the subject.

I have sent to the recorder of Albany, a bill relative to
the Albany land lottery, and Mr. Yates will deliver you a 100
copy of it. I need not inform you of the importance of that subject. It will require your watchful attention, and I trust that nothing will prevent your keeping it in constant view during its progress.

I am, Rev dear sir,
With very sincere respect,
Your most obedient servant,
ARCH. McINTYRE.

Rev. Eliphalet Nott, D. D.

XII.

J. B. Yates to E. Nott.

[*Under anxious apprehension—drawing disastrous—not yet insolvent, nor will be if sustained—whether anything further in E. N.'s power—presence of H. Y. solicited.*]

New-York, *January* 23, 1826. 101

Dear Sir : Since my visit to Schenectady, my mind has been in a very perturbed state, in consequence of *my anxious apprehension* for ourselves and our friends. The lottery of New-York has proved *as disastrous* to us as we would have anticipated by the drawing, yet the result of the Washington and Connecticut class, drawn in Washington, was so much better than we expected, that the two together have not much disappointed us. *On reviewing* our situation, it is evident that we are NOT INSOLVENT.
We have determined on not paying our prizes until they 102
are due, which will throw us beyond the Philadelphia drawing; after which we may know with some degree of certainty, what will be our situation on a view of the whole ground. In the meanwhile, we will use as little of the paper of Mr. James as we can do with. As yet, we have need of none of it. I AM SATISFIED, IF WE ARE SUSTAINED FOR SIX MONTHS, or, *at the furthest for one year, we can save our friends, the college, and our reputations. Our golden dreams, for ourselves, have vanished,* and with them, all the
imagined good I thought of doing with it. Still, a com- 103
fortable competency is far from hopeless. *I do not know what further* you may have in *your power*, should it become requisite. On mature reflection, I am convinced that our safety requires that I should go south, if we continue operating; and in that event, I KNOW THE PRESENCE OF MY BROTHER AS TREASURER OF THE COLLEGE, *during the whole time, to see to things and aid with all the energy he possesses, is positively necessary for a variety of reasons.* You may not think yourself authorized to make him a sufficient allowance from the contingent expense fund, to enable him 104

to come down; but allow him as much as you think you
can with justice, and we will add enough to save him
harmless, at least. We not only want him here, a while,
but all the time, and to be actively engaged supervising
and aiding in the detailed direction of our affairs. Mr.
McIn. and I must now, necessarily, both be often and long
absent, and often unexpectedly, and we will need his active
aid, besides the *beneficial public effect it would have, that he is*
known to be here as the treasurer of the college. I wish it
105 were possible for you to accompany him when he comes
down again, to see and judge of the full state of our affairs.

With respect, I am yours, &c.,

J. B. YATES.

XIII.

Whereas an indenture was made on the 29th of July,
1822, between the trustees of Union College, of the first
part, and Archibald McIntyre and John B. Yates, of the
second part, together with a supplement made on the same
day, and forming, together, one whole contract; and
whereas it was found *to be impossible* for the party of the
second part to procure, at the time, securities *to the amount,*
106 *and of the kind* originally contemplated; and whereas the
best interest of the college required that no farther delay
should take place in the drawing of the lotteries, it was
verbally admitted, by the party of the first part, that the
party of the second part *might proceed, for the time being,*
on such security as was given, which *relaxation,* it was
supposed, would promote the interests of both the parties,
by expediting the progress of the lottery. And as it has
been agreed that the terms of payment should, *in conse-*
quence of such relaxation, be more favorable to the college,
107 *to prevent* any future *doubt or dispute* concerning the import of the written contract, it is hereby *mutually stipula-*
ted and declared, that the real payments to be made to the
party of the first part, by the party of the second part, is
eleven per centum on each class drawn, viz, eight and three-
quarters per centum to the treasurer of Union College, and
two and one quarter per centum to the president of the
college; the same to be *made immediately* after the drawing
of each class, by deposits in banks as agreed on, until four
million four hundred and ninety-two thousand two hun-
108 dred and eight dollars worth of tickets, reckoned at the
selling scheme price, shall have been drawn, when this
whole written contract will have been cancelled; *and the*
rebate of interest spoken of in the supplement, to have effect
only in cases where the said eleven per centum shall have
been paid *before the drawing* of the classes out of which the
same is to arise.

The CONTINGENT RESIDUE of the lottery to be the subject of a new contract, the terms of which have been already discussed and *verbally settled* between the parties.

ARCHIBALD McINTYRE,
J. B. YATES. 109

NEW-YORK, *January* 24, 1826.

XIV.

NEW-YORK, *May* 31*st*, 1826.

To Dr. E. NOTT,

Rev. Sir—Having made a contract for the drawing of the lottery under the act entitled, "An act to enable the mayor, aldermen and commonalty of the city of Albany, to dispose of tickets in a lottery heretofore granted, and to limit the continuance of the same, passed April 13, 1826;"
and being desirous to mix the tickets of the same with the 110
tickets in the lotteries authorised by the act to limit the continuance of lotteries, on condition that you will consent thereto: *We stipulate*, that after having drawn, for the college, 2,004,099 dollars worth of tickets, reckoned at their scheme price, at the present stipulated rate of drawing and payments; and 1,654,497 dollars worth of tickets, reckoned at the same rate, for our benefit, as the assignees of the Fever Hospital Lottery—to deposit to your credit, in such bank as you shall designate, six and thirty-one
hundreth per centum on the gross amount of money prizes 111
in each scheme or class, immediately after the drawing of the same, so long as we shall be permitted to continue to operate under said act of 13th April, 1826, or any future act that may be obtained, modifying the principle therein contained. It being understood that the annual average rate of drawing the money tickets shall not be, hereafter, less than it has heretofore been, unless prevented by unavoidable necessity, satisfactory to yourself, or by mutual consent. The schemes of all classes to be hereafter drawn, when made out, to be regularly transmitted to you.

YATES & McINTYRE.

XV.

YATES AND MCINTYRE TO THE TREASURER OF UNION COLLEGE.

[Asking consent to mixing prizes.] 112

NEW-YORK, *June* 2*d*, 1826.

To HENRY YATES, Esq., *Treasurer of Union College.*

Sir—We have, pursuant to the terms of a law of last winter, a copy of which you have received, made a contract with the corporation of the city of Albany, to pay them the entire amount of the valuation of their lands, equal to two hundred and fifty thousand dollars, in five

equal annual payments, with the power to mingle them with the money prizes of the lotteries yet to be drawn; and to commence as soon as convenient, if the literary institu-
113 tions, interested in the grant, shall consent thereto. You will, therefore, perceive that we have taken the entire burthen of this load upon ourselves, together with all the hazards attending it. We believe this measure was necessary from every consideration of policy, and for the purpose of conciliating the good feelings of the citizens of Albany. We have asked from them no compensation arising from any sacrifice of their lands for our benefit.

We will continue to perform the terms of our engagement with you in the same manner as heretofore, as assidu-
114 ously as shall be in our power, and have no doubt that we can and will conduct the business without any disadvantage to the institutions.

In order, therefore, that we may commence our operations under the contract with the corporation of Albany, as soon as convenience will warrant, we ask from the literary institutions, their assent to the mixing the land prizes with the money prizes of the lotteries we are now conducting under our contract with them.

You will perceive by the law, that the person having the supervision and direction of those lotteries must con-
115 sent. This, we believe, is the president of Union College. Will you hand to him this application, which we make to you as treasurer of that institution, to whom we consider it ought to be officially addressed.

Yours respectfully,
ARCHIBALD McINTYRE,
J. B. YATES.

XVI.

E. NOTT TO YATES AND M'INTYRE.

[Accepts on his own behalf, the terms of the second written stipulation.]

UNION COLLEGE, *June* 10*th*, 1826.

Gentlemen—To the written propositions submitted in
116 your letter, dated May 30th, in regard to the contract you have made under an act entitled "An act to enable the mayor, aldermen and commonalty of the city of Albany to dispose of tickets in a lottery heretofore granted," and to limit the continuance of lotteries, passed April 13th, 1826, I hereby communicate my acceptance; and you will consider this as the evidence of my consent, and the pledge of my co-operation granted on the terms contained in the proposition submitted.

Very respectfully yours, &c.,
E. NOTT.

Messrs. YATES & McINTYRE.

XVII.

PRESIDENT OF U. C. TO YATES AND M'INTYRE.

[Consents on behalf of the institution to mixing of tickets.]

UNION COLLEGE, *June* 10*th*, 1826.

Gentlemen—To the proposition submitted in your letter
of the 2d inst., relative to the mixing of the tickets, authorised by the "Act to enable the mayor, aldermen and commonalty of the city of Albany, to dispose of tickets in a
lottery heretofore granted," with the tickets in the lotteries
authorised by the "Act to limit the continuance of lot- 118
teries," I reply, that since it is understood and agreed that
the stipulations entered into with Union College shall, not-
withstanding the proposed mixing of tickets, be fully complied with, in behalf of the institution, my consent to the
measure, on the terms proposed. And this I do the more
cheerfully, as the trustees of the college are not made parties to the contract under the aforesaid act of April 13th,
1826, and will not, therefore, be considered responsible for
the hazard which may arise from proceedings had under it.

Very respectfully yours, &c.,

E. NOTT, *as Pres.* 119

XVIII.

YATES AND M'INTYRE TO E. NOTT.

NEW-YORK, *May* 30, 1826.

Rev. Sir—In order to bring all the lotteries of the State
of New-York to a close, within the time for closing the
Literature and Fever Hospital Lotteries, the Legislature
have passed an act holding out strong inducements to the
subscribers to accept of the conditions of the same, entitled 120
"An act to enable the mayor, aldermen and commonalty of
the city of Albany to dispose of tickets in a lottery heretofore granted, and to limit the continuance of the same,"
passed 13th April, 1826, under which act the subscribers
have made a contract, in the execution of which they hope
to be able to indemnify themselves for the heavy losses
they have heretofore sustained; which, contract, however,
they cannot execute without your *consent and co-operation*, as
it will require a further *continuance* of the *heavy personal responsibilities assumed by you on our behalf*. And on condition that such consent and co-operation is granted by you, 121
we hereby STIPULATE AND ENGAGE that, (after having drawn
for the college 2,004,099 dollars worth of tickets, reckoned
at their scheme price, of actual sales, and 1,654,497 dollars
worth, of actual sales, for our own benefit, as assignees of the
Fever Hospital Lottery,) we will, within ninety days after the

drawing of each subsequent class, after the drawing of said
two sums, *deposit to your credit*, in such bank as you shall
designate, SIX AND THIRTY-ONE ONE HUNDREDTHS PER CENTUM,
on the gross amount of all tickets actually sold therein, to-
122 gether with *the interest* accruing thereon from the day of
drawing; which deposit shall, at all events, (and whether
the Fever Hospital grant be completed or not,) be made to
your credit, on all classes to be drawn from and after the
second day of June, 1829, so long as we shall be allowed
to operate under said act of April 13th, 1826, or any future
act that may be passed modifying the principles therein
contained.

It is to be understood, however, that 6$\frac{31}{15}$ *of the Albany
lands* drawn to tickets remaining on the hands of the sub-
123 scribers, or otherwise taken by them in furtherance of the
lottery, shall, at the *end of the same, be turned over to you*,
at the price said lands shall cost us; that is to say, the
original corporation appraisement thereof (when drawn on
hand by us,) and when purchased from others, at the price
paid therefor, together with the interest accruing thereon,
in lieu of an equal amount of money.

It is further to be understood, however, that the whole
amount of Albany lands, turned over, shall not in any
event exceed one-fourth part of the whole amount of the
124 money to be deposited in bank as aforesaid to your credit,
or that may be paid to your order, on accouut of the said
6$\frac{31}{100}$ per cent.

And it is also to be understood, that the *rate of drawing* shall not *be less* hereafter than it has *heretofore* been, unless from unavoidable necessity, satisfactory to yourself, or by mutual consent.

The schemes of all classes, and the returns of *tickets sold*, to be, in all cases, *forwarded to you*, as early as practicable.

We have the honor to be, with
high respect, your obedient serv'ts,
125 YATES & McINTYRE.

XIX.

A. M'INTYRE TO E. NOTT. (*Extract.*)

NEW-YORK, *May* 15, 1830.

*It gives me sincere pleasure, that we have been able at
length, to get released your property, which you kindly hypothecated to raise funds for us in* 1826, *to save us at a critical
moment from ruin. The papers necessary to give you legal
126 possession of your property, you will receive herewith. And
now, that this is accomplished, be pleased to accept of my sincere thanks for the important service you rendered us in this*

particular, and to be assured that I shall never cease to hold the favor in grateful remembrance.

I am, rev. dear sir,

with sentiments of profound respect and esteem,

your most obedient servant,

A. McINTYRE.

P. S.—Having concluded to send you this by mail, the certificates of stock, &c., &c., will be kept until Charles 127
Yates goes up, which will be in a few days, by whom they will be sent.

A. McI.

Rev. E. Nott, D. D.
President Union College.

PART OF XVIII.

[The following stipulation, modifying that of May 30, 1826, which is printed at folio 125, *ante*, should have been inserted immediately after it.]

Stipulation of July 15, 1830.

Whereas the claims of Union College against the subscribers, Yates & McIntyre, arising out of their contracts under the law to limit the continuance of lotteries, passed the 5th April, 1822, have been fully paid, or provided for, by notes given August 1, 1828, when said contract was cancelled: and whereas the stipulation of the subscribers, entered into with Eliphalet Nott, on the 30th May, 1826, under the "Act to enable the mayor, aldermen and commonalty of the city of Albany, to dispose of tickets in a lottery heretofore granted, and to limit the continuance of the same," passed April 13th, 1826, was for and in consideration of personal services rendered, or to be rendered, and hazards run, on our account; and whereas the hazards are diminishing, while the difficulties of conducting the lotteries are increasing; therefore, in lieu of said stipulation entered into on the 30th May, 1826, and of all the personal demands arising as aforesaid, out of services rendered and hazards run by said Nott for us, in regard to so much of the Consolidated Lottery as shall have been, or be drawn from and after the first day of May last, the subscribers promise to pay to said Eliphalet Nott, within ninety days after the drawing of each class, drawn as aforesaid, after the first of May last, five per centum on the gross amount of tickets sold therein, after deducting therefrom the contained amount of land, if any, in any of the schemes: It being always understood, that the said Eliphalet Nott is to take an equal share with us of the Albany lands that may fall into our hands, by purchase or by drawing them on hand, at the price they may cost us, and allowing us interest on the cost from the time of payment; and also that we are to continue to be authorised to sell any such Albany lands, when we can do so, we to be accountable to him therefor.

YATES & McINTYRE.

New-York, *July* 15, 1830.

XX.

SCHEDULE D.—Final Settlement with Yates & McIntyre.

bill of A. McIntyre and J. B. Yates.]

Dr. *Trustees of Union College.* *College Fund, (8¾ per ct. on each scheme.)* *Cr.*

Date	Day		Payments.	Int. at 7 per cent to 1st Aug. 1828.	Class when drawn.	Day			8⅜ per ct. on each scheme.	Int. at 7 per cent, to 1st Aug. 1828.
1823,					1823,					
May	31	To Cash paid Henry Yates, Treasurer,	$4,450 60	$1,609 46	May	20	By Literature Lottery,	1 class,	$4,581 50	1,666 77
July	30	" do paid by A. E. Brown,	1,035 30	362 50	July	23	" do	2 "	8,575 00	3,014 59
"	"	" do do	4,330	2,915 50	"	26	" Albany,	1 "	1,065 75	374 62
Aug.	2	" do paid Treasurer, $1,000—3,000,	4,000		Oct.	15	" Literature Lottery,	3 "	9,432 50	3,165 64
Oct.	18	" do do	9,163 00	3,069 86	Dec.	3	" do	4 "	12,005 00	3,916 96
Dec.	11	" do do	11,662 00	3,786 80	1824,					
1824,					Jan.	7	" do	5 "	8,575 00	2,741 14
Jan.	22	" do	8,330 00	2,638 53	Mar.	17	" do	6 "	14,971 25	4,582 10
Mar.	29	" do	14,543 50	4,417 17	June	16	" do	7 "	23,954 00	6,912 06
July	4	" do d'ft to J. W. Francis,	5,311 00	1,514 96	Aug.	18	" do	1, 1824,	14,971 25	4,142 48
Sep.	1	" do remitted H. Yates,	17,958 60	4,923 63	Oct.	20	" do	2 "	14,971 25	3,961 97
1825,					Dec.	15	" do	3 "	14,971 25	3,801 24
Apr.	13	" do do	103,492 72	23,886 66	1825,					
1826,					Apr.	6	" do	4 "	14,971 25	3,475 81
May	8	" do paid H. Yates,	3,000 00	486 41	July	20	" do	1, 1825,	23,954 00	5,081 58
1827,					Sep.	20	" do	2 "	20,020 00	4,009 55
Jan.	31	" T. Gardiner's Bond and Mort. dated,	7,000 00	735 00	1826,					
		" Isaac Riggs' note, due 17th Feb.,	1,500 00	157 50	Jan.	19	" do	3 "	49,665 00	8,807 26
		" Archer's Bond and Mort. with int. fr. 7th Dec., 1827,	16,000 00	726 98	Feb.	22	" do	1, 1826,	11,977 00	2,040 09
May	25	" Three Bonds of Coll. of Physicians and Surgeons pay't assumed by us, with int. fr. 26th Oct. 1826.	20,000 00	1,656 66	Apr.	5	" do	2 "	8,982 75	1,458 43
					June	1	" do	3 "	14,971 25	2,270 32
June	5	" Bond and Mort. of Rob't Richardson,	4,000 00	322 78	July	19	" do	4 "	11,977 00	1,704 72
Aug.	4	" do do A. B. Shankland,	4,000 00	277 66	Aug.	30	" do	5 "	8,982 75	1,206 91
"	15	" D'ft of L. Bebee, due 17th Sep, $2,500			Nov.	29	" do	6 (or Con.		
		" do do " " 1,182			1827,			1, 1826,)	23,516 50	2,752 73
		" do do " 21st " 1,200			Jan.	31	" New-York Consol.	2 "	11,539 50	1,213 90
Sep.	6	" do do " 9th Oct., 700			May	23	" do	1, 1827,	14,271 25	1,187 67
		" do do " 15th " 1,500			June	12	" do	2 "	11,736 37	931 08
		" do do " 19th " 2,000			"	27	" do	3 "	8,484 52	648 35
		" do do " 24th " 683			July	18	" do	4 "	8,462 65	613 63

Date		Particulars		Principal	Interest	Date		Particulars	Principal	Interest
Nov.	1	" do do " 25th Nov..........	3,000			Aug.	15	" do 5 " ...	8,462 65	569 34
		" do do " 20th "	750			Sep.	5	" do 6 " ...	12,759 60	806 33
		" do do " " "	550			"	26	" do 7 " ...	10,851 75	641 46
		" do do " " "	582			Oct.	17	" do 8 " ...	10,676 75	589 59
		" do do " 15th "	1,000			Nov.	10	" do 9 " ...	18,665 94	943 67
		" do do " 20th "	700							
		" do do " 21st "	2,383							
		" do do " 25th "	800							
				19,530 00	1,025 22					
Dec.	31	" 2½ per ct. on $19,530 paid L. Bebee,...............		488 55	19 93					
1828,										
Feb.	11	" Cash paid L. Bebee, bal. int. due 25th Dec.,........		329 53	10 69			8¾ per ct. on $4,948,597, is	$433,002 23	$79,231 39
1827,										
Oct.	15	" Bond and Mort. of John B. Yates,................		55,000 00	3,052 81					
Dec.	31	" Our note to A. Terhune, due 14th July, 1827,.......		2,000 00	146 52			By Balance, Princip.,..........	115,877 73	
		" Balance,....................................		115,877 73	21,506 16			Interest,..........	21,506 16	
				$433,002 23	$79,231 39					$137,383 89

Received notes for the above Balance, according to the annexed list, which when paid, will be in full of all demands against Yates and McIntyre, arising out of their original contract with the Trustees of Union College, made on the 29th day of July, 1822, under the act to limit the continuance of Lotteries, passed April 5th, 1822; and also, out of a special stipulation by them made, to provide for the payment of prizes in the class No. 3, for 1825, of Literature Lottery, drawn 19th January, 1826, and in consideration of the personal responsibilities to be assumed by the President and Treasurer of Union College, in order to sustain the contractors in the further performance of their contracts.

(SIGNED.) ELIPHALET NOTT.

For the College Fund. Notes given—dated 1st August, 1828.

Note		Interest to			Interest	Total	Note		Interest to			Interest	Total
$5,000	with interest to	1st Feb. 1830,	18	mo's	$525	$5,525	$5,000	with interest to	1st April, 1831	32	mo's	933 33	$5,933 33
5,000	"	1 Mar. "	19	"	554 16	5,554 16	5,000	"	1 May, "	33	"	962 50	5,962 50
5,000	"	1 April, "	20	"	583 33	5,583 33	5,000	"	1 June, "	34	"	991 66	5,991 50
5,000	"	1 May, "	21	"	612 49	5,612 49	5,000	"	1 July, "	35	"	1,020 83	6,020 83
5,000	"	1 June, "	22	"	641 65	5,641 65	5,000	"	1 Aug. "	36	"	1,050	6,050
5,000	"	1 July, "	23	"	670 82	5,670 82	5,000	"	1 Sep. "	37	"	1,079 16	6,079 16
5,000	"	1 Aug. "	24	"	700	5,700	5,000	"	1 Oct. "	38	"	1,108 33	6,108 33
5,000	"	1 Sep. "	25	"	729 16	5,729 16	5,000	"	1 Nov. "	39	"	1,137 50	6,137 50
5,000	"	1 Oct. "	26	"	758 33	5,758 33	5,000	"	1 Dec. "	40	"	1,166 66	6,166 66
5,000	"	1 Nov. "	27	"	787 50	5,787 50							
5,000	"	1 Dec. "	28	"	816 67	5,816 67	$115,000						
5,000	"	1 Jan. 1831,	29	"	845 84	3,845 84	22,383 89		1 May, 1828,	45	"	5,875 80	28,259 69
5,000	"	1 Feb. "	30	"	875	5,875							
5,000	"	1 Mar. "	31	"	904 17	5,904 17	$137,383 89	Prin. and Int. to 1st Aug. 1828.				$25,329 89	$162,713 78

SCHEDULE D.—Final Settlement with Yates & McIntyre.—(*Continued.*)

Dr. *Trustees of Union College,* *President's Fund.*

		Payments.	Int. to Aug. 1828.			2½ per ct. on Classes.	Interest.
1822, May 31	To Cash	$1,309	$473 42	1823, May 20	By Lit. Lotery, 1st Class, ...	$1,178 10	$428 58
July 30	To do	304 50	106 63	July 23	By do 2 "	2,205	775 18
" "	To do	2,450	857 97	" 26	By do Albany, 1 "	274 05	96 19
Oct. 18	To do	2,695	902 89	Oct. 15	By do 3 "	2,425 50	813 85
Dec. 11	To do	3,430	1,113 79	Dec. 3	By do 4 "	3,087	1,007 23
1824, Mar. 29	To do	2,450	744 11	1824, Jan. 7	By do 5 "	2,205	704 86
" "	To do	4,277 50	1,299 17	Mar. 17	By do 6 "	3,847 75	1,178 26
Sep. 1	To do	6,844	1,876 39	June 16	By do 7 "	6,159 60	1,778 59
1825, Jan. 11	To do	9,173 25	2,283 13	Aug. 18	By do 1 " for 1824, ...	3,849 75	1,065 17
April 13	To do	3,849 75	888 28	Oct 20	By do 2 "	3,849 75	1,018 78
Aug. 6	To do	6,844	1,430 57	Dec. 15	By do 3 "	3,849 75	977 59
Oct. 10	To do	5,148	1,012 01	1825, April 6	By do 4 "	3,849 75	893 76
1826, Mar. 18	To do	3,079 80	510 81	July 20	By do 1 " for 1825, ...	6,159 60	1,306 70
June 18	To do	6,936 60	1,029 10	Sept. 20	By do 2 "	5,148	1,031 07
July 3	To do	7,000	1,018 11	1826, Jan. 19	By do 3 "	12,771	2,264 72
1827, Jan. 31	To do	5,000	525	Feb. 22	By do 1 " for 1826, ...	3,079 80	524 58
				April 5	By do 2 "	2,309 85	375 02
				June 1	By do 3 "	3,849 75	583 88
				July 19	By do 4 "	3,079 80	438 38
				Aug. 30	By do 5 "	2,309 85	310 32
				Nov. 20	By do 6 "	6,047 10	707 82
				1827, Jan. 31	By N. Y. Con'd 2 "	2,967 30	312 13
				May 23	By do 1 " for 1827, ...	3,669 75	305 39
				June 12	By do 2 "	3,017 93	239 42
				June 27	By do 3 "	2,181 74	166 62
				July 18	By do 4 "	2,176 11	157 81
				Aug. 28	By do 5 "	2,176 11	150 61
				Sep. 5	By do 6 "	3,281 04	207 34
				Sep. 26	By do 7 "	2,790 45	164 94

			Oct. 17	By do	8 "		2,740 45	
			Nov. 10	By do	9 "		4,799 81	242
Balance,	70,791 40	16,071 39					$111,343 44	$20,378 48
	40,552 04	4,307 09						
	$111,343 44	$20,378 48		Balance Principa.,			$40,552 04	
				do Interest,			4,307 09	
				Interest on Notes, added thereto,			4,321 49	
				Total amount of Notes,				$49,180 62

Rec'd New-York, December 6, of Yates & McIntyre, their nine several Notes of hand to me, dated 1st August, 1828 according to the annexed List thereof and amounting to forty-nine thousand one hundred and eighty 62-100 dollars which when paid will be full of this account current. ELIPHALET NOTT.

LIST OF NOTES,

Given to Dr. Nott, dated 1st of August, 1828, for the President's Fund, viz:

Principal,					Interest,	Am't Notes.
$5,000	with interest to 1st	June, 1829,	10	months,	$291 66	$5,291 66
5,000	1	July,	11	"	320 83	5,320 83
5,000	1	Aug.	12	"	350	5,350
5,000	1	Sept.	13	"	379 16	5,379 16
5,000	1	Oct.	14	"	408 32	5,408 32
5,000	1	Nov.	15	"	437 49	5,437 49
5,000	1	Dec.	16	"	466 66	5,466 66
5,000	1	Jan. 1830,	17	"	495 82	5,495 82
4,859 13	1	Jan. 1832,	41	"	1,171 55	6,030 68
$44,859 13					$4,321 49	$49,180 62

XXI.

REPORT OF SILAS WRIGHT AND WILLIAM JAMES—July 26, 1851.

(Records, Book B, p. 163.)

The finance committee of the trustees of Union College, pursuant to a resolution of the board of trustees, of the 28th July, now last past, beg leave respectfully to report:

That the first object of the committee has been to ascertain with precision the funds which have at any time been contributed, either by individuals and corporate donations, or by public appropriations, or from any other source, to aid in founding or sustaining this institution. The result
143 of this inquiry is, that the following sums have been appropriated to the benefit of Union College, and have either been received and made available, or are still in prospect, to wit:

1. Subscriptions to the funds of the college, actually received, ... $2,707 42
2. Old academy granted to the college by the Dutch church of Schenectady, actual receipts thereof, ... 571 89
3. Bonds given to the college by the trustees of the Schenectady patent, actual receipts therefor, ... 38,357 98

144

$41,637 29

4. Grants by the State as follows to wit:
   - By § 20 of Supply bill of 9th April, 1795, ... $3,750 00
   - By § 26 of Supply bill of 11th April, 1796, ... 10,000 00
   - By act, chap. 65, § 3 of 30th March, 1797, ... 1,500 00
   - By act, chap. 19, § 1 of 7th
145 March, 1800, ... 10,000 00
   - By act, chap. 62, of 1805, to be received by lottery $80,000, but from which there was received but............. 76,138 01
   - By act chap. 120 of 1814, amended by chap. 113 of 1822, to be received by Literature lottery not yet closed, ... 200,000 00
   - By act chap. 19 of 1800, ten lots in the Military tract, re-
146 served for the promotion of literature, 5,500 acres of

land, the principal money of the sales to the present time amounting to........	32,912 38	
By act, chap 105, § 2 of 1802, garrison land at Fort George, Ticonderoga and Crown Point, 1,449 acres, all sold, and principal amounting to	9,378 20	
		343,678 59
		$385,315 88

To be added to the above, are two of the ten lots of land 147
granted by the act of the 7th of March, 1800, to wit: lot 41 Solon, and lot 18 Manlius, yet remain unsold. But as the committee have no means of ascertaining the actual value of those lots, and as they still remain the property of the college, it is not material for the purpose of the examination to be made, that they should be considered at all. It should also be remembered that although the grant made by the act of 1814, of $200,000, to be raised by lottery, has been settled with the managers, so far as the
principal and interest of that sum is concerned, and their 148
obligations, and the obligations and securities of other persons taken for the amount, which are exhibited as part of the funds of the institution, yet that but very little money has as yet been received upon the principal of that grant, and upon the payment of those obligations or not depends the justice of exhibiting as above the $200,000, as part of the funds granted to the college. Yet for the purpose of comparison, which the committee wish to present to the board, no variance in result will be experienced from this
consideration, inasmuch as while the $200,000 is charged 149
as received on the one side, the obligations are credited as funds on hand on the other.

They assume therefore, that the statement before made shows all the funds which have come to the hands of the trustees or their agents, separate from the ordinary revenues of the college itself, and that this board is properly chargeable, and bound satisfactorily to account for the amount of those funds, $385,315.88.

To do this in a way the most simple and best calculated
to satisfy the mind with the past management, and at the 150
same time to give a view of the present state of the funds, they first present the existing means as they now find them, separate from the property in the college itself and its appurtenances.

These means consist of the following items, to wit:

Stock in solvent chartered companies, ...	$89,105 00
Obligations receivable, being the principal moneys due upon bonds and mortgages, contracts and notes, ...	251,457 98
Making together, ...	$341,556 98
To this should be added the investments which have been made in the stocks of the 151 Bank of Hudson, the Franklin Bank of New-York, and the Water-works, and turnpike company, which stocks are still held, but the companies have since the investments were made, become wholly insolvent, or the stocks wholly unproductive, .	15,675 00
	$357,231 98

The sum above charged as having been received, is
152 $385,315.88, from which, if the above amount accounted for be deducted, there will remain $28,083.90, being the balance to be accounted for of the principal moneys charged to the institution.

This, however, is upon the assumption that the amounts received from contributions from the old academy and from the bonds of the trustees, were not converted to the immediate use of the institution, but were kept and have remained productive funds regularly and constantly invested. This assumption the committee by no means
153 adopt, as there can be no doubt from the most slight examination of the order of time in which these donations were received, compared with the dates of the respective grants from the State, that these sums were at once expended as the first aids in helping this institution into life and action. There should therefore be deducted from the above amount of supposed productive funds, the total of these items, amounting to $41,637.29, and sinking that amount to $133,428.59.

But another and principal consideration in this view of
154 the subject remains to be taken. More than half of the whole sum charged to have been received by the trustees, and for which they are accountable, to wit: the sum of $200,000, granted by the act of 1814, was granted with the condition that no more than six years interest should be demanded until the whole principal was paid and the lotteries closed. That principal has been liquidated, together with the six years of interest due thereon, and is now held by the trustees in obligations against the managers of the lotteries, and in securities taken from them,

but it has not been paid, and therefore, beyond the six 155
years for which the act making the grant allowed interest, the whole of this $200,000 has necessarily in a legal sense remained unproductive.

It is believed that this view of the receipts and expenditures of the college, coupled with the single statement before made of the amount of funds on hand, the losses sustained without any fault on the part of the trustees or their agents, and solely through investments which resulted unfortunately, would be sufficient to satisfy this board,
the Legislature and the public, that not only good faith, 156
but great care and uncommon prudence have been constantly exercised in the management of the funds of the institution.

But as an examination of the unexpended funds will be calculated to present in a stronger light the full extent to which the benevolent designs of the Legislature in endowing this institution have been kept in view, and as such an examination becomes necessary, to acquaint the board with the present state and condition of those funds, the
committee are emboldened to ask further indulgence while 157
they go through this task, as cursorily as it can be done without a forfeiture of the object in view.

And here it becomes necessary to remark, that all the former observations and statements have been founded upon the assumption, that the whole amount of the $200,000, granted by the act of 1814, had been received. This in a literal sense is true to a very limited extent only; and it will be seen that so far as the objects designed by that grant have, as yet, been accomplished, it is by the aid of
the other funds. 158

The following is a classification of the items of the existing funds denominated "Obligations Receivable," with reference to the source from which the respective amounts were derived.

Securities for lands ceded by the State.—Ten lots by the act of 1800.

Bonds and mortgages, ...	$4,774 16		
Contracts, ...	1,265 52		
Garrison lands by act of 1802.			
Bond and mortgage,..........	2,485 60		159
		$8,525 28	

Securities for lands conveyed by the city of Schenectady in exchange for the old college.

Bonds and mortgages,........	$18,622 20	
Contracts, ...	838 44	
Notes, ...	47 98	
		19,508 62

Securities taken from Stephen N. Bayard for a debt due.

	Bond and mortgage, ...	$5,952 79	
	Note, ...	1,379 70	
160			7,322 49

Securities for money loaned.

	Bonds and mortgages,........	$20,838 69	
			20,838 69

Securities received in payment taken with guarantee, and taken on settlement of the amount due under the act of 1814.

	Bonds and mortgages taken in payment,.................	$100,921 51	
	Note, ...	1,500 00	
161			102,421 51
	Bonds and mortgages guarantied,.....................	$36,350 00	
	Notes for balance due, ...	57,475 39	
			196,246 90
	Making the total given before of..........		$252,451 98

Thus it will be seen that the amount now due from the
162 managers of the lotteries, and upon securities which they have assigned to the College is $196,246.90, a sum less than the principal of the grant made by the act of 1814, by only $3,753.10. But it should be taken in mind, as well in justice to the managers as for the correct understanding of the means which have been received to sustain the expenditures hitherto made, and to continue the funds as they at present exist, that the six years' interest allowed by the act of 1814, upon the money granted by it, has in this mode of viewing the subject, been received and appropriated to
163 the expenses of the institution, and to the existing funds.

To the above amount of obligations receivable should be added the investments in stocks now held by the Trustees, and amounting to $104,780. These two amounts, on the present funds of the institution to be made available for any purpose of expenditure, or to be credited to the Trustees, as so much of the amount entrusted to them whenever they are called upon to account.

It must be gratifying to know that the expenditures under the different classifications have been—

164	For support of officers, beyond the whole receipts from tuition applicable to the payment of officers,	$113,060 38
	In aid of indigent students,...............	47,401 86
	For the classical library,.	5,947 31
	For the library and apparatus,............	18,102 55

For buildings and grounds,............... 221,401 01
For incidental exenses, ... 10,433 89

Making a total of,................. $416,347 00
A sum larger than the whole amount of the funds granted to the college by the state, and by individuals and corpo- 165
rations, by $31,031.12.

One other comparison shall close this part of the subject. The whole amount of funds received by the Trustees, and for which they are chargeable, as above is, $385,315 88
The amount of the capital of the several funds it is now proposed to institute, and which if no further losses are sustained, there will be means to institute, when the lotteries are closed, over and above all existing debts, and after sinking the insolvent stocks, is.. 286,356 98 166

A sum less than the whole fund received by only $98,958 90

In the meantime, separate from the loss sustained between the expenses of the Old College and the sum realized for it, the following property, estimated from its cost, has been accumulated, to wit:

New College buildings and grounds,........ $186,181 09
Library and apparatus, ... 18,102 55
Classical library,........................ 5,917 31 167

In all $210,230 95
Add to this the above amount of funds on hand, after deducting all ascertained losses and paying all debts, ... 286,356 98

and you will have..................... $496,587 93
From this deduct the whole amount of funds received, as before given,............... 385,315 88
168
And there will remain............. $111,272 05

Thus showing the actual accumulation of property, at cost, to this extent, instead of a sinking of any part of the capital of the fund bestowed. If to the above be added the following items:

Loss upon the Old College, ... $35,219 92
Loss of stocks,.............................. 15,675 00
Payment in aid of Indigent students,........ 47,401 86

In all $98,296 78 169

The conclusion must follow, not only that the finances of the institution have been well conducted, but that a singular good fortune has attended that management which could by possibility enable these funds to produce these results, and annually to sustain the excess of the ordinary expenses of the institution over its income, separate from the auxiliary funds.

Indeed these results are of a character which nearly
170 defy credulity; and as their explanation becomes almost entirely personal as to one member of the committee, the other members find it indelicate and improper to introduce that explanation into this report. They have, therefore, embodied in an appendix those facts which they deem it important the board should understand, and which at the present time at least, partake so much of the nature of confidential communications, as, in their opinions, to justify them in making the communication in that shape, and in submitting the disposition of the facts disclosed to the
171 better discretion of the trustees. To that document the majority of the committee threfore refer for such explanations as every investigating mind will require, with the single observation that nothing contained in it, and no examination of the fiscal affairs of the college which they have been able to make, whether confidential or not, will have any other tendency than fully to establish the disinterestedness, integrity and vigilance with which every act in relation to these funds, on the part of that member of the committee, who does not join in the appendix, has been
172 characterized.

But the committee feel impelled here again to recur to the fact, that this flattering state of affairs of the college funds is not beyond the reach of contingency and hazard. Nearly sixty thousand dollars of the funds of which they have been treating, and upon which their fair calculations are based, exist in unmatured notes against the managers of the lotteries, *and we shall not disguise from ourselves the probable fact that their punctual payment, and perhaps it would not be too much to say, their payment in any event,*
173 *must depend upon the success with which these very uncertain and hazardous institutions shall be finally brought to a termination.* Thirty-six thousand dollars more of these funds exist in securities assigned by the managers, and guarantied by them, and so far as the securities shall prove bad, and this board be left to call upon guarantors, this part of the amount cannot be considered exempt from the same contingency. One hundred thousand dollars more exist in securities received from the managers in payment of so much of the claim upon the lotteries. These securi-
174 ties were taken at a time when heavy misfortunes and heavy losses seemed to render the final success of the lotteries doubtful, and when therefore the securities were

considered of more value than the claims for their amounts, dependent as it was upon the future efforts of the managers to regain their former losses, and to accomplish the original purpose for which the lotteries were instituted.

The securities are, with one exception, bonds and mortgages, and little or no loss, it is hoped, will be sustained 175
upon them; but the obligors are widely scattered, some of the demands are very large, and a knowledge amounting to certainty, as to the value of the property mortgaged, or the personal responsibility of the individual debtors, cannot be had.

Losses may also be experienced upon some of the other securities, and indeed are, to a very limited extent, already anticipated. Other investments, though now considered perfectly secure, may prove unfortunate, and in short these funds yet require the same vigilance and the same guar- 176
dianship which has hitherto been extended to them, or all our favorable anticipations will fail us.

The notes taken from the managers upon the final settlement with them, all fall due between the first of the now next month and the first of May next, but the amounts are large, and they fall in so rapidly, that it is not reasonable to expect the payment of all at the day. If success is experienced by the managers, some indulgence will no doubt be required, but the committee recommend that as little be given as shall be found consistent with a due re- 177
gard to the interests of the debtors and to the safety of their operations.

Appendix.

Having investigated the matters on which this report is founded, the subscribers deem it part of their duty to notice the result exhibited in the last statement, because that from a general knowledge of the resources and expenditures of the institution during the past twenty-five years,
under ordinary management of its concerns, a different re- 178
sult might be expected. If, in explanation, their remarks shall bear on an officer of the college, they are free to say that the other member of your committee of finance had no part nor act in framing either the report or this note. This is not the occasion, neither is it the intention of the signers to eulogize individuals who are in the full enjoyment and exercise of high and distinguished faculties, and from whom so much good to the college is yet hoped for and expected; when that time shall arrive, an ample source
for commendation will be found in reviewing the exertions, 179
with the wise and well directed force of talent and influence that procured the greater part of the funds which your committee have been examining. They will there-

fore confine themselves to the abstract point mentioned. From the report it may be perceived that donations to the college were to be received in years after the grants, and that the greater part of them had been encumbered with
180 conditions that absorbed much of their nominal value, and that further diminutions became necessary from the wants of the establishment, which required that the avails should be anticipated, at cost of interest, &c., &c. It may also be observed that donations in the best lands had been unproductive for years, and that such, in lands of inferior quality, remain useless at this day. It will further be seen from the report that the faculty have expended on benevolent objects an amount exceeding legislative requirements, and that they have also met a great amount in losses on stocks,
181 &c., &c. Such considerations are calculated to check the hopes of the friends of the college in finding a balance over the endowment; and if the institution has been raised to its present high character without diminishing the capital, it appears plain to your committee that that all important result could only have been effected by indefatigable attention to prudence, economy and wise measures; but after having met expenditures and losses there appears to be an excess of more than $100,000, which forms a problem that must be solved on principles different from ordinary, or
182 even intense assiduities to official duties. Individual enterprise or parental anxieties, under the guidance of rare and experienced minds, can only afford instances of such increase of property under different and expensive establishments, and to such solicitude and sympathies for the institution, the subscribers have traced about $90,000, which now makes part of the balance in its favor.

This amount is aggregated partly by relinquishments of stipulated salaries from principal officers; $8,500 of it appears to have been a fortuitous result of a speculation in
183 chances, which had been generously added to the funds many years ago. The residue is composed of the net gains on various speculations and contracts made on individual account (or names) and responsibility, in the course of years; all which had been applied to the sole use and benefits of the college. *A sum of $42,000 out of the last mentioned sources has been added to the fund since the last annual meeting of the board.* The statement shows a large capital on paper exclusive of edifices, and also that the funds are no more than will be required to attain the important and interesting objects contemplated by the friends of Union
184 College. All which is respectfully submitted,

SILAS WRIGHT, Jr.,
WILLIAM JAMES,
Committee.

XXII.

TREASURER TO EFFECT SETTLEMENT WITH PRESIDENT.

Resolved, That the Treasurer be authorised to receive
from the President of Union College the balance in his
hands after deducting the expenses incurred, in conformity
to the original resolution of this board in relation to the 185
supervision and management of the Literature Lottery, and
to make a final settlement of the whole concern whenever
the same shall be desired by the President. Book of
Minutes B, page 197. July 27, 1831.

XXIII.

CONCLUSION OF THE REPORT OF GOV. MARCY, SILAS WRIGHT AND JOHN P. CUSHMAN.

[November 24, 1834, Minute Book C., p, 10.]

In view of all the preceding facts, it has appeared to your 186
committee—

1. That the embarrassments of Messrs. Yates & McIntyre, according to their own statements, arose from speculations entered into by them, apart from the lottery business, and wholly unconnected with Union College.

2. That such was the nature and extent of their embarrassments, that they would have been ruined, but for the timely and efficient and continued aid afforded them by the president of the college.

3. That the contracts made by them with the president, 187
were upon adequate and full consideration; and that the
frequent changes complained of by Yates & McIntyre, were
in fact made at their urgent request; and that the repeated
modifications have invariably been in their own favor.

4. That the president has furnished extensive means, performed important services, and run great personal hazards,
for the contractors on their repeated applications, and this
evidently without any sinister motive, without the design
of personal gain; but for the sole purpose of aiding the
contractors, and of securing and advancing the interests of
Union College, or some kindred institution connected there- 188
with.

In conclusion—it has appeared to your committee that Messrs. Yates & McIntyre have received the benefits of a steady and faithful performance of these contracts, and that the interests of the college, and of science, as well as the claims of justice, require that the trustees should unite with the president in the proceedings which have been commenced, or which may become necessary and proper, to obtain a full performance on the part of Yates & McIntyre.

189 That the course of the president throughout all the novel and difficult emergencies which have occurred in conducting this whole business, has been marked by fairness and liberality towards the contractors, and by firmness, sagacity, and disinterested zeal for the interests of the college and of education.

That the full powers with which he was invested by the trustees, have been exercised with wisdom and success; and from the information they have received of his views in relation to this whole subject, your committee are of opinion
190 that the interest of the college and of science requires that these plenary powers should be continued.

Your committee, therefore, recommend, that the Finance Committee be instructed to take the charge and supervision, of all suits with the contractors, in which this board is a party, now pending, or which may hereafter be instituted, or by them be judged necessary for asserting or maintaining the rights of Union College, with authority to employ such professional aid as may by them be deemed proper, and that they be authorized to draw on the treasurer for the expenses
191 which may be incurred in the premises.

Your committee further recommend, that the present treasurer of College be authorized, by and with the advice of the financial committee, to perform hereafter, in any transactions springing out of the supervision of the lotteries, all the acts that the former treasurer was authorized to perform. That by and with the advice of the financial committee, he receive from the president any bonds and mortgages, or other property, taken by him during the supervision of said lotteries, and co-operate with him as far
192 as may be, in the investment and management of any funds that have been or may be hereafter received by him in consideration of personal services rendered and hazards run; but which funds are intended for the ultimate benefit of Union College, or some kindred institution connected therewith.

All which is respectfully submitted.

W. L. MARCY,
SILAS WRIGHT, Jr.,
JOHN P. CUSHMAN,
Committee.

193 [The recommendations of the Committee, approved by the Trustees. Minutes, Book C., p. 15, &c.]

XXIV.

REPORT OF MESSRS. CUSHMAN AND DIX, 1837.

[Records, Book C, page 53.]

Whereas Yates & McIntyre, in addition to the entire amount due to Union College under their contract of July

29th, 1822, have stipulated to PAY TO ELIPHALET NOTT certain additional amounts, in consideration of subsequent services rendered, moneys advanced, and responsibilities assumed in behalf of Yates & McIntyre, either singly by himself, or jointly by himself and the college; and whereas, a portion of said additional amounts so stipulated to be
paid has already been received by the said E. Nott, and 194
by him invested, in part in lands, and in part in bonds and mortgages on land lying on the East river in New-York, immediately above Twelfth-st., or on Long Island opposite thereto, at Bushwick or Hunter's Point; and

Whereas, Dr. Nott has signified to this committee his readiness to transfer to Union College, not only its entire portion of said lands and bonds and mortgages, to hold in its own right, but also the portion belonging to himself, on the terms heretofore set forth in his reports to this
board, for the years 1831 and 1832, as soon as the same 195
shall be definitely ascertained;

Therefore, your committee recommend that this board agree to a final settlement with Dr. Nott, based on a division between him and the college, of said additional amounts so received under such several stipulations pro rata, according to the services rendered, moneys advanced, and responsibilities assumed by each in behalf of Yates and McIntyre, as the consideration on which said stipulations were entered into, and that the treasurer, by and
with the approbation of the other members of the finance 196
committee, be directed to consummate such settlement with Dr. Nott.

And that when such settlement shall have been consummated, the treasurer shall be authorised to receive from Dr. Nott the portion of said amounts found to belong to said college, in the bonds and mortgages aforesaid as by him received or to be hereafter received of Neziah Bliss and others, on his or their undivided right in said land, or in a transfer of his own undivided right or any part thereof,
the same to be estimated at the rate the other rights were 197
estimated at when said bonds and mortgages were received by him on settlement with the said Neziah Bliss and others.

And that the treasurer be also authorised to receive from Dr. Nott, in like manner, the remaining portion of said additional amounts which shall be found to belong to him, and enter the same in a separate fund to be denominated Dr. Nott's fund, and to be held and applied conformably to the aforesaid report of Dr. Nott to this board of July,
1831, and that a separate annual report be made hereafter 198
thereon to this board.

And further, that the treasurer be authorised by and

with the advice of the president, to settle with the assignees of H. Nott & Co., for any balance which may be found due from that firm, and to accept in payment thereof either stock, notes, or other personal property belonging to said estate, and held by said assignees, according as shall be deemed most for the interest of this board, and to give therefor under the seal of this board, if necessary,
199 a receipt in part or in full, as the case may be.

JOHN P. CUSHMAN,
JOHN A. DIX.

SCHENECTADY, *July* 25, 1837.

XXV.

Comparative statement of responsibilities assumed.

Responsibilities assumed by Union College in behalf of Yates & McIntyre, ...	$140,000 00
200 Responsibilities assumed by E. Nott in behalf of Yates & McIntyre,..................	338,000 00

Certificate of Treasurer.

The board of trustees having at their last meeting, (July 26, 1837,) directed the treasurer, by and with the approbation of the members of the finance committee, to effect a final settlement with the President of college, on account of the per centage received by him under the stipulations above referred to, assuming as a basis of such settlement, the services rendered, and responsibilities assum-
201 ed by him and the college respectively, in behalf of Yates & McIntyre; which respective responsibilities, exclusive of advances made on securities by the President, are believed to be correctly set forth in the above statement, the same having been compared with the President's bank books and other documents relating thereto in the possession of the undersigned.

JONAS HOLLAND,
Treas. Union College.

Approval of finance committee.

The undersigned, members of the finance committee, hereby approve of the treasurer's effecting a settlement
202 with the President, as directed by the board, on account of the per centage in question, on the terms above set forth, conformable to the resolution of 26th July, 1837.

JOHN P. CUSHMAN,
A. C. FLAGG.

XXVI.

Extracts from reports of Attorney-General Bronson.

In 1832, the Attorney General made a report to the Assembly on the subject of these lotteries. Assembly Docs. 1832, No. 292, p. 10 and 11. In this, he computes the
amount of tickets that might be sold annually at $389,800, 203
and the total in eleven years at $4,287,800. He thinks that the institutions might draw more than the average amount in any year, so as to hasten the conclusion of the lotteries, but that they could not exceed the total amount.

In 1833 the Attorney General made another report. Assembly Docs. of 1833, No. 13, vol. 1.

The result of rejecting the Owego lottery is thus stated :

"The Literature lotteries could in no event be extended beyond a period of eleven years, which would expire on
the 21st of April, 1834. During that period the institu- 204
tions might annually sell and draw tickets to the amount of $335,800 ; amounting in the eleven years to $3,693,800. When that amount of tickets has been sold and drawn, these lotteries were to cease, whether the eleven years had expired or not."

XXVII.

REPORT OF MESSRS. MARCY AND FLAGG, NOV. 15, 1838.

[Records, Book C, p. 74.]

The committee appointed for the purpose of settling by 205
compromise the suits pending between Union College and Yates & McIntyre, report,

That by the indenture entered into on the 29th July, 1822, between Union College and Yates & McIntyre (Doc. § 36) as modified by certain subsequent stipulations (Doc. § § 81, 94, 111,) the said Yates & McIntyre covenanted to pay the Treasurer of Union College for its entire right, title and interest in the literature lottery, $8\frac{3}{4}$ per cent., and to pay to the President of Union College for the supervision
and management thereof $2\frac{1}{4}$ per centum on $4,948,597 206
worth of tickets reckoned at their scheme price, which was the amount computed to have been authorised to be drawn in said Literature Lottery under the act "to limit the continuance of lotteries," passed April 5, 1822.

Subsequently however, to wit, in the year 1832, on the agitation of the lottery question by the Legislature, in consequence of the presentment of the grand jury of the city of New-York, it was adjudged by the Attorney-General, to whom the question was finally referred (see his report dated Jan. 7th, 1833, page 9), that in place of $4,948,597

207 worth of tickets, the whole amount of tickets authorised to be drawn under the act to limit the continuance of lotteries was only $3,693,800 worth, being $1,254,795 worth less than the amount which had been previously assumed.

The percentage paid on this amount of tickets by Yates & McIntyre, to wit, the $8\frac{3}{4}$ to the Treasurer, and $2\frac{1}{4}$ to the President of Union College, amounted exclusive of interest, at the time ef settlement, Aug. 1, 1828, to $138,027.45, and the interest for nine years thereon, to Aug. 1, 1837, amounted to $86,957.37, making a total of $224,984.82.

208 For the recovery of this amount, claimed to have been paid in error, Yates & McIntyre filed their bill before the Chancellor.

Your committee further report, that after the drawing of the Literature Lottery had closed, Yates & McIntyre entered into successive stipulations with Eliphalet Nott, the last of which was dated July 15, 1830, covenanting to pay him for individual services rendered, hazards run and moneys advanced in their behalf, a certain percentage on all tickets to be drawn in the consolidated lottery after the 22d day of
209 June, 1829, when it was calculated that the Fever Hospital Lottery would be closed.

Your committee further report, that under the stipulations so entered into with the President of Union College, he claimed that there remained due to him from Yates & McIntyre a larger amount even than the amount claimed to have been paid in error to Union College; for the recovery of which amount he had filed a bill before the Chancellor, in which bill the trustees of Union College had without their knowledge been joined by him as complain-
210 ants.

That to this bill Yates & McIntyre had demurred on the ground,

1. That the trustees of Union College have no interest in the issue of said bill, they having transferred all their right, title and interest in and to said lottery to Yates & McIntyre by an indenture entered into between the parties July 29, 1822.

That said stipulations in question were entered into with Eliphalet Nott personally, for services rendered, hazards
211 run and moneys advanced by him, in which Union College could therefore have no interest.

That such was the state of things when it was proposed to stop all further litigation, and bring this whole complex controversy to a close, by a mutual relinquishment between the parties concerned, of a portion of what had hitherto been deemed to be their legal rights, the same to be set forth in a triplicate agreement to be entered into between Archibald McIntyre, Henry Yates and John Ely, Junior,

surviving partners of the house of Yates and McIntyre, of the first part, the trustees of Union College, in the town of Schenectady, of the second part, and Eliphalet Nott, of the 212
third part; one of the conditions of which agreement to be, that the party of the second part thereto should relinquish their claim to the bond and mortgage of John B. Yates, for the payment of $55,000, with the interest due thereon, and also their claim to certain promissory notes of Yates and McIntyre, amounting to $19,448.47, and also their claim on the party of the first part for the payment of $20,000 with the interest paid thereon to the New-York Insurance Company; another condition of said triplicate agreement to be that the party of the first part thereto exe- 213
cute their bond for the further sum of $150,000, the same to be in full of all demands against the party of the first part by the parties of the second and the third; and another condition of said triplicate agreement to be, that all the parties thereto suspend the suits already commenced, and relinquish their right to the commencing of any other suits in the future prosecution of their respective claims in the premises.

In reference to such triplicate agreement and as a condition precedent on the part of Eliphalet Nott to his assent- 214
ing thereto, it was agreed that the bond given by the party of the first part to the party of the second part, should be given and held on condition that the said amount should be considered as received on the suit pending at the time between Union College and Eliphalet Nott, President, and John B. Yates, Archibald McIntyre, Henry Yates, James McIntyre and John Ely, Junior, before the Chancellor, as per bill filed by said college and said Eliphalet Nott 26th May, 1834; and that the portion of the avails thereof which on a settlement to be made between the said Eliphalet Nott 215
and Union College according to a resolution passed July 28, 1837, approving of the report of the finance committee, shall be credited to the said Eliphalet Nott in the fund specified in said report; after which the said triplicate agreement was executed, and the whole controversy amicably disposed of.

W. L. MARCY,
A. C. FLAGG,
Committee.

Dated Nov. 15, 1838. ELIPHALET NOTT.

XXVIII.

SETTLEMENT WITH YATES, M'INTYRE, ELY AND M'INTYRE, FOR LOTTERIES, WITH COPY OF BOND. 216

Henry Yates, Archibald McIntyre and others, the trustees of Union College, acting through a committee appointed for that purpose, and Eliphalet Nott, agree,

That Yates, McIntyre and others pay to the trustees of Union College one hundred and fifty thousand dollars, for which they are to give a bond.

That the trustees of Union College assign to Yates, Mc-
Intyre, &c., the bond and mortgage of John B. Yates, for
$55,000, surrender certain unpaid notes amounting to $19,-
217 448.47, and pay a certain debt of the college of physicians
and surgeons, amounting to $20,000, for which notes had
been given to the New-York Insurance company, upon the
payment of the bond for $150,000.

The parties release each other from all suits, controversies, actions and claims of actions.

Signed and sealed by

HENRY YATES,
ARCH. McINTYRE,
JOHN ELY, Jr.,
218 A. McINTYRE, Jr.

ELIPHALET NOTT.

W. L. MARCY, *Gov.*,
A. C. FLAGG, *Comp*.,
JOHN A. DIX, *Sec. of State*,
Committee of Union College, and under College seal.

XXIX.

Know all men by these presents, that we, Henry Yates,
of the city of New-York, Archibald McIntyre, of the city
219 of Albany, John Ely, jr., of the city and county of Philadelphia, and Archibald McIntyre, of the county of Mont-
gomery, and State of New-York, are held and firmly bound
unto the trustrees of Union College, in the town of Schenectady, in the State of New-York, in the sum of three hundred thousand dollars, lawful money of the United States
of America, to be paid to said trustees of Union College or
their certain attorney, successors or assigns, the which
payment, well and truly to be made, we bind ourselves,
our heirs, executors and administrators firmly by these
220 presents, sealed with our seals, and dated the 27th July,
1837. The condition of this obligation is such that if the
above bounden Henry Yates, Archibald McIntyre, John
Ely, jr., and Archibald McIntyre, jr., their heirs, executors, administrators, or any of them shall and do well and
truly pay, or cause to be paid unto the above mentioned
trustees of Union College, or to their certain attorney, exe
cutor, administrators or assigns, the just and full sum of
one hundred and fifty thousand dollars, as follows: Ten
thousand dollars, part thereof, on the first day of Septem-
221 ber next, and the remainder of said sum being one hundred and forty thousand dollars, in ten equal annual payments, with lawful interest from the first day of August

next on such sums as may be unpaid yearly, with a right to pay any part thereof before due, and to have interest allowed for the same, without any fraud or any delay, then this obligation to be void, or else to remain in full force and virtue.

Signed, HENRY YATES, [L. S.] 222
A. McINTYRE, [L. S.]
JOHN ELY, Jr., [L. S.]
A. McINTYRE, Jr., [L. S.]

Sealed and delivered in the presence of J. V. N. Yates.
Arch. Campbell.

XXX.

Resolution of 1845.

Resolved, That the treasurer be authorised to affix the 223
college seal to a conveyance, and execute a conveyance to the President of such pieces or parcels of land heretofore conveyed by him or by Neziah Bliss, Esq., to this institution, as shall be necessary (when reckoned at the prices stated in the annual report) to cancel any cash balance that may be found by the finance committee to be due to the said President on a final settlement with him; and that the items forming the basis of such settlement, having been attested, be entered on the minutes of this board. Minutes,
book C, page 192, July 22, 1845. 224

XXXI.

Extract from report of President Nott to the Trustees, July 1831.

(See Minutes, p. 213.)

That although contingencies might yet arise, that would prove ruinous alike to the contractors, the college and himself, still that they were apparently so far out of dan-
ger as to justify him, perhaps, in communicating to them 225
what he had previously more fully communicated to their committee of finance, to wit:

That he had been obliged, in order to prevent the failure of Yates & McIntyre, and to enable them to go on with the lotteries, to render in their behalf, personal services, to assume personal responsibilities, and to raise moneys for their use, at different times, and to very large amounts, for which he was entitled by stipulation, to receive a portion of the profits of the lotteries, should any arise; as
there was now reason to hope would be the case, and per- 226
haps to a large amount; which amount, be the same more or less, it was, and ever had been (after providing for the

services rendered and hazard run), his intention to appropriate to the use of Union College, or some kindred institution, connected therewith.

That, with a view to this, he had procured the passage of a law for founding, in connexion with the college, an Institute of Science, the material provisions of which are as follows:

(See § 4, 5, 6, 7, of act of April 3, 1831, Chap., 273, p. 342.)

XXXII.

227 *Extract from the report of the President of Union College, in relation to the lotteries for the year* 1832.

It has been usual for the subscriber, while acting under a resolution of the board, investing him with the entire supervision of the literature lottery, to report, from time to time, the progress made therein, and the prospect of ultimate gain or loss therefrom. Although the original contract with Yates & McIntyre required from them adequate security, this not being furnished, they were allowed,
228 by the subscriber, to assume for the time being, the management of said lottery on their own responsibility.

For a time they were prosperous, and their prospect of ultimate success was great.

Early in 1826, however, they became exceedingly embarassed. From a statement made by them, at the time, it was apparent, that a loan, to a very large amount, was requisite to save them from ruin.

One hundred thousand dollars was, therefore, raised for their use, by the president and treasurer of Union College,
229 as heretofore reported to the board.

The consideration allowed for the procurement of this loan, after providing for the expense and hazard incurred thereby, was, and is intended to be, in some way, applied to the use of Union College.

Soon after the procurement of this loan, and while the affairs of the contractors were in the most unpromising state, an act passed the legislature, authorising the mixing of the land prizes in the Albany land lottery, with the money prizes in the Literature and Fever Hospital lotte-
230 ries, provided the consent of the institutions interested therein could be obtained.

This act of the Legislature, in the opinon of Yates & McIntyre, afforded an opportunity for making a contract which, though attended with the hazard of great loss, held out as the alternative, the prospect of corresponding gain.

To enable them, however, to execute the contemplated contract, the consent of the subscriber, in behalf of the college, was necessary, as the mixing of the land and money prizes, as proposed, would greatly increase and perpetuate the hazards to which the institution must be exposed, and his consent and co-operation in his own behalf, was also necessary, as the heavy responsibilities already assumed by him, in behalf of the contractors, must not only be continued, in case such contract was to be executed, but still greater responsibilities must also be assumed, in order to sustain their credit during the execution of the same.

To induce the consent and co-operation of the subscriber, a specific share of the profits, whatever the same might be, was proffered to him by the contractors.

Though fully aware that they were deeply involved, and that very large additional amounts must be furnished for their use, in order to sustain their credit during the prosecution of the contemplated undertaking, the subscriber, in the hope of ultimately benefiting the college thereby, made up his mind to put everything at hazard, by consenting to share with them the responsibilities, and the losses or profits of the enterprise, in conformity to the stipulations then made and provided.

This he did, however, with the intention, expressed at the time, and often since repeated, of appropriating, after providing for the expense and hazard by him incurred, his share of the profits, should any accrue, to the use of Union College, or some kindred institution connected therewith; an intention never relinquished, and which he still purposes to execute, reserving to himself the right of determining the objects to which said profits shall be applied, and the time and manner of their application. In conformity to which intention, certain expenses have already been incurred by the subscriber, as others may hereafter be, in the enlargement and improvement of the college site, or the buildings thereon erected, or in furtherance of those arts and sciences which it is the object of the institution to promote.

Had it not been for the passage of the act under which the contract, just alluded to was made, the amount of tickets belonging to the Literature and fever Hospital Lotteries, having been disposed of, said lotteries would, before this time, have been completed.

How long the Consolidated Lottery, in which the aforesaid lotteries were merged, will be allowed to continue, or what will be the result of its continuance, as the contractors have ceased to report to the subscriber, is, of course, unknown. Had the same closed on the first of May last, it is believed that the entire amount to which Union College would have been entitled, would not differ materially from the entire amount of principal and interest on the original grants made to said college, and to other institutions whose rights have been severally purchased out by that institution.

This, considering the great and long continued exertions
236 which have been made, and the mighty hazards which have been run, is indeed less than might have been hoped for; and it is less, perhaps, than will, ultimately, be received. Should the present lottery be continued during the time suggested by the Attorney-general, in his report, losses may yet occur that will be ruinous alike to the subscriber and the college, or gains may be realized alike advantageous to both.

For whatever profits shall arise from tickets sold in the Consolidated Lottery, over and above the original amount
237 of tickets in the Literature and Fever Hospital Lotteries, reckoned at their scheme price, the subscriber will be entitled, by contract, to share the same with Yates & McIntyre; and whatever the amount, so shared by him may be, it is still, as it ever has been, his design to appropriate the same in manner aforesaid; a design thus formally expressed, that the trustees may be induced to take measures for obtaining any contingent residuary benefits that may accrue to them conformably to provisions that will be found in the will of the subscriber, should his own life not be spared till said
238 lottery is closed, and a settlement effected between him and the contractors, agreeably to stipulations formally entered into by them, and which will be found on file among his papers.

All which is respectfully submitted.

ELIPHALET NOTT.

XXXIII.

President's Report for 1833.

The Annual Report of the President of Union College to
239 *the Board of Trustees.*

Gentlemen: No material alteration has taken place in the concerns of the Consolidated Lottery, since the last report, except that the time of its continuance has, by consent, been limited to the year 1833.

In relation to the president's fund, held in trust for the institutions interested therein, and which arose out of the Literature Lottery, afterwards merged in the Consolidated Lottery, it is only necessary to observe that one portion thereof has already been paid into the treasury of this
240 board, another portion deposited in the Mohawk Bank, and the residue invested in bonds and mortgages.

As to the additional lottery avails, arising out of the act, authorising the mixing of Albany land prizes with the mo-

ney prizes of the other lotteries, passed 1826, little need be
said, as the rights and claims of the respective parties interested therein, remain the same as stated at length in
the last report; no further payments having been since
made to the subscriber by the managers, under a special
contract entered into with him, by virtue of the act aforesaid, for personal services rendered, hazards run, and monies advanced.

Of the several amounts previously received by the sub- 241
scriber under said personal contract, and held by him in
his individual right, though appropriated to public purposes, in the manner heretofore stated, the principal part
has, with the approbation of the financial committee, been
invested in real estate, situate for the most part in the city
of New-York, and on Long Island or elsewhere, or in bonds
and mortgages, or stocks of some sort, and the residue appropriated to repairs and experiments.

The old college purchased and repaired by the president,
remains still in his possession; but he has not thought 242
proper to proceed to the founding an institute on the
amended charter of the old academy, to be connected with
the college, as was contemplated; because it yet remained
uncertain whether the amount to be received by him, from
the source aforesaid, will be equal to his former expectations.

The subscriber is aware that the best devised human
plans may be frustrated, and that uncertainty attends all
things future. He is aware that contingencies may occur,
that will not only refute the calculations of profits he has 243
made, but also involve him, the college and the managers,
in one common ruin. Still, appearances are more favorable than on any former occasion; and even though the
residue of the percentage, stipulated to be paid the subscriber for personal services, hazards and advances, should
not be fully received; still there is reason to hope that
something handsome will eventually be realized by the
college, from the investment aforesaid already made, and
besides, even though there should be some deficiency in
the final payment of the percentage stipulated, still the 244
subscriber may, if prospered in some other way, make up
therefor, and this, if in his power, it would afford him
pleasure to do; nor will anything but necessity reconcile
him to the ultimate disappointment of expectations, which,
though not founded in any legal claim, he has contributed
to raise.

All which is respectfully submitted.

ELIPHALET NOTT.

Union College, July, 1833.

XXXIV.

CHANCELLOR WALWORTH'S CERTIFICATE.

245 "I was consulted some years since by Dr. Nott, the President of Union College, as to the manner of conveying or devising certain property, to a very large amount, which he desired to give to the college, in trust, to establish certain professorships, or otherwise, to promote the cause of education in that institution, which property had risen from a certain percentage, which Yates & McIntyre had agreed to give him on the proceeds of certain lotteries, as compensation for his services and risks in raising moneys to save them from bankruptcy. I came to the conclusion
246 that he could not convey or devise the property to the institution legally, upon the proposed trusts, which were not such as the Revised Statutes authorised. And as he expressed the apprehension that he might possibly die before he could get a law passed authorising the proposed trusts, I therefore advised him to convey the property absolutely, taking such a writing from the treasurer or other proper officers of the corporation that he was entitled to control or direct the application of the property at any time during his life, and that he could, in that case, after
247 he had obtained the passage of the proposed law, take a reconveyance of the property, and convey or devise it to the corporation upon the contemplated trust. I also know Judge Paige was also consulted on the subject, and that he concurred with me in my opinion.

REUBEN H. WALWORTH."

SARATOGA SPRINGS, *Nov.* 21, 1851.

Judge Paige's certificate

248 "I do hereby certify, that after the President of Union College procured the passage of the act of May 14, 1840, authorising literary incorporated institutions to receive grants of real and personal property to be held in trust to found and maintain professorships and scholarships, and for other purposes, he applied to me to prepare, under the advice of Chancellor Walworth, a conveyance from him to the trustees of Union College of certain real and personal estate to be held by the latter upon the trusts authorised by said act. And I do further certify, that I accordingly
249 prepared such a deed of trust and submitted the same to Chancellor Walworth for revision and correction, and that the Chancellor revised and corrected the same; and that such deed of trust, after it was so revised and corrected, was delivered by me to Dr. E. Nott.

"*Nov.* 19, 1851. A. C. PAIGE."

A. Holland's certificate.

"I hereby certify, that President Nott, after having procured the passage of the act of May 14, 1840, authorising literary institutions to hold real and personal estate in trust, did employ Judge Paige to make out under the ad- 250
visement of Chancellor Walworth, a trust deed to Union College of certain real and personal estate to a large amount, in accordance with the annual reports to the trustees, made by him in the years 1831, 1832 and 1833; and that such deed was duly executed, acknowledged and placed in possession of the treasurer of said college, with written instructions to deliver the same to the board of trustees on the event of his death; and that such trust deed has been, and continued and still remains deposited
in the office and in the keeping of the treasurer of said 251
College. ALEX. HOLLAND,

Treasurer of Union College."

November 11, 1851.

[The acts referred to by Judge Paige, are the following: Chap. 318, passed May 14, 1840, "An act concerning certain trusts," p. 267. This act authorises real and personal property to be conveyed to any incoporated college, to be held in trust, to establish an observatory; to found professorships and scholarships; to provide a place for the 252
burial of the dead; and for any other specific purpose comprehended in the general object authorised by their respective charters.

Chap. 261, passed May 26, 1841, p. 245, in addition to the above act. It authorised, devises and bequests of real and personal property, to be made in trust for any of the purposes, specified in the above act of 1840.]

XXXV.

STATEMENT APPENDED TO THE REPORT OF THE TREASURER OF 253
UNION COLLEGE, MADE TO THE TRUSTEES, APRIL 27, 1853.

Statement No. 1, of the original cost of the Old College building and site, and of its subsequent sale and repurchase.

To cost of original site,	$10,544	28
To cost of building,	50,101	18
To cost of incidental expenses on its purchase by the county,	1,388	93
To cost of repurchase of E. Nott,	11,500	00
	$73,534	39

254

	By receipts for parts of original lots,................		$14,400 00	
	By receipts from the lands taken from the county on its sale to them, principal,.........:	$40,722 06		
	Interest,........	37,795 63		
	Rents	249 10		
			78,766 79	
255	By receipts for materials sold,.		2,061 41	
	By building now on hand at original cost,.		50,000 00	
	Amount to balance, being the profits on the West College,			71,693 81
			$145,228 20	$145,228 20

Statement No. 2, of the original cost of the New College buildings and site, and of the sales of portions of the site.

256	To cost of the lots purchased for the site of the New College buildings,.............................		$38,961 97
	By amounts realized on lot sold,	$38,031 16	
	By amount estimated as to the value of lots yet to be sold,	25,677 45	
	By amount estimated as the value of the site remaining for college use 223 acres, $100 per acre,...........	22,300 00	
257		$85,998 61	$38,961 97
	By amount to balance, being the profits on the New College sites,................		$47,036 64
		$85,998 61	$85,998 61

	Profits on transactions connected with the West or Old College,...................	$71,693 81
258	Do. on do. connected with the East or New College,...........................	47,036 64
		$118,730 45

XXXVI.

RESOLUTION DIRECTING THE AUDITING COMMITTEE TO EXAMINE REPORT.

[Records, Book C, page 482.]

Resolved, That the auditing committee examine, on rigid principles of law and equity, the profit and loss account 259
now submitted, of the president's agency in the financial affairs of the college, since his first connection with it as president, in 1804, and that they report the same to this board at its annual meeting, with any alterations that they have to suggest.

REPORT OF THE AUDITING COMMITTEE ON PROFIT AND LOSS ACCOUNT, JULY 27, 1853.

[Records, Book D, page —.]

The subscribers, the auditing committee, under the resolution of April 27, 1853, as follows:

(Here follows the above resolution.)

Find that to comply with its spirit and details will require more of their time than it is possible for them at present to bestow. But they report that it appears from 260
the profit and loss account submitted by the treasurer, of President Nott's agency in the management of the fiscal concerns of Union College, while acting under the plenary powers conferred on him by the board, that irrespective of funds gratuitously placed with the treasurer of Union College, referred to in the report of Silas Wright and William James, and irrespective of other large amounts placed with the treasurer without consideration, and irrespective of $30,000 which inured to the benefit of the college from the purchase by the agency, and with means furnished by the 261
president, of the rights of the other institutions in the Literature Lottery, there has inured to the benefit of the college, from the sale, purchase, and resale of the college by the president of the West College, and from the purchase and sale of lots in connection with the sites of the several college edifices, including lots yet on hand, for sale, $118,-730.45.

The college has lost, on loans and investments made by or with the advice of the president, (as chairman of the finance committee,) during the same period, as follows: 26

Edward James' bond and mortgage,........	$14,000 00
William Anderson's bond and mortgage,...	5,000 00
Philo Stevens' bond, ...	1,295 77
Joshua Monroe's bond and mortgage, ...	2,305 10

Rens. and Saratoga Ins. Co. stock, ...	930 00
B. Nott's bond, ...	700 00
	$24,230 87

263 To which may perhaps be added a small contingent loss on the amounts held by the college in the following stocks, viz:

In the Schen'y and Saratoga Plank Road,...	$2,459 17
the Schenectady Steam Mills,...........	2,509 66
the Schenectady Locomotive Manufactory,.	2,490 83
the Schenectady Marble and Cement Co...	655 75
	$8,115 41

264 But even though this should be the case, the college would, as appears from the statement of the treasurer, be more than compensated for such loss, by the increased value which has been given to lots belonging to the institution, by thus opening a plank road through property belonging to the college, and the establishment of an important manufactory on lots adjoining said road.

Submitted July 27, 1853.

JAMES BROWN,
265 R. M. BLATCHFORD,
J. L. LANE,
Auditing Committee.

XXXVII.

DOCUMENTS RELATING TO THE STOCK IN THE COMMERCIAL BANK OF ALBANY.

Extract from assignment of H. Nott & Co., Dec. 20, 1836.

In the second place, to pay the Delaware and Hudson
266 Canal Company the sum of six thousand one hundred and twenty-nine dollars, the same being a debt due said company and originally secured by certain stock of the Commercial Bank of Albany, and which stock was surrendered under an arrangement for the immediate payment of said debt. (This debt may stand in the name of J. H. Williams, who is the treasurer of said canal company.)

And whereas, E. Nott, President of Union College, has from time to time placed in the hands of H. Nott & Co. certain funds, part whereof was the property of Union Col-
267 lege, and part his own property; and whereas from the mode in which the transactions took place there may be difficulty in tracing the specific funds of said college into our hands, the same having generally passed through the said

Eliphalet Nott, and for which he is answerable to said institution; and whereas we have this day accepted E. Nott's order upon us to pay the trustees of Union College the amounts which we owe on both accounts to the extent of his and our indebtedness to said college as the same shall be found on the adjustment of the accounts relative to said
funds, in trust, seventhly, to pay the trustees of Union Col- 268
lege so much of the existing indebtedness of H. Nott & Co., whether the said indebtedness be to the said Eliphalet Nott individually or to Union College, as will pay the amount for which the said H. Nott & Co., or Eliphalet Nott are found indebted to said college for funds received from said college on an adjustment of the accounts relative to said funds.

Statement of Edward James, Esq.

Messrs. Stratton and Seymour			269
To assignees of H. Nott & Co.			
For amount of Novelty Works inventory,..................	$61,419 30		
For amount of bricks to be delivered,....................	6,000 00		
		$67,419 30	
For amount of Water-st. inventory,......................	38,617 47		
Less goods sold,..............	135 18		
		38,482 29	270
		$105,901 59	
Discount 20 per cent.,...............		21,180 32	
		$84,721 27	
To receive from Water-street debts,........		21,000 00	
To receive 105 tons castings at 44 pr. lb.,..		8,400 00	
		$114,121 27	
			271
CR.			
By amount paid Union College,.	$78,214 27		
By amount paid Jonas Holland,.	20,913 86		
By amount paid Alonzo Potter,.	5,964 20		
By amount paid John Nott, ...	2,178 10		
By amount paid Edward James,.	6,723 24		
		$113,993 67	

Treasurer's receipt to assignees of H. Nott & Co. 272

Received 1st of September, 1837, of James Brown, James Hall and John Delafield, assignees of H. Nott & Co., the

sum of seventy-eight thousand two hundred and fourteen dollars and twenty-seven cents, on account of the indebtedness of said firm, or of Eliphalet Nott (for moneys advanced by the trustees of Union College to the said Howard Nott & Co., or to the said Eliphalet Nott, and by him passed into their hands, and for the payment of which in either case, to the extent of his or their indebtedness, provision is made in said assignment) the same being in full of all de-
273 mands of every sort under said assignment, the said Eliphalet Nott having himself satisfactorily provided for the payment of the further sum of about fifty-six thousand three hundred and ninety-eight dollars seventy-eight cents, including interest; also advanced by Union College to Howard Nott & Co., through the said Eliphalet Nott, on the 10th day of June, 1835, and for which he stands charged in the books of said college, which receipt in full is given by virtue of a resolution of the board of trustees of Union College, at a meeting held in the college hall 26th of July,
274 1837, a copy of which is hereunto annexed.

In witness whereof I have hereunto affixed the [L. S.] corporate seal of the trustees of Union College the day and year first above written.

JONAS HOLLAND, *Treasurer.*

XXXVIII.

INTERROGATORIES TO HON. JOHN A. DIX AND HON A. C. FLAGG, AND THEIR ANSWERS.

275 In the matter of the enquiry into certain pecuniary affairs of Union College: Interrogatories to be put to Gen. John A. Dix, and to the Hon. A. C. Flagg, respectively, in behalf of Eliphalet Nott, President of the said college.

1. Was you an ex-officio trustee of Union College, and during what years?

2. Did you ordinarily attend the meetings of the trustees and become acquainted with the financial condition of the college? and did you serve on any committees of the trustees charged with the duty of enquiring into and
276 reporting upon the financial affairs of the college, or any of them?

3 Have you any knowledge from your acquaintance with the affairs of the college, or from your communication with the trustees, whether the allowance made by law for the supervision and management of the literature lotteries, drawn for the benefit of Union College and other institutions, was claimed by the trustees of that college as belonging of right to it? or if any expectation of receiving the amount of such allowance was indulged,

how, when, and from whom was it to be received, and 277
upon what was such expectation founded?

4. After the original contract made with Yates & McIntyre, on the 29th of July, 1822, were there other and subsequent stipulations between them and the president of Union College, on or about the 4th of January, and the 24th of January, 1826?

5. What were the inducements and consideration of the
said stipulations, and what disposition was to be made of
the profits arising therefrom, over and above the sum originally agreed to be paid by Yates & McIntyre, for the pur- 278
chase of the lotteries? If such profits were to be divided among any parties, who were the parties, and on what
principles, and in what proportions was such division to
be made?

6. Have you any knowledge of the subsequent stipulations made between Yates & McIntyre, and the president
of Union College, on the 30th May, 1826, and July 15,
1830, in relation to the Albany land lottery, and the Fever Hospital lottery? Had Union College any interest in
those stipulations, or did the trustees, to your knowledge, 279
ever claim any interest in them?

7. Were you as members of a committee of Union College, parties to a settlement with Yates, McIntyre, Ely
and McIntyre, made on or about the 27th day of July,
1837, in which among other things, Yates, McIntyre & Co.,
agreed to execute a bond to Union College for the payment of $150,000, and the college agreed to assign a bond
and mortgage of John B. Yates, for $55,000, to the said
Yates, McIntyre & Co., and to surrender certain notes and
to pay a certain debt to the College of Physicians and Sur- 280
geons? if so, please to state what and whose claims were
embraced in the said settlement, and particularly, what
was the consideration for the said bond of $150,000, and
for whose benefit it was given? and in reference to the securities assigned and surrendered by the college, and the
debt assumed by it to the College of Physicians and Surgeons, what was the consideration and inducement for
such assignment, surrender and assumption? Did such
assignment, surrender and assumption, form any part of
the consideration of the said bond of $150,000? please to 281
state fully the circumstances, causes and objects, of the
said settlement, as you then understood them?

8. Were you, as such trustee, acquainted with the fact that moneys and securities had been and were deposited with the treasurer of Union College, by Dr. Nott on account, and subject to future settlement?

9. Is there any other matter or thing within your knowledge, concerning the interest and care taken by Dr. Nott,

as president, and as a member of the finance committee of
282 the college, in the management, improvement, and promotion of its funds? if any, please to state the same.

10. Were you or either of you knowing to the purchase by the college, in 1838, of the one-half of the Stuyvesant cove property, and of the Hunter farm? Did you, or either of you form any opinion of the value of those tracts at the time, from personal observation or enquiry? and if so, what was that opinion? how were the purchases of the said tracts regarded by the trustees at that time, in respect to their value as investments?

283 11. Were you consulted about, and acquainted with the loans and investments made by the Treasurer of Union College, under the general supervision of the finance committee of the trustees, while you was a member of that committee? And if so, were the acts and proceedings of the President, as chairman of that committee, approved by you and the other members of the committee?

12. On the resignation of Henry Yates as Treasurer of Union College, did you, as a member of a committee charged with that duty, make a very thorough examination of the
284 fiscal affairs of the college? What other member of the committee, if any, co-operated with you? What was the general result of that examination, in respect to the management of the pecuniary affairs of the college, and particularly so far as the same had been conducted by the President?

13. Are you acquainted with the fact that similar examinations were made by other committees and at other times, and particularly by committees of which William James, William L. Marcy, Silas Wright and John P. Cushman, or
285 either of them, were members? What were the results of such examinations, in the respects mentioned in the last interrogatory?

J. C. SPENCER,
for E. Nott.

Answers by John A. Dix, to interrogatories propounded to him in the matter of the enquiry into certain pecuniary affairs of Union College.

286 1. I was, as Secretary of State, a Trustee of Union College from Feb., 1833, to Feb., 1839.

2. I think I attended the annual meetings of the Trustees, as I will state more particularly, in 1833, 1834, 1835, and 1837. I was a member of the Committee of Finance for several years, commencing with 1833, and for nearly a week, from the 14th to the 21st Aug. of that year, I was at Schenectady, in company with Gov. Wright, then U. S. Senator, and also a member of the committee, constantly

engaged in the examination of the financial affairs of the college. I remember our examination was very thorough 287
and minute, extending to the calculation of interest on all the securities belonging to the institution. I was at Schenectady on the 24th and 25th days of July, 1833, on the 25th of July, 1834, on the 21st and 22d July, 1835, and on the 25th and 26th days of July, 1837. I presume the annual meetings of the Trustees were held on these days, though I cannot speak with absolute certainty. At the corresponding periods of the year, in 1836 and 1838, I was at Sachem's Head in Connecticut. In fixing these dates, I have consulted a series of memorandum books, which I 288
have been in the habit of keeping, and by which I can ascertain where I was on any day during the last twenty-five years.

3. After the lapse of more than fourteen years, since my connection with the college was dissolved, I can only speak in general terms of its financial affairs. My recollection is, that the allowance made by law for the supervision and management of the lotteries, was never claimed as matter of right by the Trustees of Union College. My understanding was, that the college was entitled under the law 289
to about $275,000, and that the only expectation it had of receiving more, was from the voluntary assurances of Dr. Nott, who had assumed very heavy personal responsibilities and incurred great pecuniary risks, for which he was to receive from Yates & McIntyre a portion of the profits to be derived from the lotteries. Dr. Nott always avowed the intention of appropriating the amount of these gains, and the allowance for management to the college, or some literary institution connected with it, but the trustees never, as I remember, claimed either these gains, or the allowance 290
for management as of right, or assumed to control him in the disposition of them; and his intended appropriation of them to the uses referred to, was always regarded as voluntary.

4. These transactions were before my connexion with the college. I have no knowledge of them otherwise, than as they became complicated with posterior transactions. I remember there were contracts between Dr. Nott, and Yates and McIntyre, subsequent to the original one. It was from these contracts, involving heavy pecuniary re- 291
sponsibilities and risks on the part of Dr. Nott, that the gains referred to were to accrue. During my connection with the college, I think payments were made to the trustees by Dr. Nott from these gains or the allowance for management, which were treated by them as donations, and not as funds belonging of right to the college.

5. I cannot give to that question a more definite answer than I have given to No. 3.

6. I have no distinct remembrance of these transac-
292 tions. My ideas all resolve themselves into a general recollection that the college was entitled by law to about
$275,000 ; that it could not, under the law, receive a larger
sum; that the profits to accrue from the management of
the lotteries and from the special agreements with Dr.
Nott, after the college had been paid the above named
amount, to advance money for the purpose of saving the
managers from the ankruptcy with which they were
threatened at very critical periods, belonged to him ; that
the college could only receive those profits as a donation,
293 but could not claim them as of right. The trustees, therefore, did not undertake to interfere with the disposition of
these profits, but left it to him to determine the time and
mode of applying them to the benefit of the college or some
institution connected with it, in pursuance of the intention
uniformly expressed by him.

7. I believe I was, as a member of a committee, a party
to the settlement between Dr. Nott and the college with
Yates and McIntyre and their representatives, probably in
the year 1837. I urged this settlement very strongly upon
294 Dr. Nott because I thought it would be better for him to
take a much smaller sum than he considered himself justly
entitled to, rather than to be engaged, at his advanced age,
in vexatious and complicated lawsuits, which might out-
live him. The amount agreed to be paid to Dr. Nott by
Yates and McIntyre was $150,000, and my recollection is
that this amount was to be paid, on a suit brought by him
under one of the special agreements entered into after the
college had received the amount it was entitled to by law.
I remember Dr. Nott thought they ought to pay him double
295 that amount. I recollect that a bond of John B. Yates for
about $55,000, on which, I believe, the interest had not
been paid for several years, was to be surrendered, and
that a debt of some eighteen or twenty thousand dollars to
the College of Physicians and Surgeons, was to be assumed
by the college. The surrender in the one case, and the
assumption in the other, were in consequence of an alleged overpayment by Yates and McIntyre, which the college
admitted. I do not remember the exact terms of the settlement. I give the principal agreements. I know Dr.
296 Nott assented to them with great reluctance, and that in
doing so he surrendered his own judgment to the earnest
wish expressed by Mr. Flagg, Gov. Marcy, Mr. Wright
and myself, to put an end to what we believed would prove
an unpleasant and protracted litigation.

8. I do not remember.

9. I do not recollect anything in particular. I was always strongly impressed with the zeal and devotion of Dr.
Nott to the interests of the college. I was associated with
him as a member of the finance committee, as I think. In 297
the pecuniary transactions with which he was connected,
I remember nothing which impaired my confidence in his
integrity and fair dealing with the college. On the contrary, I considered him as deserving the highest praise in
the purpose avowed by him of devoting to the institution
a large sum of money, which he might, without any impropriety, have appropriated to his own use and that of
his family.

10. I remember going with Dr. Nott to the Stuyvesant
Cove property in the neighborhood of Novelty works, and 298
that he pointed out to me a purchase he had made on
the opposite side of the East river near Green's Point,
known as the Hunter farm. I do not remember the value
attached to them by the trustees. I think I was there at
a period of great pecuniary embarrassment and depression,
probably in 1838, and I remember distinctly that I considered the property very valuable, and certain, if retained, to enrich the proprietors.

11. I cannot say how far, as a member of the finance
committee, I was consulted in advance as to the loans and 299
investments made by the treasurer. I think I was usually
acquainted with them soon after they were made, and that
they were approved by the trustees. I remember this
whole subject was brought before them at a meeting in the
Governor's room at the Capitol in Albany, (should say in
1837 or 1838) in consequence of some enquiries which had
been made, and that it was thoroughly and satisfactorily
explained by Gov. Wright, who was then a member of the
U. S. Senate.

12. I do not remember the year in which Mr. Henry 300
Yates resigned as treasurer of the college, and therefore,
cannot say positively, whether a thorough examination of
its affairs, at that time, was made by me as a member of
the finance committee. My impression is, however, that
the examination of August, 1833, by Gov. Wright and
myself, which was very minute, was consequent on Mr.
Yates's resignation, though I do not venture to speak with
absolute certainty.

13. I know there were repeated examinations by the finance committee. I have just referred to one by Gov. 301
Wright and myself, in August, 1833, and I remember
there was a laborious one by Mr. Cushman, of Troy. All
these examinations, as well as I can recollect, were satisfactory to the trustees, and I remember nothing growing

out of any one of them, which impaired their confidence in the integrity, zeal, or good faith of Dr. Nott.

Cross-examination of Gen. Dix by Mr. Vanderheyden.

In reference to the second interrogatory, he says: The
302 committee minutely examined the securities of the college, cast interest on them, and ·scertained the amount of the funds of the college; they had the college books and the treasurer before them; can not say that they looked at any thing but the books.

They examined into the avails of the lottery, that was a particular subject of enquiry. Can not state in detail the mode of proceeding; as to the seventh interrogatory, he says there were a number of suits; there was a suit by Yates & McIntyre, against the college for overpayments;
303 and Dr. Nott sued Yates & McIntyre on their stipulations; thinks there was another.

He does not think he was particularly engaged in the examination of the matters embraced in the settlement of 1837; but he had a general knowledge of them; has no knowledge of any argument by Mr. Butler respecting Dr. Nott's right to recover; never had any such argument before him.

He does not recollect whether the trustees or the finance committee authorised Dr. Nott to buy the Stuyvesant Cove
304 property or the Hunter farm.

It is not my recollection that the trustees gave Dr. Nott general powers to manage the affairs of the college, or permitted him to do so. The finance committee were very particular; the financial affairs of the college were managed by them. The committee always met once a year, and sometimes oftener, but can not say how frequently. He does not recollect that Dr. Nott exercised any powers as chairman of the finance committee, without their instructions or authority. Whatever was done by him, was re-
305 ferred to the committee, and sanctioned by them.

In answer to questions by the counsel for Dr. Nott, he says he has no recollection of any indebtedness by the college to Dr. Nott, or of any special deposit by him while he was a trustee.

He has no knowledge of any funds belonging to the colledge having been appropriated to his own use by Dr. Nott, and he never saw any thing in the conduct of Dr. Nott but what was strictly honest and upright.

NOTES *of the testimony of* HON. A. C. FLAGG, *given before the committee in answer to the same interrogatories above,*
306 *October* 13, 1853.

To the 1st, he says: He was appointed Secretary of State

in 1826; in 1833 was appointed Comptroller, and as such,
was a trustee. He retired from office in 1839, and was re-
appointed Comptroller in 1842, and continued in that office
until 1847. While holding these offices, he was *ex officio*
a trustee of Union College; he was a trustee 19 "com-
mencements" of the college.

To the 2d, he says: That he believes he always attended 307
the meetigns of the trustees while he was thus in office at
Albany, but may have been absent a few times. He was
on committees as afterwards mentioned.

To the 3d, he says: From 1826, for a number of years,
he did not get any particular information of the affairs of
the college; he was not on the finance committee until
after 1833. As a trustee, I derived the information that
a certain percentage, which I supposed was given by law
to the college, was, by the trustees, agreed to be given to
Dr. Nott for the management of the lotteries. About the 308
time that Yates and McIntyre got through paying up the
sum they were to pay, $276,090.14, it then came to my
knowledge, as a trustee, that there was a large amount
that had accumulated in Dr. Nott's hands from the President's fund. It was conceded by all except Henry Yates,
that this sum was Dr. Nott's, he saying all the time that
he intended to give it to the college or some kindred institution. This fund the trustees did not pretend to control; it was left to the Doctor's control, and considered as
belonging to him.

Answering the 4th interrogatory he says: This fund 309
was the amount allowed for management; besides this,
there were agreements or stipulations by Yates and McIntyre, to pay him large sums for the risks, hazards and responsibilities he had incurred. The percentage derived
from these stipulations and agreements, were conceded by
the trustees to belong to Dr. Nott.

The trustees did not claim any percentage on any agreements or stipulations beyond the $276,090.14, except that
the treasurer had pledged the credit of the college in aid
of Yates and McIntyre, and the college was entitled to a 310
portion of the percentage in proportion to the liabilities
assumed by the college and Dr. Nott respectively. He is
speaking of percentage that arose long prior to the giving
of the $150,000 bond, and having no connection with it;
and this proportion was fixed after the settlement of
1837. (He refers to his certificate approving the proportions settled by the treasurer. See folio 202 of Doc'mts.)

The 5th interrogatory he has already answered.

To the 6th he says: He never learned that the college
had anything to do with these lotteries or any stipula- 311
tions concerning them.

To the 7th he says: There had been considerable litigation. There was a suit brought by Yates & McIntyre against the college for alleged over-payments; then there was a suit by Dr. Nott against Yates & McIntyre, to recover a large amount which he claimed. The verbal part of the compromise was made in my office. Gov. Marcy, James McIntyre, Mr. Ely, and he thinks Archibald McIntyre, and Dr. Nott were present. The meeting was brought about in consequence of a suggestion by Mr. McIntyre or Yates,
312 of a willingness to settle on surrender of certain securities and being paid a certain sum Yates & McIntyre were to give a bond for $150,000, for the use of Dr. Nott. The college was to surrender a bond and mortgage of J. B. Yates, for $55,000, release the assumption of Yates & McIntyre to pay the Comptroller's bonds for $20,000, to A. H. Lawrence, and the college original responsibility to revert; there were some notes of $19,000 of Yates & McIntyre, which were also to be given up. These securities were given up to pay for a conceded error in consequence
313 of an erroneous estimate by the Comptroller, of the amount of tickets to be drawn, which was corrected by the Attorney General.

The college had received their portion of the profits of this lottery, arising from that over estimate. The bond of $150,000 was given to settle the suit of Dr. Nott against Yates & McIntyre, to recover the percentage they had agreed to give him in consequence of liabilities he had in-
314 curred in behalf of Yates & McIntyre, and which the college conceded belonged to him.

To the 8th interrogatory, he says: He has no recollection of knowing about deposits by Dr. Nott There was some of the percentage that belonged to Dr. Nott, that was paid over by him to the college.

To the 10th interrogatory (the 9th being passed for the present), he says: The knowledge of the purchases referred to came to the trustees, as far as he knows, after they were made by Dr. Nott. This was before he was a mem-
315 ber of the finance committee. From the representations he received, he thought it was a very valuable property.

The Doctor always avowed his intention to give all that he derived from the lotteries to the college, in such form as Chancellor Walworth, who was a Trustee, should say was legal.

To the 11th interrogatory, he says. He was frequently consulted by Dr. Nott; and the general management of affairs was with the President and Treasurer. The Doctor was anxious to consult the committee, and when he
316 had acted, he was in the habit of reporting to the committee. Thinks he succeeded Gov. Wright on the committee,

though his predecessor may have been Gen. Dix; cannot state the year when he was a member of the finance committee; he had as much to do with the settlement of 1837 (when the $150,000 bond was given) as any one.

To the 12th, says: He thinks he was not on the committee at the time referred to.

To the 13th interrogatory and questions founded thereon,
he says: There were thorough examinations made by Mr.
James and Mr. Wright, and by Gen. Dix and Judge Cush- 317
man. The yearly accounts and reports of the Treasurer
were generally examined by the committee; but these were
not so thorough as those he has spoken of. He considered
Wm. James a sagacious man; he was not a regular accountant, but was a remarkably shrewd and sagacious man, and
with Gov. Wright, who was a thorough accountant, there
were not two men in the State, whom he would sooner se-
lect to investigate the affairs of the college. Wm. James
was a close, scrutinising man. He was a trustee, and died
a few years after the report by him and Gov. Wright was 318
made.

To the 9th interrogatory, he says: He considered Dr. Nott very much devoted to the interests of the college; as much as any man could be; it was owing to his efforts, his sagacity and labor, that the college was enabled to realise even the sum of $276,090.14. He never saw anything in Dr. Nott, but what was perfectly upright; he was entirely devoted to the interest of the college; he was always doing extra work for it.

On his cross-examination by Mr. Potter, who appeared 319
for the college, witness says: He does not know or recollect
that Dr. Nott was paid a salary for managing the lottery, in
addition to his salary as President.

The witness is asked the names of the Trustees who conceded that the President's fund, or the 2¼ per cent fund,
belonged to Dr. Nott? The witness said he never heard
any one question it, but Henry Yates; does not recollect
any one in particular, who acknowledged it belonged to
Dr. Nott. He knows of no written agreement to give that
fund to Dr. Nott, and knows nothing about it but the con- 320
cessions that were made when the matter came up.

On his cross-examination by Mr. Vanderheyden, he says: He cannot define the amount that was received from the President's fund.

He might have looked at the law in 1837, but does not
now recollect whether he did or not; he presumes he
looked at the law and the documents that were necessary
to enable him to perform his duties as a member of the
committee; he got his information from Dr. Nott, the Treasurer, and the books of the college; he did not get the terms 321

of the settlement with Yates & McIntyre in 1837, from Dr. Nott; the Doctor was decidedly averse to it, and thought that he could recover a larger amount than $150,000. Yates & McIntyre were anxious for a settlement. Is asked, whether it was not considered, at the time, that Dr. Nott could not recover against Yates & McIntyre? Witness answers, No; Gov. Wright was decidedly of opinion that Dr. Nott could recover, and Dr. Nott obstinately insisted he
322 could recover a great deal more.

XXXVIII.

TESTIMONY OF NEZIAH BLISS, INTRODUCED AS A WITNESS BY MR. VANDERHEYDEN.

Says he lives in Kings county; knows about the Hunter point property; it consists of about 140 acres of land, is narrow, and surrounded partly by water; he exhibited a map of it. He got Gen. Johnson to purchase the property
323 for witness and Dr. Nott, at the request of the Doctor. The original agreement was for $100,000; the sum of $4,800 besides, was paid for fishing rights and interest; and $1,000 was agreed to be paid Gen. Johnson for his commissions; this was not paid; it was forgotten, I suppose.

The property was bought with the view of selling it to the government, to enable the navy yard to be extended so as to get a rock foundation. Thinks it would have been sold to the government for a large sum if he had had the
324 management of the business. The reason he purchased was because he knew from the government officers that they wanted to buy this property. This was intended to be kept secret; but does not know that the government wished it kept secret.

Dr. Nott said he had $100,000 college funds, which he would like to invest in the purchase. There was a prospect of making several hundred thousand dollars for the benefit of Union College and Dr. Nott; but it was broken up by Mr. Van Buren.

355 Witness believed a great deal of money could be made by selling the property to any one. Gen. Johnson told him it could be sold the next day for $50,000 advance.

When it was purchased, supposed advances would be made to improve it. The agreement between him and Dr. Nott is given in the pamphlet appended to Mr. Beekman's resolution of April 8, 1853, Senate Doc. 68., at p. 12, 13. It was made in 1831, but not reduced to writing until 1834. The agreement at p. 14, was also signed by Dr. Nott. Witness never took the title to the property; Dr.
326 Nott took it in his own name; he was glad to get rid of it,

because no money was advanced to improve the property, according to agreement. Dr. Nott said he had no money, all the trouble came from Dr. Nott's skepticism.

In 1832, he bought the Stuyvesant cove property, for which $1,500 was paid down, and he gave a mortgage for $16,000 payable in eight years. He made an agreement with Dr. Nott, respecting it, who was to have one half of it at the original price, and advance the money to improve it, according to the agreement before mentioned. The real 327
consideration was $8,750. He does not know what the consideration was in the deed from him to Dr. Nott, for the one-half; he did not mind what consideration he put in the deed; he never objected to the Doctor putting in any consideration; he did not care what consideration was in the deed. The next step was, Dr. Nott wanted to raise money, and he took my bond and mortgage on the undivided half; and considering this like the other papers, I did not care what sum was put in the bond and mortgage. I had full confidence in the Doctor; I did not expect the 328
Doctor would transfer or record it; I supposed it would come back to me. It was not executed for my benefit; Dr. Nott never advanced me any money for it; I did not so consider it.

Years rolled around, there was no money advanced for ten years after the purchase. Dr. Nott did nothing, and in 1842 I made a settlement because I wanted to have something of my own. This settlement related to several matters, viz: 1st, we bought the sand hill April 15th, 1831, for $15,000; 2nd, Sept. 1, 1832, we bought the 329
Stuyvesant Cove property; 3d, October 12, 1834, we bought the Griffin property, 30 or 40 acres, for $13,800; 4th, March 8, 1836, we bought the half of the Prevost property for $3,357.85; 5th, Nov. 10, 1835, we bought of John Meserole, 30 acres of land, for $40,000; of which $10,000 was paid and a mortgage given for $30,000; for interest and expenses $7,200 was paid, and then it was given up; it is now worth $150,000; 6th, June 12, 1839, the Bushwick and Deveaux meadows, containing 23 acres, were bought for $2,000. We sold it for $2,300; the purchaser 330
was offered $60,000 for the property, but refused it, considering it worth $100,000. 7th, Sept. 28, 1839, we bought stock in the Hallet Cove and Ravenswood turnpike, and there was paid on it $5,500 in all. 8th, the Hunter farm.

Does not recollect that any money was laid out on the Stuyvesant Cove property between 1832 and 1839; very little, if any. Mr. James resided there.

When Dr. Nott got the mortgage he said he wanted it to raise money upon, to carry on the improvements. He did not give the mortgage for any thing he owed Dr. Nott, did 331

not consider it in that light. Did not suppose the mortgage would be transferred or recorded, but would come back. He finds it was recorded at the request of Robert Stratton, who was Dr. Nott's agent, the same month it was given. Dr. Nott said it should never be recorded. He applied to Dr. Nott to give up the mortgage and advance the money. He did not tell witness what he had done with it He declined giving it up until 1842, when they settled and ex-
332 changed releases. I told him they had better divide, and I gave up my right to all the property, except two-thirds of the sand hill. I gave a deed, at the same time, to Dr. Nott for one-half of the Stuyvesant Cove property. When he gave the mortgage and those deeds, he gave up the agreement with Dr. Nott, and they signed general releases. He would not have given up the property but for the mortgage, and the failure to furnish the money advances, and his anxiety to know what was coming to him. When he gave up the property in 1842, he considered it worth
333 $500,000, if properly managed.

The Ravenswood and Hallet Cove turnpike stock was subscribed for by Dr. Nott in behalf of the owners of the Hunter property. It was taken as investment for revenue, and for the improvement of the property; if well managed, it would be a good investment.

On his cross-examination by the counsel for Dr. Nott, he says that Dr. Nott generally paid the sums mentioned by him as having been paid on the purchase of the lands and for expenses; but he had about $10,000 of his own money
334 that arose out of his business in Ohio, which he thinks he paid. He had no accounting with Dr. Nott, no footing up of accounts, because they were in the hands of Mr. James. He never had any settlement with Mr. James, that he ever knew of. Mr. James figured up something, but I did not know any thing about it. My mind at that time was in such a state, that I knew very little what I did. The cause of this, was the not fulfilling by Dr. Nott of his agreement with me. He received moneys from Dr Nott, and from Howard Nott & Co., as his agents, from 1828 up to 1842; does not know how much. He received moneys
335 also on account of the Novelty steamboat.

The witness was asked by the chairman, whether he had stated on any occasion that the consideration of $50,000 was inserted in the deed to Dr. Nott for the one half of the Stuyvesant Cove property, at the particular request of Dr. Nott? He said he did not recollect He added that he did not consider the consideration of any importance.

XXXIX.

TESTIMONY OF EDWARD JAMES, WHEN BEFORE THE COMMITTEE, OCTOBER 18th AND 20th.

EDWARD JAMES, called by Mr. Vanderheyden, and sworn,
says: From 1830 to 1835, he had charge of the business of 336
Howard Nott & Co., and was partly in business on his own
account; was employed by Dr. Nott, many years ago, in
preparing his papers for patents; otherwise has never been
in his employ; he never was connected with Dr. Nott in
any business or enterprise, nor in any business in which they
participated in the profits or losses. He, Dr. Nott and
Mr. Staples once endorsed a note for a man in Canada;
property assigned by the maker, was held by Mr. Staples;
witness and Mr. Staples were connected in the management
of it; Dr. Nott advanced money in that transaction. 337

About the year 1834, I purchased property in Saratoga
county, of John F. King; I purchased his interest in the
water power, and some 70 or 80 acres of land attached to
it; I paid between eight and nine thousand dollars, by assuming to pay his debt to the firm of Nott, Wing & King,
and agreed to employ him at a large salary, eight or nine
hundred dollars a year. These were the considerations for
the purchase. Some small sums, but does not recollect
the amount, were charged on the property. After he purchased it, he erected on it a building that cost him $2,000, 338
and he built a machine shop also.

In 1838, a gentleman from New-York examined the property, and offered him $20,000 for the one-half of it, and an agreement was concluded so far, that he gave his note for the amount, to be held until the writings were completed, and then to be given back to him. He was a responsible person, so much so that Mr. Staples often endorsed notes for him; the arrangement, however, fell through.

The first firm that owned the Waterford property, was
Nott, Wing & King, consisting of H. Nott & Co., and Messrs. 339
Wing & King, this was in 1831; he assumed the debt of
Wing & King to H. Nott & Co., and bought them out for
eight or nine thousand dollars. He mortgaged the premises to Dr. Nott for $14,000, and the payment of it was guar-
anteed by H. Nott & Co.; Dr. Nott had placed money in the
hands of H. Nott & Co. The witness was indebted to H.
Nott & Co. for the debt of Wing & King, which he had assumed on the purchase of the property, and he gave the
mortgage in consideration of that indebtedness, and of three
or four thousand dollars in money which they had advanced
to him, and which they had received from Dr. Nott; he 340
executed the mortgage to Dr. Nott, instead of H. Nott &

Co., and thereby cancelled their debt to him to that amount.
It was taken by Dr. Nott in payment of so much due to
him by H. Nott & Co., and was therefore guaranteed by
them to him.

He afterwards procured $6,000 from Dr. Nott, to purchase
the half of the land that King owned individually, and
he paid the money to King. Witness, at first, said he had
given a mortgage for $6,000 to secure this sum, but on re-
341 flection, he said it was in a bond and mortgage for $20,000
that he gave, to include this $6,000 and the $14,000 in the
previous mortgage. He might have paid interest on the
mortgage, but does not recollect doing so more than once;
was not called on to pay the interest. Dr. Nott never had
any interest whatever in the purchase of this property, or
in the business carried on there; the witness held the property for his own benefit, and not for the benefit of Dr. Nott;
he never heard that Dr. Nott had any interest in Wing's
patent water-wheel; he advanced money to H. Nott & Co.,
342 which they may have employed in that way.

The mortgage for $14,000 was guaranteed by H. Nott &
Co., and they made ample provision for its payment, by
their assignment; he believed the property was worth many
thousand dollars more than the amount of the mortgage,
and he represented to Dr. Nott that it would be good security for that amount.

On his cross-examination by the counsel for Dr. Nott,
the witness said there was an amount of between 6 and
7,000 dollars of Commercial Bank stock of Albany, that
343 came into the possession of Howard Nott & Co., from Union
College. It was hypothecated by them and sold, and they
provided for its payment in their assignment. It was paid
for to Union College by their assignees, and a receipt given
for it by the treasurer of the college. He has a statement
of various stocks received by H. Nott & Co., from Union
College—Mohawk bank, Farmers' bank and Commercial
bank stock amounting to $51,000. He stated an account
with Stratton and Seymour, (a copy of which is presented
to him, and he says is the same, it is printed among the do-
344 cuments annexed hereto at folio 269, No. 37) in which he
credited them $78,214.27, paid by them to Union College
for H. Nott & Co. This amount included the above stocks,
and he believes also the amount of his bond and mortgage
for $14,000. He says so, because there was no account
between Union College and H. Nott & Co., the college never
loaned any money to that firm; and there was nothing due
from H. Nott & Co. to Union College but the amount of
those stocks, which had been received through E. Nott, and
their guarantee of his bond and mortgage. The difference
345 between the $51,000 for the stock and the $78,000 paid

by the assignees, amounting to $26,000 about, can not be
otherwise accounted for than as a payment of his bond
and mortgage for $14,000, and the interest on it and on the
loans of stock. He was in the employ of H. Nott & Co.
until December 1836, and was then employed by their assignees until 1839.

Dr. Nott placed money with Howard Nott & Co. to be
paid over to Neziah Bliss, and which they paid to him.
Seeing the large sums that had been advanced to Bliss by 346
H. Nott & Co., and which had been received from E. Nott,
before the year 1833 he went to New-York to effect a settlement with Bliss: he took with him a statement of the
amount, and compared it with Bliss, who brought out
his books, a number of small memorandum books, to compare them with me. Bliss admitted the accounts were
correct. They were for money advanced for the purchase
of lands, part of which came through the hands of H. Nott
& Co. from Dr. Nott, and the residue of which he knew to
have been advanced by Dr. Nott. After they had agreed 347
on the amount for which Bliss was indebted for the money
advanced for the Novelty steamboat and the lands in which
Dr. Nott and Bliss were interested, Bliss and witness settled upon a sum which was the claim of H. Nott & Co.
against Bliss and Dr. Nott. It was finally agreed that a
bond and mortgage should be given by Bliss for $75,000
on the Stuyvesant Cove property, and one for $50,000 on
property purchased, or that was to be purchased on the
other side of the river; a part, he thinks about $30,000,
on the Sand Hills or Bushwick Hills, and about $20,000 348
on other property to be purchased. These securities were
to discharge Bliss for the advances made by H. Nott & Co.
Until he got a settlement with Bliss, he could not charge
Dr. Nott with his proportion. These securities were charged to Dr Nott by H. Nott & Co. in their account with him
for his advances. This settlement did not include the
steamboat Novelty; each of them, Dr. Nott and Bliss,
owned one half of the boat, and were to own their halves
after the settlement.

The monies advanced to Bliss by H. Nott & Co., were 349
received from Dr. Nott.

Bliss did not leave him to insert what sum he pleased
in the mortgage; the sums were proposed by him, and
agreed to by me. He gave as a reason for putting the
$75,000 on the Stuyvesant Cove property, that he consid-
ered it so very valuable Bliss was also to give Dr. Nott
a deed for one half of the Stuyvesant Cove property, and
this, with the mortgage, settled the account. Dr. Nott was
not present at this settlement with Bliss, and did not know
that witness went down to New-York to effect it until his 350

return. Bliss was so well satisfied with this settlement,
that he said we (Bliss and Dr. Nott) could afford to lose
a Novelty steamboat every year.

Witness is by profession an accountant, and has been
employed in the Canal Department, (the Auditor's office)
since 1839. He has examined the report of Mr. Vanderheyden contained in the printed book, with a good deal of
care. It is the most difficult report to understand, he has
351 ever seen that was sent to the Legislature. I can not make
out a statement from this book. I can not understand it,
and can not make out how Mr. Vanderheyden has stated
it. He has receipts and then I find the same things charged.
Specifies an entry of $78,000 received from Stratton &
Seymour, which he finds at different places at p. 140, at p.
39, and notes of the same persons at p. 35, amounting to
$13,712 33; he can not tell how to apply them, or whether
they form a part of the other or not. The bond account at
p. 186 contains two things entirely distinct; it is confused
352 because it embraces two accounts. It purports at the head
to be an account with the $150,000 bond, and yet in the
body, it drops that bond and debits three different items,
and then gives the balance $29,000 to Dr. Nott, without
any reason; if a part belonged to him the whole did. Mr.
Vanderheyden has given the college the benefit of $120,000,
part of this bond, in this account, and has also given it the
same amount in the sum of $355,000, the proceeds of the
lottery, because the same items, J. B. Yates' bond, the 19
notes and the $20,000 for the College of Physicians, were
353 included in the sum of $433,000 at the settlement of 1828,
and the $355,000 is the portion of the $433,000 which the
accountant says belongs to the college. He has thus made
this sum of $120,000 answer twice, and I think he has
used it a third time, in not treating it as it was, a surrender
by the college to Yates & McIntyre of the securities given
for an over-payment. The accountant has expressed a
doubt whether the balance of $29,000 should be credited
to Dr. Nott, and has left it to the Commission to decide; at
354 pages 133, 135, he has done the same thing in respect to
the Hunter farm and the Stuyvesant Cove property. These
items, of which he had doubts, should have been placed
in a suspense account, and should not be charged, as they
have been in the accounts of actual transactions.

The accountant at p. 6, makes Union College have property to the amount of $1,279,000, which was never given
the college in any way; and by the acts of the Legislature
given in the appendix to his book, the grants were only
$385,000. This large sum of $1,279,000 is made up so as
to make it necessary to bring Dr. Nott in debt, $855,000.
355 Deducting this $855,000 from the $1,279,000, leaves

$393,213.23, which is only $7,000 more than the sum stated by Mr. James and Silas Wright, in their report of 1831, to be the amount of the college property, and it has not been increased since.

The accountant's balance sheet (No. 2), is different from any balance sheet I ever saw. A balance sheet takes the name of the account as it stands at the head of the ledger, and the total amount of the debits and credits of each account, not the items. 356

This balance sheet No. 2, and the account of receipts and expenditures No. 3, are duplicates from p. 8 to p. 22. They are duplicates for all practical purposes, except the heading. This does not prove the account wrong, but it confuses. After p. 22, he is at a loss to find the same items in No. 2, and No. 3.

Cross-examined by Mr. Vanderheyden.—When Bliss agreed to give the bond and mortgage for $75,000, not a word was said about its being given to enable Dr. Nott to raise money upon. 357

Witness engaged in the undertaking of breaking up the concern of Nott, Wing and King, in order to protect H. Nott & Co., and in that way he got into the transaction.

Howard Nott and Benjamin Nott, composed the firm of H. Nott, & Co. Dr. Nott had no interest in it. If he furnished capital, he would be allowed interest like any other person. Witness can not tell what capital Dr. Nott furnished them. H. Nott & Co., had great credit, it was undoubted, their business being considered a good one.

H. Nott & Co., never looked into or examined the busi- 358
ness conducted at Waterford, Saratoga co., after witness purchased the property. He made the purchase at the instance of John F. King, who was the owner of it. King had become embarassed by being indorser for others, and it became necessary that this property should be sold.

No papers or receipts were passed between him and Bliss when they settled; thinks he left his account with Bliss.

Witness is asked if the $1,279,000 appear by the college 359
books or otherwise to have been received, what objection is there to the account so stating it? Why is it incorrect?

The witness says, because mere receipts are not evidence of the property on hand. The accountant, in No. 3, gives the total receipts at $4,469,000; this is a different account. A summary is a condensation of accounts—it is not necessarily a condensation of balances. A summary is a proper paper if correctly drawn up. The form of this summary is correct, but the substance appears to me to be very 360
incorrect.

The balance sheet No. 2 is confused in itself and by comparison with No. 3.

He says the accountant furnished him, at his request, with a statement of the deductions he had made from the $433,002.14 to produce the sum of $355,593.26, that he had charged, as received from the lottery; and that in tracing these items, he found the interest paid College of Physicians, at p. 33, short by $600; when he was directed
361 to p. 32, debtor side shows the college is charged with receiving $606 from the Comptroller. He never could have discovered this without personal information from the accountant.

The account at p. 186 of the $150,000 bond, is the most mysterious statement I ever saw; it is a palpable absurdity.

Re-examined, and shown a statement furnished by the accountant for the item in No. 3 at p. 41, and in No. 2 at p. 12, "interest from Yates & McIntyre," (this statement
362 follows) and the witness says it is a most extraordinary statement, and utterly unlike a regular accountant.

XL.

STATEMENT *of Accountant* (*above referred to*,) *in answer to the question, where he finds the item of interest received from Yates & McIntyre*, $45,572.08, *charged by him?*

The accountant has heretofore testified, as regards the interest received from Yates & McIntyre, and is now again
363 required to give testimony to the same fact. He now presents all that he is informed under this head, and if there should appear any disparity between this and his testimony already thrice given, he relies on the present statement as the correct one, and revokes all former testimony incompatible with this.

Before giving this statement, he would call attention to page 179, printed book, which succeeds the settlement by E. Nott, as agent, and under authority of the resolution of the board of Trustees, passed 24th July, 1822, to the words,
364 viz: *The above settlement, adopted by the accountant, in the accounts presented.*

At page 177, statement No. 35, the balance of interest on account, is stated at, ...	$21,506 16
At the same page, the interest on notes taken in settlement, ...	25,329 89
	$46,836 05

The college books do not enter the Beebee draft, ... $19,530 00
Nor the succeeding two entries of Beebee,.............. 488 35 365
And, ... 329 53

$20,347 88

But enter, as is supposed, in lieu of the above, J. Averell's bond and mortgage, as of .. 20,536 34

$188 46

Showing a disparity of $188.46, which is supposed to be accruing interest,.......... 188 46 366

$47,024 51

Of the above 1st item of $21,506.16, being interest on the account, up to 1st August, 1828, the accountant carried to the account of six years interest, on the original grant, to make that account the amount actually raised under the grant, $10,552.60, say.............................. 10,552 60
367

$36,471 91

The accountant then derives from Mr. Hemingway, the accountant of Yates & McIntyre, the interest on seven notes, received 2d February, 1830, being the notes as stated in statement No. 35, page 177, due from 4th March, 1830, to 4th Sept., 1830, and which interest was, ... $1,583 78
From which he deducts the interest on Yates & McIntyre's notes, due, as stated on page 368
177, above referred to, and due 4th February, to 4th July, and which notes were paid 23d July, 1830; less interest on Terhune note,................ 1,326 67

257 11

Also, interest on renewals of notes, due 4th Nov., to 4th Jan'y, as stated on page 177, 1,882 47
Also, interest on renewal of notes, due from 369
4th Aug., 1831, to 4th Dec., 1832, also interest on renewals of notes, due from 4th May, 1832, ... 5,660 18

	And the accountant enters the amount of interest on the 17 notes of Yates & McIntyre, as stated at page 186, printed book, ...		3,226 40
			$47,498 07
	Against which he charges, disallowed E. Nott		
370	on two notes, discounted by him 26th Nov., 1833, ...	$15 64	
	" " "		
	" " "		
	discounted by him 17th Jan'y, 1834, ...	467 12	
	Paid E. Nott interest on five notes, discounted by him, 17th Jan'y, and now returned, ...	1,443 23	
			1,926 99
371			
			$45,572 08

Testimony of Mr. Vanderheyden, in relation to the item of $45,572.08, *interest received from Yates & McIntyre.*

On the 27th of September, 1853, at Schenectady, he says: This interest is the item credited the college at p. 186, 187, as having been received on the bond of Yates, McIntyre & Ely; afterwards, corrects this, and says it is the interest on
372 the $150,000 bond, until it was paid, as appears by the college books.

[The foregoing written statement, makes it the interest on the amount due at the settlement of 1828, and on notes taken for the balance then found:—totally different transactions from the bond for $150,000.]

On being enquired of subsequently, he says: These items included all the interest provided for on the settlement of 1828, and subsequent renewals of the notes then given, the total of which is $56,124.68, from which he deducted $10,-
373 532.60, and added it to previous receipts, to make out the $84,000 of interest received from the State, leaving the exact sum of $45,572.08.

[It will be seen by the above written statement, that there was no such total of interest as $56,134.58—or the written statement is equally incorrect with the verbal explanations.]

XLI.

[The following resolution of the Trustees of Union College upon the report of Messrs. Cushman and Dix, Doc. XXIV, should have been inserted immediately after that report, at folio 199 *ante.*]

Resolved, That the foregoing report be accepted and
adopted by this board, and that the Secretary and Treasu- 374
rer be directed to carry into effect the recommendations
therein contained. Book of Minutes C, page 55.

XLII.

Original agreement in full, on which the bond for $150,000 *was given*; Doc. XXVIII, folio 216 *ante, being a mere abstract.* [*This original was produced after the abstract or memorandum was printed.*]

Articles of agreement tripartite, made this 27th day of 375
July, 1837, between Henry Yates, John Ely, Junior, Archibald McIntyre, partners of the firm of Yates & McIntyre, of the first part: The Trustees of Union College, in the town of Schenectady, in the State of New-York, of the second part, and Eliphalet Nott of the third part.

Whereas, the said Trustees of Union College and said
Eliphalet Nott, president of said college, in the month of
May, 1834, filed their bill in the Court of Chancery, against
the said John B. Yates, Henry Yates, Archibald McIntyre,
James McIntyre, and John Ely, Junior, claiming, among 376
other things, that the said defendants were indebted to the
complainants in the sum of $31,004.00 by them borrowed.
And also a large amount under certain agreements and
stipulations, as in said bill set forth, and praying, among
other things, that the said defendants might be decreed to
pay over to said complainants, such amount, as should
appear on settlement, that they should be entitled to receive.

And whereas, also, Archibald McIntyre, Henry Yates,
James McIntyre, now deceased, John Ely, Junior, and John 377
B. Yates, now deceased, in August, in the year 1834, filed
their bill in the Court of Chancery, against the Trustees
of Union College, and Eliphalet Nott, a Trustee of said
college, claiming among other things, that in consequence
of alleged mistakes in a settlement previously made, as in
said bill was set forth, the defendants should be decreed
to deliver up to be cancelled, certain promissory notes,
amounting in the aggregate to the sum of about $19,448.47;
and also, that a certain bond and mortgage, given by said
John B. Yates, to secure the payment of the sum of $55,000, 378

should be assigned and transferred to the said complainants, and praying, among other things, that by a decree of said court, said complainants should be discharged from a certain promise to indemnify the Trustees of Union College against a verbal guarantee to said trustees, to provide for the payment of $20,000, due from the College of Physicians and Surgeons, in the city of New-York, to the New-York Insurance Company.

And, whereas, also the board of trustees of Union Col-
379 lege did, at their stated meeting on the 26th day of July, inst., pass a resolution in the words following, to wit:

"The committee appointed at the last annual meeting of the board, for the purpose of settling, by compromise, the suits pending between the college, and Yates & McIntyre having communicated the terms of agreement on which a settlement can be made, and the committee recommend to the board the acceptance of the terms as an arrangement which under all the circumstances it would be prudent to accede to;

380 "*Therefore Resolved*, That the said committee, or any three of them, be authorised to arrange a settlement of the said suits on the terms proposed, and to cause the corporate seal of the college to be affixed to any articles of agreement which may be made for that purpose."

And whereas, also, under and by virtue of the foregoing resolution, the parties of the first part and the committee referred to in the said resolution for and on behalf of the said trustees of Union College, and the party of the third part, have come to an arrangement and settlement of the
381 matters in controversy.

Now therefore, for carrying into effect the said arrangement and settlement, the said parties of the first and second part do agree, as follows:

§ 1. The said party of the first part, and the said party of the second part, do hereby mutually release the one to the other, the said parties of and from all suits, controversies and actions now pending by and between them respectively, and all claims, demands and causes of action out
382 of which these suits have arisen.

§ 2. The said parties of the first part in consideration of the premises (together with Archibald McIntyre, jun., son of James McIntyre, deceased), have simultaneously with the execution of these articles, executed to the said parties of the second part, a bond in the penalty of $300, 000, conditioned for the payment of $150,000, as follows: $10,000, part thereof, on the first day of September next, and the remainder of said sum, being $140,000, in ten equal annual payments, with lawful interest, and from the
383 first day of August next, on such sums as may be unpaid

yearly, with a right to pay any part thereof before due, and to have interest allowed for the same; which said bond is given for the claims and demands set up by the said parties of the second part, as well as the third part, against the said parties of the first part.

§ 3. The said parties of the first part, do also hereby assign to the said parties of the second part, and their successors, certain bonds and mortgages, and certificates of
stock, particularly described in schedule A, hereto an- 384
nexed; but such assignment is merely made as collateral security for the payment of the bond mentioned in section two, of these articles.

§ 4. From time to time, as payments shall be made on the bond last mentioned, the parties of the first part shall be entitled to receive from the parties of the second part such part of the securities mentioned in schedule A as shall be equal in amount to such payments, and thereupon such securities so given up and returned shall be discharged
from the assignment hereby made of them. 385

§ 5. If the parties of the first part shall at any time be disposed to sell or assign any of the securities mentioned in schedule A, while held by said parties of the second part, then and in that case such securities so selected by the said parties of the first part shall be returned to them by the said parties of the second part, on their receiving the amount due thereon, or on their receiving other full and adequate security which shall be equivalent thereto in value and amount in the opinion of the said parties
of the second part, in security as aforesaid, the said parties 386
of the first part shall nevertheless be entitled to receive any interest that is now due or may become due thereon, which any of the debtors in schedule A may be disposed to pay, and the said parties of the first part are hereby fully empowered and authorized to receive the same.

§ 7. The said parties of the second part hereby agree to surrender and give up to the said parties of the first part the said bond and mortgage now held by them against John B. Yates, deceased, and which shall be duly assigned
by the said parties of the second part to the said parties of 387
the first part, as soon as the bond in section two of these articles shall be given and accepted by the said parties of the second part.

§ 8. The said parties of the second part shall surrender and give up to the parties of the first part promissory notes hereinbefore referred to, given by Yates & McIntyre, now held by the said parties of the second part, amounting, without interest, to about nineteen thousand four hundred and forty-eight dollars and forty-seven cents, or in case
they, or any of them, shall not be given up, the parties of 388

the second part shall indemnify and save harmless the said parties of the first part against them and every of them, and also against the payment of three several bonds given by the Comptroller in June, 1817, to Augustine W. Lawrence—one for ten thousand dollars, one for six thousand dollars, and one for four thousand dollars, which bonds are now held by the people of the State, and the parties of the second part hereby assume and take upon them-
389 selves the payment of the same; the above bonds being the same debt as referred to in the preamble to these articles, as the twenty thousand dollars due from the College of Physicians and Surgeons to the New-York Insurance Company.

§ 9. The said party of the third part, and the said parties of the first part, do hereby reciprocally, in consideration of the foregoing premises, release each other jointly and severally of and from all claims, controversies, suits, actions, causes of action and demands whatever, which the
390 one party has, have or may have against the other.

In witness whereof, the parties to these presents have hereunto set their hands and seals, the day and year first above written; and the parties of the second part have also affixed the seal of Union College.

Sealed and delivered in the presence of

The name of "John Ely, Jr.," interlined in the third line.
391 J. V. N. YATES,
ARCHD. CAMPBELL.

HENRY YATES, [L. S.]
A. McINTYRE, [L. S.]
JOHN ELY, Jr., [L. S.]
A. McINTYRE, Jr., [L. S.]
ELIPHALET NOTT, [L. S.]
W. L. MARCY, *Gov.*,
A. C. FLAGG. *Compt.*,
JOHN A. DIX, *Sec. of State.*

Schedule A.

	Delaware and Chesapeake canal bonds, ...	$24,000 00
	Union canal bonds, ...	10,000 00
392	Anthony Rosier's bond and mortgage on lands in New Jersey, ...	16,500 00
	Francis Morris' bond and mortgage on lands in Jersey City, ...	4,500 00
	James W. Winne's bond and mortgage, in Albany, ...	2,800 00
	J. W. Dundas' bond and mortgage on house and lot in Rochester, ...	1,600 00
393	Pittsburg city loan, and Pittsburg Gas Company stock, ...	17,000 00
		$76,400 00

XLIII.

Letter of Rev. Jacob Van Vechten, admitted in evidence, with the same effect as if verified by the oath of the writer.

ALBANY, *Oct.* 29*th*, 1853.

Rev'd and Dear Sir—In a conversation with me, in Mr.
Pease's book store, about the 1st of May, 1852, Doct.
Campbell said that Doct. Nott need feel no uneasiness, re- 394
specting the fairness with which the investigation of the
fiscal affairs of Union College would be conducted by the
commissioners appointed by the Senate, and of which he
was chairman; that after the accountant had finished his
work, and before the commissioners reported, Dr. Nott
should have an opportunity to see what was done, with a
view to explain any difficulties, and to correct any mistakes;
and that he should have the benefit of those explanations
and corrections in the report to be made to the Senate.
With very great respect 395
and esteem, Your serv't,
(Signed) JACOB VAN VECHTEN.
Rev'd DOCT. NOTT.

P. S. At a meeting of Trustees, before the books were
given up, Chancellor Walworth expressed the opinion, that
they ought not be taken away from the college, saying that
the accounts would be garbled; in this opinion, the whole
board seemed to acquiesce. My own opinion was decidedly on the same side, and when I heard of the books being 396
taken to Albany, I felt convinced, and still feel so, that it
was without the sanction of the board, and that the President must have complied with Doct. Campbell's request
solely on his own responsibility. J., V. V.

XLIV.

TESTIMONY OF GEN. GEORGE R. DAVIS.

[Gen. Davis was introduced as a witness by Mr. Vanderheyden, and examined by him in relation to his charac- 397
ter, as a man of truth, and as to his integrity and skill
as an accountant. As no part of the testimony on those
subjects, by the other witnesses is given; that portion of
Gen. Davis', relating to it, is also omitted. But the following, brought out by Mr. Vanderheyden, has an important bearing on two of the points in the case.]

The witness is asked by Mr. Vanderheyden, to state a
conversation between them, about an article Mr. Vanderheyden had published in the Albany newspapers, in which 398

he charged Dr. Nott with having endeavored to induce Mr. Vanderheyden to alter the books of Union College?

No objection being made, the witness answered.

Gen. Davis: I began by asking him (Vanderheyden) what he alluded to by the charge mentioned, what Dr. Nott had done to justify that charge? Vanderheyden said that Dr. Nott claimed that he should be credited for the Bliss bond and mortgage; he insisted, that by the books
399 of the college, he was entitled to be credited the amount. I remarked, to Vanderheyden, that the fact stated by him, did not justify the broad charge he had made; that he ought to have stated it as it was. To which he answered, that it might have been better to have done so; but that the article was written under excitement, in consequence of a previous article that had been published, in which Dr. Nott charged him (Vanderheyden) substantially with perjury. I think he (Vanderheyden) said, that the Doctor insisted that he was entitled to the credit of the Bliss bond,
400 and if he (Vanderheyden) did not give him the credit, he should not submit to it, and he would have a re-investigation in the Senate. (*a*)

Witness has thought that Vanderheyden was prejudiced, that he was under some strong feeling against him (Dr. Nott), but he always disclaimed any hostility to the Doctor, and asserted his desire to do him justice.

In answer to questions concerning the ability of Mr. Vanderheyden, as an accountant, he said: I mean by an accountant, a man that takes up the books, and states what
401 is in them, without going beyond them. As such an accountant, I would have as much confidence in Vanderhey-

(*a*) The following is the passage referred to in the question and in the answer, contained in an address, signed Levinus Vanderheyden, dated Albany, 24th March, 1853, and published in the Albany Evening Journal, of the 26th March, 1853, and in the Daily State Register on the 28th of the same month.

"In the month of February, 1852, the President met me by his own appointment, at the Troy house. He asked if we could not retire to some private place, as he had matters of importance to talk about, and I invited him to my house. On our arrival there, he unfolded the object of his visit, which was, to induce me to make sundry new entries in the books of the college, then in my custody, the effect of which would have been to produce a change in his favor, and that to a large amount. He continued in earnest labor with me, to accomplish this purpose, until two o'clock the next morning, and, among other things, urged in substance, that unless I yielded,
402 a counter report would meet me in the Senate, charging me with falsehood in my statements. I declined to consent to his solicitations."

It will be seen, by his own statement, as proved by Gen. Davis, his own witness, what an atrocious falsehood he coined out of the interview with Dr. Nott.

The only ground for the pretext, that "he had been substantially charged with perjury," as alleged by Vanderheyden, is the following passage, in the memorial of Dr. Nott to the Senate. Speaking of his suspending the printing of an answer to Mr. Beekman's report, and of his having delivered the books of the college to the accountant, he says:

"Both these acts were performed by the undersigned, on his own responsibility, and contrary to the expressed opinion of the legal members of the board, who insisted that an examination of the same, by an accountant entirely ignorant of the transactions concerned, exposed to the influence of the accusing party, and in the absence of the party accused, could not be expected to be either correct or impartial."

There must have been a sad want of pretext, to compel a resort to this passage to
403 find "a charge substantially of perjury."

den, as in any man I know. But if the stating of an account depends upon the construction of an argreement, or of a statute, or a principle of law, I should not have as much confidence in him, for he does not pretend to be a lawyer.

On his cross-examination, he said: I was in the room in the State hall, where Vanderheyden was at work, a week or ten days before his report was made, and asked him
when he would get through? he said, in a week or so; and 404
he would then go over to Schenectady, with his memorandums. I inferred his purpose was to see Dr. Nott about explanations. I saw Dr. Nott, or wrote to him, and told him what Vanderheyden had said; Dr. Nott asked me if I knew the day Vanderheyden would come over? I said I did not. Dr. Nott then wished me to ascertain the day when Vanderheyden would come over, as he wished to be at home when he came; I saw Vanderheyden afterwards, and inquired of him; he said he was not able to fix a day,
and promised me he would inform me what day he would 405
go over, so that I could inform Dr. Nott, that he might be ready to meet him; Vanderheyden did not afterwards name any day to me, before the report was made.

XLV.

ANSWER AND STATEMENT OF ALEXANDER HOLLAND, TREASURER OF UNION COLLEGE, TO THE FOLLOWING QUESTION—BY MR. VANDERBILT, CHAIRMAN.

What amount do the college books show to have been 406
received under the Lottery acts of 1814, and 1822, or under any contract made under or in consequence of said acts, or either of them—and give the time of receipt and amount—and time, and date, and amount, of any note, &c.

Ans.—The books of the college show the following amounts to have been received.

1. Under the act of 1814, there was received from the State, on account of the six years interest belonging to the grant, the following sums:

1819.	July 8.	Cash,........	$14,823 00	407
1820.	Jan. 19.	"	19,000 00	
	June 16.	"	1,505 15	
1821.	Apr. 3.	"	9,579 08	
	Aug. 14.	"	12,302 88	
1823.	Jan. 9.	"	606 00	
	May 31.	"	5,355 98	
	31.	"	6,844 98	
1824.	July 21.	"	2,436 33	

Amount carried over,.......... $72,453 40 408

	Amount brought over, ...			$72,453 40
	2. Under the act of April 5, 1822, the college received from Yates & McIntyre, under their original contract of July 19th, 1822; and their stipulations of January 4th, and 24th, 1826, as follows:			
409	1823.			
	May 31. Cash,....		$4,450 60	
	July 30. "		1,035 30	
	30. "		4,330 00	
	Aug. 2. " $1,000, $3,000,		4,000 00	
	Oct. 18. "		9,163 00	
	Dec. 11. "		11,662 00	
	1824.			
	Jan. 22. "		8,330 00	
	Mar. 29. "		14,543 50	
410	July 4. "		5,311 00	
	Sept. 1. "		17,958 60	
	1825.			
	Apr. 13. "		103,492 72	
	1826.			
	May 8. "		3,000 00	
	1827.			
	Jan. 31. " F. Gardner's B. and Mort'ge,		7,000 00	
	31. " I. Riggs' Note,.		1,500 00	
411	31. " Archer's B.&M.		16,000 00	
	May 25. " 3 bonds Coll. P. & S. assumed,		20,000 00	
	June 5. " R. Richardson's Bond & Mort.,		4,000 00	
	Aug. 4. " A B Shankl'd's Bond & Mort.,		4,000 00	
	15. L. Beebe, dft.,	$2,500		
	15. do	1,182		
	15. do	1,200		
412	Sept. 6. do	700		
	6. do	1,500		
	6. do	2,000		
	6. do	683		
	Nov. 1. do	3,000		
	1. do	750		
	1. do	550		
	1. do	582		

Amount carried over,.

413

Amount brought over,	$	$	$72,453 40	
Nov. 1. L. Beebe, dft.,.	1,000			
1. do	700			
1. do	2,383			
1. do	800			
			19,530 00	
Dec. 31. Beebe, 2½ per cent,.			488 25	
1828.				414
Feb. 11. Beebe, balance,....			329 53	
1827.				
Oct. 15. B. & M., J. B. Yates,			55,000 00	
Dec. 31. Note to A. Terhune,			2,000 00	
			$317,124 50	
Interest received at time of settlement,...............			57,725 23	
			374,849 73	

In Dec., 1828, a settlement was made 415
with the President of the college, of August 1st, 1828, under said original contract and under said stipulations, when it appeared, that the college had received under said original contract of July, 29, 1822, the above sum of $374,849.93, and that there remained due on the same $4,314.06, and that there also remained due under said stipulation of Jan. 4 and 24th, 1826, $133,069.83. For which balances, amounting together to $137,383.89.
Yates & McIntyre gave their notes, amount- 416
ing, with interest to maturity, to $162,713.78, as appears by the receipt of the President, given at said settlement, as set forth at page 177 of the accountant's report. Of the notes, *the college* received from Dr. Nott, including interest to maturity, $95,165.09, as follows:

Barrington's B. and mortgage,		$18,654 17		
Van Schaick's	do	1,373 62		
Newell & Dyer's	do	2,062 33		
Payne's	do	8,579 33		
Van Dyke's	do	6,020 00		417
S. & M. Smith's	do	1,000 00		
Notes of Yates & McIntyres,..		57,475 64		
			95,165 09	
			$542,468 22	

In all, therefore, the college received, under the acts of
1814 and 1822, the above sum of $542,468.22. 418

The precise times when each of the bonds and mortgages and the notes were received from Doct. Nott by the college, in conformity to said settlement of Aug. 1st, 1828, cannot be given in detail from the books. The reason is, that Mr. Henry Yates, the Treasurer at that time, having become a member of the firm of Yates & McIntyre, was most of the time in New-York, and did not, therefore, make these entries in detail, in the college books, but in mass, at
419 a subsequent period, and as of a single date.

(Signed) ALEX. HOLLAND.

[On his examination by the counsel for Dr. Nott, he was asked to state the NETT sums received by Union College? To which he furnished the following written answer.]

	From the above total of		$542,468 22
	Should be deducted the amount paid by Union College to the other institutions,	$75,331 94	
420	And the amount repaid to Y. & McIntyre, ...	94,448 87	
	Making, ...	$169,780 81	169,780 81
	Leaving actual amouni retained, ...		$372,687 42
	Deducting from the above, the amount received by the college on the stipulation of Jan. 4, 1826, ...		95,165 09
421	Leaves the amount received by the college, under the acts of 1814, and 1822, including the principal of the grants, and the interest received on the grant of $200,000,		$277,522 33

XLVI.

Alexander Holland was examined at intervals on various subjects as they were presented, and at the close of the investigation reduced his answers to writing and presented them in the following form:

422 During the time I have acted as Treasurer of Union College, I have also acted as Secretary of the Board of Trustees, attended their meetings and kept their minutes. From the books and documents of the college, which I have examined extensively, as well as from the conversations and acts of the trustees, I have learned that when Dr. Nott was elected President, the college was in debt between three and five thousand dollars, and had not the means of paying the same.

423 When the act of 1814 was passed, granting Union Col-

lege $200,000, the college was in debt thirty thousand dollars; and in 1822, when the act of April 8th was passed, authorising the institutions to assume the management of the Literature lottery, two years interest (on the grant of $200,000) remained unpaid; and the whole of the principal remained unpaid.

So far as my knowledge extends, or as I have learned from the books, vouchers and records of the college, *and from conversations with individual trustees*, (a) it was the 424
uniform and admitted understanding of the board, that the $2\frac{1}{4}$ per cent fund was entirely under the control of the President and belonged to him.

From the documents, as well as from the acts *and conversations*(a) of the trustees, I have understood that the avails of the stipulation of January 4, 1826, entered into to induce the President and Treasurer to raise a large amount of money to save Yates & McIntyre from ruin, were to be divided between the President and the college *pro rata* according to the advances made, services rendered and ha- 425
zards run by each in behalf of Yates & McIntyre.

Great gains have arisen to the college from the purchase of the rights of the other institutions in the lottery granted, by estimating the time required for drawing the same at eleven years. Great gains also arose to the college, from the sale and repurchase of the old college buildings, and from sales of portions of the new college sites, of which I have furnished a statement, as treasurer, to the trustees, (Doc. XXXV, folio 253 to 258.) These purchases were made by the advance of the private means of 426
Dr. Nott, which was repaid to him years afterwards, at cost, and he has not participated in the profits thereof. Besides which, he has expended, gratuitously, considerable sums on the grounds, gardens, houses and out-houses belonging to the college, so that were all the losses on loans and bad debts charged to Dr. Nott, which are, by the accountant debited to him, and all the gains that have enured to the benefit of the college from the use of the private funds of Dr. Nott in its behalf, credited to him, he would, on a final settlement, be found to be not a debtor, 427
but a creditor to the college, and to a large amount.

The moneys charged to Dr. Nott as loans, by the accountant, have usually been amounts delivered to him for investment, or to be expended on the premises purchased by Dr. Nott, near New-York, and destined by him for the benefit of the college. And the moneys deposited with Stillman, Allen & Co., have been temporarily deposited on call, at 7 per cent, for the purpose of saving interest to the college, and not for the benefit of Dr. Nott. These trans- 428

(a) The words in *italic* were objected to, and decided to be not competent; when the witness said that he could make the same declarations without those words.

actions were either authorised or approved by the finance committee, and on several occasions the same have been reported to the board in terms of commendation.

Dr. Nott's acts in relation to loans, investments and the management of the college funds generally, have been examined and approved by the finance committee, and reported to and approved by the Board of Trustees.

I have never known of Dr. Nott's being engaged in any
429 speculations other than those intended for the benefit of Union College, nor have I ever heard it intimated by any trustee, that he had made use, for private purposes, of any lottery funds belonging to the college.

Had the accountant credited Dr. Nott's salary account with all the extra pay that the resolutions of the board would warrant, for extra services, for supplying the chapel pulpit, and for fire-wood, candles, and the amount allowed for repairs to buildings, as allowed and paid to other officers, and to which he was equally entitled, he
430 would have found the balance largely in favor of Dr. Nott.

I have personally examined the account of expenses incurred and charges made by Dr. Nott in the supervision and management of the Literature lottery, and have compared the same with the vouchers, and find it correct.

I gave the certificate printed at folio 250, (Doc. XXXIV) of the documents printed in behalf of Dr. Nott, at the time it bears date, and it is true. The trust deed therein referred to, is still in the keeping of the acting treasurer of the college.

431 The statement of the accounts of Union College which Levinus Van Derheyden has made out, I have carefully, frequently and fully examined, and have not been able to understand many of the accounts, from the fact of their being so mixed up with charges *not found* in the "books of account as delivered to him," or in "the vouchers" referred to in those books. I could not have understood the accounts, owing to the manner in which they are made up, and to this introduction of other matter, without the verbal explanations of Mr. Vanderheyden.

432 The entire tendency of these accounts, it seems to me very apparent, is to deceive and mislead, and give an appearance to matters the very reverse of what was contained in "the books of account delivered to him." Take, as an example, the account against Eliphalet Nott of over $800,000. Neither "the books," "the vouchers," nor any thing else, except the deceptive combinations of Mr. Vanderheyden, drawn from *other sources* than are mentioned in his affidavit, show any such thing.

The witness was then cross-examined by Mr. Van Der-
433 heyden, and in answer to the question who received credit

for the notes of Stratton and Seymour, for which the treasurer gave his receipt to the assignees of Howard Nott & Co?

The witness answered: The transaction was before my time. By the books of the college it appears that E. Nott received credit for those notes in his general account, amounting to $78,214.27. H. Nott & Co. had no account with the college in their own name; being received from Dr. Nott, they were credited to him as agent for H. Nott 434
& Co.

I do not know from the books of the college or otherwise, that Dr. Nott ever paid Union College for the Commercial Bank stock.

Dr. Nott has sold lots, parts of the Stuyvesant Cove property, to the amount, perhaps, of $200,000, which has been expended in improvements on the property, and paying incumbrances; and the property has been very much enhanced in value, so that when the improvements are complete, the property or its proceeds will be worth much 435
more than the original property.

He has understood that Dr. Nott has parted with portions of the Hunter farm to Jonathan Crane and Mr. Ely; large tracts have been added by them to the Hunter farm, and extensive improvements have been made on the joint property. Dr. Nott has an interest in that property. His interest in it now is considerably more valuable than his original interest in the whole of the Hunter farm alone.

He received the note of J. A. Yates from Dr. Nott, who endorsed it, but it was not protested. The circumstances 436
of the loan to Mr. Yates were such that it was not proper to protest it.

Witness is asked to show the evidence in support of a statement made by him to the committee of the Assembly in 1850, contained in Mr. Beekman's report, No. 146, in which he says that upon a settlement with Dr. Nott, the college owed him $41,340.57? And is asked to show the account of that settlement in the books of the college?

The witness answered, that the account spoken of never was in the books of Union College. There was no such 437
account on settlement. In reports made by him, he had stated a balance in favor of Dr. Nott, on account of the moneys received on the $150,000 bond, which the witness had estimated by applying to those payments the resolution of the Board of Trustees of July 26, 1837, (see Doc. XLI and Doc. XXIV,) directing a settlement with Dr. Nott for lottery percentage, according to services rendered, responsibilities incurred and hazards run. This estimate was erroneous, because it was based upon an entire mistake. The resolution, I find, was passed before the bond 438

was given, and in its terms, connected with the report of Messrs. Cushman and Dix, on which it was founded, referred only to sums received on stipulations made with Yates & McIntyre for percentages on the lottery.

The sum of $41,340.57, with the interest, $5,309.28, was paid Dr. Nott 1st September, 1848.

Dr. Nott has given the college credit for it, in the deposit account certified by Messrs. Brown, Blatchford and Lane.

He did not charge Dr. Nott the same price for the Far-
439 mer's Bank stock that the college paid for it, because he expected it would be returned. It was all returned except $5,000. The reason he did not charge any premium on the stock, was, that as agent for Dr. Nott, he sold it at par, and for all that it could fetch; he made enquiries respecting its value, and could get no more.

There is no account separately of the classical library fund; they have a library account, and what there is belonging to the classical library fund, is in that account. Former treasurers kept a distinct account of the classical
440 library fund; entries of expenditures appear on the books before the grant for this fund was realized or any part of it. It was mixed up with interest paid for a series of years, on loans in anticipation of the grant being realised, so that it would be difficult to tell whether the college realised any thing from it or not; and in 1850 he reported, as he believed, that nothing had been realised from it. In respect to the indigent grant of $5,000, he makes the same answer.

In previous examinations of this witness, he testified
441 that it appeared from the books of the college that Henry Yates was treasurer from 1807 to 1833; that during the latter part of his term, he was absent in New-York, and his duties were performed by clerks, one of whom, his son, was incompetent. That the books of the college were not well kept by him at any time; and that when he resigned, they were imperfect and in great disorder, and that no vouchers, receipts or memorandums, calculated to explain the college transactions during his term of office, ever have
442 been or can now be found. A committee of the trustees were for a long time engaged in the examination of his accounts after his resignation, and found many errors in them, and a large balance against him. I have often, as treasurer, been embarrassed in explaining transactions during his term, from the want of means to explain his accounts.

Jonas Holland was appointed treasurer upon Mr. Yates' resignation in 1833, and continued such until 1839, when he died unexpectedly. I was requested by the President to come to Schenectady and take charge of the books, which
443 I did at first temporarily. I was appointed to the office

soon after, and continued until 1851, when I removed to New-York, and although I am still treasurer, the active duties have been performed since that time by Jonathan Pearson, one of the professors.

XLVII.

Jonathan Pearson, Acting Treasurer of Union College, was also examined at intervals, and at the close of the investigation he reduced the substance of his testimony 444
to writing, as follows:

1. That for two years past there has been lying in the safe of the Treasurer's office, an instrument in writing, purporting to be, and as he believes is, a deed of trust from Eliphalet Nott to the trustees of Union College, of certain real estate lying on the East river, near the Novelty Iron Works, in the city of New-York, called the "Stuyvesant Cove property," and of certain other parcels of land lying opposite to the above on Long Island, called the "Hunter 445
farm," &c., [he produces the original deed executed by Dr. Nott and his wife, duly acknowledged and re-acknowledged several times, the last time in October, 1853.]

2. That he has made long and diligent searches for vouchers of payments made during the treasuryship of Henry Yates, Esq., and has been able to find none.

3. That the whole amount of bonds, mortgages, notes, contracts and leases, belonging to Union College on Jan. 1, 1853, was $103,100.26, and that he has verified this amount by an actual comparison with the obligations on hand at 446
that time.

4. That the account books in daily use during the year 1852, were at Mr. Vanderheyden's request, put into his hands, that he might bring his accounts down to the first day of Jan. 1853.

5. That several times during the year 1852, he, the said Vanderheyden, informed him, the witness, that when he came to the lottery accounts, which he reserved till the last, he should visit Schenectady to consult Dr. Nott upon matters connected therewith. 447

6. That between the 30th day of September, 1822, and the 2d day of April, 1833, the trustees of Union College were indebted to the Mohawk Bank for interest on overdrafts, $54,520.12, of which the sum of $36,877.87, was charged to and paid by H. Yates, Treasurer; and that the rate of interest charged by said banks, was 7 per cent.

The witness produced a statement of the account of Union College with the Mohawk Bank for interest on overdrafts, which is hereto annexed. He was then examined, and answered orally. The first column he says, was 448
taken from the books of the Bank. The second col-

umn was made from old original papers in the Bank, of the dates referred to, and from information given by its officers. From other papers produced, it appeared that the Bank charged 7 per cent. The third column was taken from the books of the bank. The fourth column was prepared by the witness, and he believes it accurate. It shows the differences between the interest paid by the Treasurer of Union College, and the interest actually due. In
449 the course of his examination, he stated that four of these items of differences correspond precisely in amount with four of the items charged by Mr. Vanderheyden, as loans to Dr. Nott, in the printed statement No. 3, at p. 86. The two items of differences due April 1, and October 1, 1826, amount to $2,238.54, which is the exact sum charged in the printed statement as the second item. The three items of differences due April 1, and October 1, 1827, and April 1, 1828, amount to $3,825.46, the exact sum charged in the printed statement as the third item. There are two
450 items in the printed statement, the first and the sixth amounting together to $3,384.35, for which no corresponding differences are found. But the statement of differences annexed, shows that they amount in all, to $17,642.25, considerably more than the amount charged by the accountant.

All these items charged by the accountant to Dr. Nott, appear on the books of the College as payments to him for interest, and in one instance, simply as a payment.

451 *Union College in account with the Mohawk Bank for interest on over drafts at 7 per cent.*

	Date.	Overdrafts.	Interest due.	Interest paid by H. Yates.	Difference.
	1822, Oct. 1,	$68,206 06	$2,247 28	$2,247 28	
	1823, April 1,	71,017 80	2,401 28	2,401 28	
	Oct. 1,	73,094 34	2,458 91	2,558 91	
	1824, April 1,	48,081 74	2,279 79	2,166 65	$113 14
	Oct. 1,	72,401 93	2,346 64	1,938 00	408 64
	1825, April 1,	84,009 79	2,728 11	2,138 27	589 84
	Oct. 1,	74,120 53	1,963 68	1,277 19	686 49
	1826, April 1,	84,660 31	2,665 67	1,493 80	1,171 87
452	Oct. 1,	84,586 89	2,682 01	1,615 34	1,066 67
	1827, April 1,	87,938 33	2,983 47	1,754 16	1,229 31
	Oct. 1,	86,125 52	2,809 00	1,399 63	1,409 37
	1828, April 1,	92,797 94	2,863 60	1,676 82	1,186 78
	Oct. 1,	96,457 19	3,067 07	1,772 12	1,294 95
	1829, April 1,	99,672 65	3,152 64	1,853 87	1,298 77
	Oct. 1,	99,813 48	3,163 21	1,834 95	1,328 26
	1830, April 1,	98,058 73	3,451 00	1,815 32	1,635 68
	Oct. 1,	102,122 57	3,382 12	1,771 59	1,610 53
	1831, April 1,	60,147 26	2,024 88	1,776 82	258 06
	Oct. 1,	52,354 53	1,852 45	1,397 91	454 54
	1832, April 1,	43,161 87	1,743 91	975 05	768 86
	Oct. 1,	33,527 20	1,336 55	679 48	657 07
	1833, April 1,	22,740 68	916 85	443 43	473 42
453			$54,520 12	$36,877 87	$17,642 25

XLVIII.

[To enable the reader to understand the next document XLIX, it becomes necessary to reprint here, in connexion with it, the summary condition of the college given by the accountant in his report; p. 5, 6 and 7.]

(No. 1.)

SUMMARY STATEMENT SHOWING THE CONDITION OF UNION COLLEGE ON THE FIRST DAY OF JANUARY, 1853. 454

Original grants and endowments, viz:

From subscriptions,......	$7,433 15½		
trustees of Schenectady patent,.....	24,954 02½		
the Reformed Dutch Church, Schenectady,...........	8,307 63		455
old academy debts,..	563 92		
		$41,258 73½	

Grants and endowments from the State of New-York, viz:

Act April 9, 1795, irrespective of interest,.......	$269 58		
Act April 11, 1796, irrespective of interest,....	10,000 00		
Act March 30, 1797, irrespective of interest,.....	1,500 00		456
Act March 7, 1800, irrespective of interest,....	10,000 00		
Act March 7, 1800, irrespective of interest,....	43,656 44		
Act April 8, 1801, Act April 3, 1802, ...	15,084 82		
Act March 30, 1805, irrespective of interest,....	80,000 00		
Act April 13, 1814, irrespective of interest, Act April 3, 1822, irrespective of interest,	355,593 26		457
Act April 5, 1822, supervision and management of lotteries,...........	104,732 54		
Six years interest received on act April 13, 1814,..	84,000 00		
Total grants from Legislature,....		$704,836 64	458

Amount carried forward,.. $

	Amount brought forward,........		$704,836 64
	Bequest from Abraham Yates jr.,............	250 00	
	Bequest from Goldsbrow Banyer,..............	500 00	
	Grant from Presbytery of Albany,.............	35 00	
			785 00
459	From proceeds of sale of West College buildings and site,................		78,766 79½
	Debts owing by Union College,.......		21,260 07
	Revenue of Union College from 1795 to January 1853, above all expenses,...		432,095 61
			$1,279,002 85

Cr.

460	West College buildings and grounds including the repurchase in 1836,....	$55,684 05½	
	New college buildings and grounds erected since 1812,................	106,904 19½	
	New philosophical hall erected in 1852,.......	6,281 37	
			$168,869 62
	Real estate other than college grounds,		2,100 99
	Library and apparatus,...	$22,748 51	
	Classical library,.........	2,807 82½	
461	Telescopes, barometers, &c,	753 00	
			26,309 33½
	Investments, viz:		
	In bonds and mortgages,..	$77,237 63	
	Bonds, ...	6,165 94	
	Notes,...............	2,042 26	
	Contracts for land,....	2,019 20	
	Accounts,...........	25,411 44½	
	Bank stocks,.........	18,332 90	
	Plank road stocks,....	2,300 00	
	Manufacturing stocks,.	1,500 00	
462	West Troy durable leases,...........	7,311 81	
			142,321 18½
	Interest accrued on above investments,		8,393 27
	Losses in investments, &c.,...........		44,727 14
	Cash on hand,..........	$73 52	
	in bank,..........	414 04	
			487 56
	Due from Eliphalet Nott,.............		885,789 62
463	Total,......................		$1,279,002 85

XLIX.

Objections to the statement presented by the Accountant, called No. 1, and entitled "Summary statement, showing the condition of Union College on the 1st day of January, 1853."

The grant under the act of 1795, is charged only at $269.58, when, in fact, $3,750 was received and expended, or accounted for by the committee.

The item charged as having been received under the 464
act of March 30, 1797, $1,500 was granted, expressly for the salaries of professors, and belonged to the revenue account, No. 4, p. 58, as an off-set to the credit given in that account for payments of salaries.

The grant under the act of March 7, 1800, stated at $43,656. 44, was, in fact, $43,483.90.

The item of $355,593.26, charged as received under the acts of 1814 and 1822, should be $200,758.20, that being the nett balance of Yates & McIntyre's note for $276,090.14,
after deducting $75,331.94, paid to the other institutions 465
on the purchase of their rights.

The item of $104,732.54, charged as belonging to the college, from the supervision and management of lotteries, was never received by it, nor was it ever claimed by the trustees; but for more than twenty years has been conceded by them in various acts, resolutions and proceedings, as belonging to the President, individually.

The item of $84,000, for six years interest on the grant contained in the act of 1814, should be $72,453.47, that
being the sum actually received. The accountant has ad- 466
ded the balance from interest received from Yates & Mc Intyre, that had accrued after the settlement in 1828, and on the renewal of their notes, and from the balance of interest against them on their payments.

He thus converts interest into capital, and departs from his own principle. Besides, there is every reason to believe, that the interest referred to is charged also in the revenue account, No. 4, at p. 58, in the item of $45,572.08. The explanations by the accountant, of this item, and of
the operation now objected to, have been inconsistent, and 467
the last is quite unsatisfactory. (See Doc. XL.)

The item of $78,766,79½, proceeds of sales of West College buildings and site, is made up of principal of $40,722.06, and $38,044,73½ interest; (see p. 159, of his report.)

Here again interest is converted into capital. But a still greater objection exists against it. A part of this sum ($78,766.79½) must have been deducted by the accountant from the cost of West College buildings, as shown
in the summary prepared by the treasurer, and this item, 468
or a portion of it, is therefore, twice charged to the college.

The item of revenue above all expenses, $432,095.61, is fictitious; it has never been received, and constitutes no part of the property of the college. It is the balance of the revenue account No. 4, page 61. This, in its turn, depends on the item on the debit side of the same account, page 60, "interest due from E. Nott, on general account, $510,024.11." And this, we are informed by the accountant in his testimony, is the balance of interest in the ac-
469 count with Dr. Nott, beginning at page 81. The committee need not be told that the interest charged in that account is upon items which are altogether denied by Dr. Nott, and which, in the course of the argument, have been shown it is believed to be without foundation.

The objection frequently made in the above remarks, against the accountant converting interest into capital, and holding the college to account for it, is founded on the obvious injustice of the proceeding. This interest was a part of the current revenue of the college, and was expended
470 in the current business of the college, and in payments for interest due on debts contracted for its buildings, improvements, repair, salaries, &c.

In his revenue account (No. 4, p. 58, &c.,) the accountant has stated the whole amount of interest received in different items, amounting to $358,744.62, and the amount of interest paid on loans (and no other is credited) at $232,-500.68, showing an accumulation of interest amounting to $126,243.94; a result contradicted by the whole history of the college. An exposition in full of this error of the ac-
471 countant, is given in the argument for the defence.

On the credit side the following items are questioned:

The charge for the cost of the college buildings is greatly below the amount actually paid. How this reduction has been effected will appear by the notes in the treasurer's summary.

West College buildings and grounds, including repurchase, are put down at page 6, at $55,684.05; in the balance sheet, page 8, they are put down at $48,039.77; at page 158, at $57.056.70½; and at page 160 the re-purchase
472 is stated at $11,500, making the two items here credited $68,556.70½, instead of $55,684.08, as here stated. Which is correct?

Real estate, other than college grounds, $2,100.99. It is claimed that this should be $26,667.45, the college actually having property on hand of that value, as proved by Mr. Holland. It is no answer to say that this sum does not appear in the books of the college. The accountant has felt at liberty to resort to other sources than the college books, and even to the private books of individuals,
473 having no connection with the college, for charges against

it. The Trustees are accountable for the actual value of this property, and no statement of the present condition of the college would be complete without it.

The items for library and apparatus, and for classical library, telescopes and barometers amounting to $26,309.33. There has been actually paid on this account, as appears by the books of the college, and shown by the treasurer, $33,817.34. No explanation has been given of the reason for the difference. 474

The items, bonds and mortgages, bonds, notes, contracts for land, and West Troy durable leases, amounting to $94,776.84, do not represent the amount on hand, which is $110,523.55, as testified by Mr. Pearson, from actual examination of those securities in his hands. The accountant has stated that in addition to his amount, there is included in his balance against Dr. Nott, a bond and mortgage for $12,000, which being added to his amount would make the whole $106,776.84, which is very nearly the amount stated by Mr. Pearson. 475

The item of accounts ($25,411.44½) is too large. It is $25,077.22.

Losses on investments, &c., $44,727.14. The list of what the officers of the college regard as losses, amounts to $57,101.79, the difference is not explained.

The last item, due from E. Nott, $855,789.62, is alleged, on our part, to be entirely fictitious; it is the result of the fabulous account at page 81.

We contend that his summary of the condition of the college, is, on its face, an absurdity. In that statement he 476
makes a deficiency in the assets of the college, to the exact amount of $885,789.62; and he makes out an account in detail against the President, corresponding to that precise sum, to a cent; evidently made up to fill this gap. No man will believe, that in the transactions of an institution for 58 years, the exact sum, to a cent, necessary to balance its accounts, is owing to it by one individual.

It is in vain for him to say that the books must balance. There is no *must* in the case. If the fact is that there is a deficiency or an excess not accounted for, let the result 477
show it. To make the debtor and credit sides equal, when they are not equal, is a falsity; and if that be the science of book-keeping, no honest man can profess it.

L.

SUMMARY OF THE CONDITION OF UNION COLLEGE ON THE 1ST OF JANUARY 1853, BY THE TREASURER THEREOF.

Statement of amounts received from the State and otherwise by Union College without interest.

1. Original gifts and endowments: 478

From original subscriptions (a)............ $7,433 15
" Trustees of Schenectady Patent (a)... 24,954 03
" Dutch Refd. Church, Schenectady (a) 8,307 63
" Old Academy (a).................. 563 93
" Bequests of Abraham Yates, G. Banyer,
and Presbytery of Albany (a)............ 785 00

$42,043 73

479 2. Grants from the State:
Under the act of April 9, 1795, (b) (1)..... $3,750 00
" " 11, 1796, (a)........ 10,000 00
" March 30, 1797, (a)........ 1,500 00
" " 7, 1800, (a)........ 10,000 00
" same (b) (2)..... 43,483 93
" Ap. 8, 1801 & Ap. 3, '02 (b) (3) 9,378 20
" March 30, 1805, (a)........ 80,000 00
" April 13, 1814, (b) 276,090 14
Less paid other in-
480 stitutions,....... 75,331 94

200,758 20

Under stipulation of Jan. 4. '26 (b) 95,165 09
Less am't repaid Yates & McI. (b) 94,448 87

716 22
On the interest granted on the act of 1814 (b) 72,453 41

$474,083 69

481 Statement of property on hand—debts and losses of Union College Jan 4, 1853.
1. Productive and available:
Bonds and mortgages, bonds, notes and contracts and durable leases (b) (4) $103,100 26
Bonds and mortgages in the hands of P. Potter attorney for collection 7,423 29

$110,523,55
Stocks, par value 18,460 (b) with premium
482 added, cost, &c........................ 22,132 90
Real estate for sale (b) 25,667 45
Due from undergraduates (b) 2,354 34
New Philosophical Hall (a) (6)........... 6,281 37
Accounts against individuals (b) (6)...... 7,084 81
Deposit with Stillman, Allen & Co, (a) (6). 15,638 07
Cash on hand and in bank (a)............ 487 01

$190,169 50

2. Unproductive and in use for College
483 purposes:

Old college buildings and site at cost, including additions and repairs (a)(7)	$73,534 39		
New College buildings and site including additions aud repairs after deducting the cost of parcels sold (a) (7)......	226,078 87		
Library and apparatus (b) (8)	33,817 84		
		333,431 10	484
Due from graduates, exclusive of in't (9) ..		44,814 01	
		$568,414 61	
Losses have occurred as follows:			
Schenectady Water Works, ...	$545 00		
Sacandaga Turnpike,..........	200 00		
United States Bank,....... ...	2,300 00		
Hudson Bank,...............	5,000 00		
Franklin Bank, ...	10,000 00		
On Mohawk Bank,............	30,000 00		485
Hallet's Cove Turnpike,*	5,500 00		
N. Y. Poudrette Co., ...	1,677 09		
S. N. Bayard's note,...........	1,379 70		
Estimated on Bayard's mort.,...	2,000 00		
	$58,601 79		
*Deduct error on Hallets Cove,	1,500 00		
	$57,101 79		
Assumed losses:			486
On E. James, B. & M..........	14,000 00		
William Anderson, ...	5,000 00		
Philo Stevens, Bd.....	1,295 77		
J. Monroe. B. & M.	2,305 10		
Rens. & Sar., Insurance Co.,....	930 00		
B. Nott's Bond,...............	700 00		
		$81,332 66	
		$649,747 27	
Less debts,........................		18,547 76	487
		$631,199 51	
Rec'd as pr. page 106,.................		474,083 69	
Difference,........................		$157,115 82	

This difference arises from various sources, among which may be named the profit arising from the sale and repurchase of the old College, the profits on sales of portions 488 of the new College site, and the profit arising from the purchase of the rights of other institutions in the lotteries.

There is no interest charged or credited in the above statement, because whatever interest was received, was expended in the ordinary business of the college.

This is shown by the accountant's statement No 4, of revenue and expenses when divested of the sum entered there to balance the account, and the sum entered as due
489 and unpaid. Thus that statement shows a total of revenue of............................ $1,462,297 92

In which is included interest due from Eliphalet Nott,....................	510,024 11
Showing actual revenue received,......	$952,273 81
It also shows a total expenditure of	$1,462,297 92
But a sum is entered to balance the acc't of	432,095 61
490 Showing the actual expenditure to be...	$1,030,202 31

Thus establishing that the actual expenditures have exceeded the actual revenue, $77,928.80. The interest received, is therefore more than accounted for.

NOTES.

(a) Indicates that the item is the same as that stated by the accountant.

491 (b) Indicates that the item is different from that stated by the accountant.

EXPLANATIONS.

(1.) This sum was received from the State, and applied to the purchase of books and apparatus, by a committee of the board; the sum stated by the accountant was a balance left in the hands of that committee, and by them paid to the treasurer, and afterwards expended.

(2.) This difference, (about $200,) arises in part from
492 the accountant not giving this fund credit for the amount repaid on account of the title failing to 50 acres of the land sold.

(3.) The accountant has charged, as principal, all that was received, whether for rent or interest, or on sales of the lands granted. The treasurer has only charged, as principal, the amount received for lands sold.

(4.) According to the accountant's summary, page 6, deducting his item " accounts $25,411.44¼ " (which is not in this charge,) and adding for West Troy durable leases,
493 $7,311.81, which is in this charge; his amount should

be $94,776.84. But the amount here stated is taken from the actual securities on hand carefully compared. The difference is explained in the previous document, objections to the accountant's summary.

(5.) A credit is given on this account by the accountant, for only $2,100, because, as he says, the residue is the profit of a purchase of land. But we claim, that as the college is to be accountable for losses, it should be
credited for its gains, in order to show its present actual 494
condition. It certainly ought to be here, or in the revenue account, No. 4, p. 58, which the accountant says is a profit and loss account; but it is not there, and thus the college is deprived of any credit for it, in any form.

(6.) The above three items amount to $25,077.22, while the accountant's is $25,411.44, (p. 66, and p. 8.) although they agree so nearly in results, they differ in details.

The items in his statement at page 60, which are deemed erroneous, are compensated by the above charge of sums
due from under graduates. 495

The above two items charged as the cost of the old and the new college buildings, amounts to......		$299,613 26
The accountant allows for the same items, (p. 6.)		162,588 25
The difference is		$137,025 01

which is thus accounted for. The accountant has apparently deducted from the actual cost of the old buildings
the amounts received on sales of common lands taken in 496
exchange, and interest there-

on, (see page 159.).........	$78,766 79½	
And amount received on sales of part of original site, (p. 159)	14,400 00	
		$93,166 79½
The accountant has credited the college for payments to Register for repairs, improvements, &c., which he admits includes expenses on buildings, $79,364.68, (p. 10.) If there be taken from this sum as applicable to buildings,......................... (497)		43,858 22
We have the above difference, ...		$137,025 01

The treasurer, instead of deducting the amounts received in the above sales, from the cost of the buildings, has carried them in the shape of money or bonds or other securities

498

received, into the general fund of the college, and credited them to it.

(8.) This is the actual sum paid.

(9.) This sum is actually due, although a part of it may not be collected.

(10.) The difference between this and the amount stated by the accountant, $21,260.07, is owing to his having charged interest on the bonds due the Comptroller, and
499 having included some small items owing to men in the college employ and others. (See p. 159.)

These last items were transient, and have been paid. The interest above mentioned is not included, because no interest is reckoned on the bonds, mortgages, notes, &c., on hand, in the above statements.

A. HOLLAND, *Treasurer.*

LI.

500 *Eliphalet Nott, in account with Union College.* (Changes in forms of gifts.)

	Date	Dr.		
	1845.			
	Aug. 1.	Consideration of conveyance of Stuyvesant Cove property to you, at this date, ...	$150,225 42	
		Less this sum never paid by the college on the purchase		
501		from Dr. Nott,...	16,367 85	
				$133,857 57
		Interest thereon from time of conveyance to Aug. 1, 1852, ...		65,590 21
	1845.			
	Aug. 1.	Consideration of conveyance of one half of Hunter farm,.		100,000 00
		Interest thereon from time of conveyance to Aug. 1, 1852, 7 yrs.,		49,000 00
	1848.			
502	Sep. 21.	Cash paid you, ...		46,649 85
		Interest to Aug. 1, 1852, 2 yrs., 10 months and 21 days,..........		12,599 31
		Balance,..........................		105,485 64
				$513,182 58

Gift of prize in lottery,..........	$8,500 00	
do amount of President's fund (1),	115,640 53	
Balance,......................	34,936 20	
	$159,062 41	

1834. Cr.

July 2.	N. Bliss' bond and mortgage, ...	$75,275 52	593
	Interest to Aug. 1, 1852,.........	95,208 34	
1837.			
July 27, to 1849, May 3.	Cash received by Treasurer between these dates from Yates, McIntyre & Ely, on their bond for $150,000,	203,091 75	
	Interest to Aug. 1, 1852, on the payments,......................	187,656 97	
		$513,182 58	504
	By balance brought down, ...	$105,485 64	
	Interest to Jan. 1, 1853, 5 mos.,...	3,076 57	
	Deposit of amount of lottery prize,	8,500 00	
	do. on account of President's fund,......................	42,000 00	
		$159,062 21	

If there be charged to Dr. Nott, what ought not to be charged, interest on what is 505

called loan 5,............	$23,344 89	
do. do. 6,............	1,160 79	
		$24,505 68
There is a balance still due him of,........		10,416 00
The amount of his balance above, ...		$34,921 68

Loans 1 and 2 are denied; 3, 4, 7 and 8, are balanced; 9 and 10 are provided for. 506

(1) As this was a gift, no interest should be credited. But in fact, the interest is absorbed by the expenses paid out of the fund.

www.ingramcontent.com/pod-product-compliance
Lightning Source LLC
LaVergne TN
LVHW050515100826
845148LV00002B/343